POWER
PARENTING
for Children with
ADD/ADHD
A Practical Parent's Guide
for Managing Difficult Behaviors

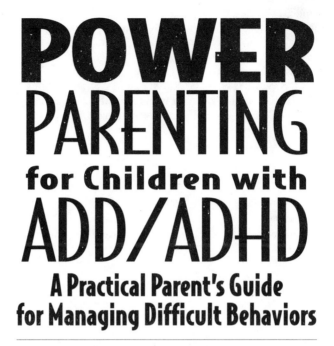

GRAD L. FLICK, PH.D.

**THE CENTER FOR APPLIED
RESEARCH IN EDUCATION**
West Nyack, New York 10994

W9-AMM-732

Library of Congress Cataloging-in-Publication Data

Flick, Grad L.
    Power parenting for ADD/ADHD children : a practical parent's guide
for managing difficult behaviors / Grad L. Flick.
        p.   cm.
    Includes bibliographical references (p.   ) and index.
    ISBN 0-87628-885-9. — ISBN 0-87628-877-8 (pbk.)
    1. Problem children—Behavior modification.   2. Attention-deficit-
disordered children—Psychology.   3. Parenting.   I. Title.
HQ773.F56   1996
649'.64—dc20   96-5133
                                                                  CIP

© *1996 by The Center for Applied Research in Education*

All rights reserved.

No part of this book may be reproduced in any form or by any means, without permission in writing from the publisher.

Printed in the United States of America

10   9   8   7   6   5   4   3   10   9   8   7   6   5   4   3   (p)

ISBN 0-87628-885-9   (C)   ISBN 0-187628-877-8   (P)

ATTENTION: CORPORATIONS AND SCHOOLS

The Center for Applied Research in Education books are available at quantity discounts with bulk purchase for educational, business, or sales promotional use. For information, please write to: Prentice Hall Career & Personal Development Special Sales, 240 Frisch Court, Paramus, New Jersey 07652. Please supply: title of book, ISBN number, quantity, how the book will be used, date needed.

THE CENTER FOR APPLIED RESEARCH IN EDUCATION
West Nyack, NY 10994
A Simon & Schuster Company

On the World Wide Web at http://www.phdirect.com

Prentice-Hall International (UK) Limited, *London*
Prentice-Hall of Australia Pty. Limited, *Sydney*
Prentice-Hall Canada Inc., *Toronto*
Prentice-Hall Hispanoamericana, S.A., *Mexico*
Prentice-Hall of India Private Limited, *New Delhi*
Prentice-Hall of Japan, Inc., *Tokyo*
Simon & Schuster Asia Pte. Ltd., *Singapore*
Editora Prentice-Hall do Brasil, Ltda., *Rio de Janeiro*

This book is dedicated to these loving people in my life:
my late parents, Peter and Olive Flick,
who gave me unending love
and support for my education and achievements;
and to my wife, Alma Lott Flick,
who is certainly
the most unselfish and most caring person
I have known.

About the Author

G **RAD L. FLICK** received his Ph.D. in Clinical Psychology from the University of Miami in 1969 with APA-approved internship at the University of Florida Medical Center. A licensed psychologist since 1971, he has specializations in neuropsychology and biofeedback, along with certification as a biofeedback therapist. He has been certified in stress management, in employee assistance, and has Fellow and Diplomatic status from the American Board of Medical Psychotherapists. He has held positions in psychology at University of New Orleans and Louisiana State University School of Medicine and has served as consultant to several hospitals in the New Orleans and Gulf Coast area. Since 1971, he has been in private practice and is currently director of Seacoast Psychological Associates, Inc., in association with his wife, Alma L. Flick, Ph.D.; they specialize in the evaluation and treatment of children, adolescents and adults with Attention Deficit Disorder, learning and behavioral problems. Dr. Flick is also the Director of the ADD Clinic (year-round and summer programs) for children, adolescents and adults with ADD where behavioral and cognitive therapies are offered as well as traditional psychotherapy, play therapy, and various group therapies.

Dr. Flick has had numerous scientific presentations and publication credits, conducted many workshops for both parents and teachers on

ADD, and has given lectures to various parent and teacher organizations on ADD and Child Management. He has over 25 years' experience in both research and clinical practice with children who present attentional, learning and/or behavioral disorders. Grad and Alma have also parented a child with learning disability and Attention Deficit Hyperactivity Disorder.

Foreword

Children with attention deficit disorder (ADD) provide both a challenge and an opportunity to those who care for them.

The challenge, of course, lies in helping them to achieve their fullest potential. Often children with ADD have difficulties with cognition and behavior which can impede their success in school as well as in family and social relationships. Problems with concentration, attention, and organization can seriously disrupt learning and academic performance leaving teachers, parents, and children frustrated and disappointed. Problems with behavior, characterized by hyperactivity and impulsivity, can antagonize and frustrate friends, teachers, and parents. Children with ADD often challenge their teachers in school who try to help them better focus and who strive to modify their behavior so that their educational performance matches up to their ability to learn. They often challenge their parents at home who worry about them fitting in with others, feeling good about themselves, and, in general, finding success and happiness in their life. Teachers and parents who accept these challenges can succeed by looking for opportunities and strategies to reach and teach those with ADD.

There has been remarkable growth in interest in attention deficit disorders in the past decade which has led to greater identification and treatment of children with this problem. Health professionals are more aware of the characteristics of children with ADD and are better trained to diagnose and treat this condition. Pediatricians, psychologists, and other health professionals are less likely to disregard symptoms of ADD or blame the child, or his environment, for his difficulties. Educational systems are more apt to identify children with ADD in school today than they were five or ten years ago and are better equipped to provide appropriate educational services to help students with ADD succeed in school. Programs are in place in many districts to provide accommodations in regular education classrooms for students and, for those students with ADD who require more assistance, special education programs are available to help.

Parent support groups offer assistance to families of children and adolescents with ADD and help to guide parents through the many challenges they face as they try to help their child succeed. Issues centering around education, medication, social relationships, behavior modification, self-esteem development, family relationships, and a myriad of other topics are of importance to parents who are raising a child with ADD. Thus, it is essential that parents of children with ADD become sophisticated and educated in the subject to help them best make decisions regarding the proper care of their child.

Power Parenting for Children with ADD/ADHD, written by Grad Flick, Ph.D., an experienced clinician who has worked with many children with attention deficit disorders and their families, will become a treasured resource. Dr. Flick provides practical information to parents which will help them make the many daily decisions they must face in caring for their child. Methods of behavior management are clearly spelled out in understandable and practical terms. He explains the principles of behavior modification simply and directly, thereby giving parents the tools they will need to better understand how to help their children. Dr. Flick takes care not only to help parents manage behavior, but to ensure that in the process the child continues to develop a positive, healthy self-esteem.

Dr. Flick also offers numerous suggestions for teaching children with ADD. His discussion of common problems such as inattention, impulsive behavior, homework management, peer conflicts, etc. will be welcome by almost any parent and teacher of a child with ADD. Once again, his advice is practical and instructive as he gives hands-on tools to care-givers to help improve the academic performance of the student with ADD.

Clinicians, researchers, and those with ADD themselves have discovered that, in many instances, this disorder does not stop after childhood. Previously thought to diminish in adolescence and be outgrown by adulthood, we now realize that a significant number of children with ADD will continue to have symptoms as adults. All the more reason for us to make sure that children with ADD get off to a good start. Perhaps through early intervention and heightened awareness we can help provide for a lifetime of opportunity for these children.

HARVEY C. PARKER, PH.D.

Co-founder and former Executive Director of CH.A.D.D., Children and Adults with Attention Deficit Disorders, a parent support organization with chapters nationally, and author of *The ADD Hyperactivity Workbook for Parents, Teachers, and Kids.*

How This Book Will Help Parents of Children with ADD/ADHD

P arents are interested and concerned about what their child will be like when he or she is grown. They also worry, at times, when their child exhibits problem behaviors that are different from the norm. When constant attention is directed towards their child—who becomes easily distracted from a task, acts before he or she thinks, has conflicts over rules, and who may fidget or exhibit blatant overactivity—there is cause for concern. While some behaviors are simply annoying, as, for example, fidgeting, other behaviors appear more serious, as when the child plays with knives, is overly aggressive with others, or repeatedly runs into a street with fairly heavy traffic. Parents find little reassurance and comfort in comments from others, such as, "Oh, he'll outgrow that stage" or "Boys will be boys." Many parents are aware from an early age and, at times, even before birth, that the identified child is somehow different. Upon reaching school age, classroom demands often seem to elicit problem behaviors, but the parents know quite well that these behaviors are not limited to the academic situation. Difficulties in social relationships and even in play behavior may be manifested by this child who appears poorly equipped to cope with the demands and expectations of daily living. Often, these problem behaviors constitute a syndrome termed Attention Deficit Disorder, or ADD. The terms ADD and ADHD (Attention Deficit Hyperactivity Disorder) will be used interchangeably in this book.

Throughout my clinical practice of over 20 years, I have evaluated and treated hundreds of children with ADD behavioral characteristics. I have also worked closely with their parents and continue to do so in current clinical practice. For parents whose children exhibited only mild ADD characteristics, there were some challenges in dealing with the children's behaviors; yet, eventually, these parents were able to achieve adequate management. Other parents whose children exhibited moderate-to-severe ADD characteristics not only seemed unable to achieve adequate management, but they sometimes appeared indifferent and more often gave in to their children's demands. In short, this latter group of parents at times felt frustrated and helpless to cope with their children's behavior, often wondering, "How could this have happened?" or "Have I done something wrong?" or "What's wrong with me?" or "Is there anything that can be done to help with these problems?"

The first step in dealing with the ADD child's "difficult behavior" is to understand its origin. This behavior is physiologically based and, as such, the child often responds to situations with automatic behaviors that are innately designed to aid him or her in adapting to that situation and to compensate for his or her internal physiological deficiencies. All children learn some form of adaptive behavior in various situations. However, the child with ADD must also compensate for deficiencies in the physiology within the nervous system that may cause him or her to engage in behaviors that simply, as many of these children put it, "get me in trouble." Without intervention, such children literally cannot control many of these behavioral patterns and thus react as "slaves to their own nervous system." Their ADD behaviors are as much "out of control" as are the behaviors of a child experiencing an epileptic seizure or delusional speech associated with an extremely high fever. For the ADD child, though, there is often no evidence of any definitive brain damage or structural abnormalities within the nervous system on conventional medical and neurological examination when such tests are indicated for other reasons. The point is that the ADD child's behavior is essentially not under voluntary control.

Initially, parents of ADD children may utilize common parental practices such as making requests of the child, giving commands, and even providing reminders to carry out specific tasks. However, when these ADD children continually and consistently fail to comply with instructions, parents then often become frustrated and increasingly emotional (i.e., angry), giving more frequent, more restrictive and emotionally laden commands that may likewise be ineffective. Ultimately, these frustrated and frazzled parents are likely to develop passive and acquiescent parental behaviors, simply giving in to the child and basically letting the child have "his or her way." This parental behavior is therefore described as a state of "learned helplessness." One parent noted, as her child was jumping up and down on the sofa, "I've tried everything and nothing works. It's easier just to let him have his way than to try to correct him."

This pervasive sense of helplessness can be overcome. Parents of ADD children may often feel inadequate, depressed and angry, and also have a poor self-concept as a parent. It is certainly time for these parents to take back the power that lies within effective parenting techniques for the ADD child. It was long ago stated that "Knowledge is power." And today this quote would certainly apply to parenting skills needed for the ADD child. Parents succeed more often when they have a good understanding of the nature of their child's ADD behavior problems *and* when they have a set of effective guidelines and strategies for managing these behaviors. I emphasize that it also takes a "strong willed parent" to deal with a "strong willed child." Many parents who have previously been unsuccessful in managing their child's ADD behavior will have a history of failure experiences and may have lapsed into a state of "learned helplessness" through their avoidance of power struggles and hassles with the child. Literally, their child has been "in control" and it will not be easy for the parent to regain control. Other parents who *themselves* are experiencing the residual effects of their own ADD may have a low frustration tolerance for their child's misbehavior, and they may consequently respond impulsively with anger. Such conditions are thus conducive to an escalation of misbehavior and angry retorts that may ultimately lead to "abusive tendencies." However, having a good understanding of the child's condition and knowing what to do and when to use these behavioral techniques—combined with support from relatives, spouse and an inner-parent voice (or self-talk)—will enable parents to begin to cope more effectively with their child's behavior. Also combined with an increased awareness of possible ADD residual behaviors of the *parent(s),* there is a further basis for avoidance of situations that may lead to either "child abuse" or "parent abuse."

This book has been written primarily for those parents who are trying to manage the difficult behaviors of the "strong willed child" with ADD. Still, the basic principles outlined apply generally to parenting of all children, including those children who exhibit "ADD-like" behavior. Clearly, ADD behaviors exist on a continuum and overlap with "normal" as well as with various deviant behavior and neurological disorders. Besides good common sense, the material in this book is based on physiological, psychological, and neurological research, along with many years of clinical experience—yet, it can be read, understood and applied by any parent with a basic education and a strong desire to learn. The book is straightforward, though it is not a cookbook. Consequently, it allows you to make decisions on the most viable alternative solutions to deal with your own child's individual behavior.

The uniqueness of this book lies in its comprehensiveness, bringing together essential information about ADD with basic principles of behavior management, while focusing on some of the typical problems you, as a parent of a child with ADD, have to deal with—notably at school, in peer and sibling relationships, at home, and with homework. Here, in one source, are all the tools needed for power parenting in a single package. In a logical, step-wise fashion, the topics include a discussion of techniques for giving commands and instructions, ways to conceptualize behavior and, ultimately, to either develop, strengthen and maintain certain specific *appropriate* behaviors **or** to weaken, decrease and remove specific *inappropriate* behaviors. The book is intended to be a useful, practical guide for you in managing difficult behaviors across various situations and in a variety of relationships that are often seriously impaired by ADD behavior. It is not intended as a substitute for therapeutic involvement, although the book may certainly complement many therapeutic programs. For many parents this book may become your sole guide to organize and plan for the management of ADD behavior. For others, it may be a good starting point for direction and support in your initial attempts to understand and more effectively manage ADD behavior.

Grad L. Flick

PEANUTS reprinted by permission of United Feature Syndicate, Inc.

How to Use This Book

My initial recommendation to parents is that before you attempt to make any changes in the manner in which you deal with your child's behavior, you first: (a) have a thorough understanding of the behavioral techniques you will use, and (b) understand some of the possible problems or reactions by your child to these changes in your interactions. Only when you are well prepared in these two areas can you expect positive results in the "long run." I emphasize "long run" since initially your child's behavior may—very often—become worse when you change how you react to the child. After all, he or she is accustomed to dealing with certain expected consequences; when you react differently, the child may be confused, shocked, even angry. Don't be surprised by any of these reactions to your changing the way you deal with your child's behavior.

Following are a series of twelve steps for you, the parent, to follow to help obtain desired results for your child and for you in successfully managing your child's difficult behaviors.

STEP 1 It is important for you, the parent(s), to read the entire book before attempting to make any changes in how you manage your child's behavior, even if your child lives with you and his or her other parent does not but shares custody. Ideally, both parents should be comfortably familiar with the behavioral procedures, understand how to use them effectively, and be willing to integrate these procedures in his or her relationship with the child. It is also best that both parents use the procedures consistently across time (and distance, if that is the case) and for there to be consistency in interactions with the child from both parents.

STEP 2   Fill out the Home Situations Questionnaire (see Appendix D) to determine in which situations the child's problem behaviors are most liable to occur. It will be much easier to deal with problems that are more restricted to one situation (e.g., only at home) compared with those that occur across a wide range of situations. Noting frequency of these problem behaviors is also important.

STEP 3   Separately, list the child's undesirable and desirable behaviors. Unless some of the child's undesirable behaviors are a danger to others, to property, or to the child him- or herself, it is best to focus initially only on two or three minor problem behaviors in order to establish some success with the implementation of these new behavioral techniques. You may be surprised that once success is felt, even with minor behavior changes, some of the other more difficult behaviors may actually be easier to deal with. Very often the child's desirable behaviors are ignored when there are many undesirable behaviors, so include the desirable ones for balance. Some of these desirable behaviors may actually be alternatives to the undesirable behaviors.

STEP 4   Realize that to modify your child's ADD behavior, it is essential for you to change your behavior in the process.

In this step you may decide to: (a) focus on more positive behaviors in the child, (b) set up a more structured environment with regular routines, posted rules, etc., and/or (c) decide to be a better role model for the child.

After deciding generally how you will begin to deal with your child's behavior, decide which changes you, as parent, are willing to make and write these down, too. Clearly it would be difficult for your child to learn self-control with regard to temper outbursts if you, as the parent, react to life's frustrations by screaming and/or being physically destructive. Now, while in this planning stage, write down these changes you plan to make in yourself, for though it is easy to remember these intended changes in yourself, over time you, too, will need reminders. Anyone who has tried to change a habit knows quite well that ongoing support and cues help reinforce these conscious changes.

Last, you may decide to be much more careful in terms of what TV programs or movies you allow your child to watch. This step obviously could be continuously reevaluated and revised.

STEP 5   Now select some of the specific techniques you wish to implement to change the unacceptable or inappropriate behavior. As Step 3 states, it is easier in the beginning to focus initially on a minor behavior change and reinforce it, for the success tends to beget more success. Then, after success is experienced by both you and the child, in this fifth step many parents select Time Out, Behavior Penalty, Ignoring, and Overcorrection for the more difficult-to-manage behavior problems. As you will learn when you read this book, physical punishment will not be endorsed.

STEP 6   You must also decide on which procedures you will use to develop or strengthen acceptable or appropriate behavior. These techniques may include Time In, Point Systems, Modeling, and Grandma's Rule. It is most important for the parent to develop a balanced system where much attention is devoted to establishing and strengthening alternative appropriate behavior, while in the process of controlling or getting rid of inappropriate behavior.

STEP 7   Once you have decided on those behavioral procedures to use for both rewards (for acceptable behavior) and punishment (for unacceptable behavior), you must review these procedures again, this time in writing. Divide a page into two columns and list in the left column any problem reactions you anticipate may occur and in the right column state exactly how you would deal with each of those problem reactions. For each anticipated problem reaction, there should be a solution. This solution may be a comment (e.g., "broken record" on the rules) or it may be another procedure (e.g., refusal to go to Time Out results in more minutes and ultimately could result in a behavior penalty). Also discuss any potential unique reactions to your new way of handling the problem behavior and what your strategy may be to such a unique reaction from your child. Planning ahead to be fully prepared makes good sense.

STEP 8 Introduce the procedure to the child by explaining the specific (problem) behavior(s) you are concerned about and how you plan to deal with these behaviors from now on (include appropriate/desirable behaviors as well as inappropriate/undesirable ones). Don't "surprise" the child with a new and different way of handling (reacting to) his or her established problem behavior(s). In fact, rehearsing the procedure to be employed (e.g., Time Out or Time In) now will teach your child what to expect from you when certain unacceptable or acceptable behavior occurs in the future. In this step, be especially careful to address your child at his or her level of understanding.

STEP 9 Now, be sure you have some way of monitoring or recording how well the procedures work and begin implementation of the behavioral program you have planned. If you have selected a point system, you will have such a record on the sheet used to track the points. For other procedures you may want to keep a kind of "diary" that records the date a given procedure was used, the circumstances (e.g., fight over Nintendo™ game), and any problems/successes encountered in using that procedure. Over time you may make a calendar for a specific behavior to show whether its frequency is decreasing, increasing, or remaining about the same. This type of information will be very useful in making decisions about any revisions or changes in your program. Last, perhaps about two to four weeks later, you may complete the Home Situations Questionnaire again and compare these responses with your first ones. Again complete the Home Situations Questionnaire at the end of eight weeks.

STEP 10 If your behavioral program is successful, then you should continue to use it and gradually allow it to be incorporated into a more natural, unstructured system. For example, on the point system, if the child receives points for some desirable behavior (specifically alternative to some inappropriate behavior), you may begin to give verbal praise along with the awarding of points, thus pairing praise with points for the good behavior. Gradually, the child may be weaned from the formal program (using the chart) so that you simply use praise without "points" (but with an occasional additional reward) to maintain the new level of the desirable behavior. Note well, though, that if you, the parent, become lax and return to earlier, unsuccessful ways of dealing with behavior (e.g., using critical comments), then the alternative to the desirable behavior may again surface. It is important for you to remember that when you get improvement (i.e., more desirable behavior), you maintain it with periodic reinforcement (i.e., praise or other rewards).

However, if the program is not succeeding, then it will be necessary to analyze it and determine what mistakes were made in carrying out the procedure. For example, one parent, after putting his child in Time Out, continued to lecture the child for the entire time. Obviously Time Out was ineffective under these conditions. To get clues as to what mistakes were made it will help for both parents to re-read the section of the book on that procedure and then jointly discuss their observations. Perhaps there was no mistake but that the wrong procedure was selected for this child. Perhaps instead of using Time Out, only threats were made to use it—a big mistake! Should you encounter continued problems it will be best to discuss these with a therapist skilled in dealing with ADD behaviors.

STEP 11 Continue to periodically review the procedures in this book even after you have successfully implemented them over a period of six to twelve months. *Remember that over time all learned skills deteriorate if they are not practiced periodically, and some variations will inevitably occur in how you implement the procedures. So even if implementation is successful, re-reading the book will refresh your memory and help keep your techniques consistent over time.*

STEP 12 This book will be used best by most parents who have an ongoing relationship with a therapist skilled in the management of ADD behavior. This book is not intended to be a substitute for therapy, nor is it totally comprehensive so as to usurp the need for professional consultation. In fact, during the course of maturation, many ADD children will encounter situations that will make them prone to more serious psychological problems. Such problems will then perhaps require other medical interventions and/or psychological or psychiatric consultation. So, even if you are initially successful with some of these behavioral techniques, don't hesitate to consult a professional regarding more serious problems that are beyond the scope of this book.

Remember, take one step at a time toward your goal and begin with Step 1: Read the book first! Next, read the section on Model Behavioral Programs to get an overview of how the behavioral procedures may be used for specific problems. After this, read and review the techniques discussed in the book. At this point you will be ready to look at how to deal with your child's behavior.

Model Behavioral Programs

F irst, you, the parents, should become very familiar with the behavior management techniques explained in this book. Then you should be prepared with ways to deal with the problems that may arise from the use of these techniques. **Only then** should you make changes in how you deal with your child's ADD behavior (as explained in the 12 steps described in "How to Use This Book").

Two specific case scenarios illustrate model programs that utilize some of the procedures described in this book. It is important to read these "simulated" cases so you can get an overview of how the techniques and procedures explained in the book can be successfully integrated into your child's and your family's daily life routines. (Read, but don't make any changes yet!) After you have read this section, follow the 12 steps, reading the book through in its entirety. Finally, come back to this section and review these model programs/cases again. (Note that although these scenarios represent probable "real life" situations, any seeming similarity to actual persons and/or situations is purely coincidental.)

These two case scenarios are representative of children at preschool age and children at mid-elementary school age who have demonstrated behaviors that are difficult (if not seemingly impossible) for the parent(s)—and for the child—to manage. The techniques and procedures

Model Behavioral Programs

illustrated do not represent a simplistic, right/wrong approach to managing behavioral problems. There are no "right/wrong" approaches—only effective and ineffective ones; and there are often several effective ways of dealing with any behavior. Many parents have been very creative in setting up lasting, successful behavioral programs for their ADD children and, using the guidelines set forth in this book, you can, too!

CASE #1: PRESCHOOL CHILD

Mother's name: Mary X

Child's name: Brent X, age 4 years

Brent's mother approached the pediatrician for help dealing with Brent's problem behaviors and the pediatrician recommended a consultation with a psychologist, noting that, This is a young child who is "out of control." What can you offer this mother and child?

During the initial meeting with the mother, she relayed to the psychologist that Brent had always been "strong willed" and often greatly defiant even very early in life, but that he had become even more openly defiant and had shown excessive temper outbursts since his parents' divorce. Mrs. X stated, "I've tried everything, but nothing seems to work." However, "everything" consisted mainly of simply scolding and yelling whenever Brent misbehaved and sometimes just threatening him with punishment. She reported very little structure in their daily routine (although she seemed to have been unaware of this lack of structure until that very moment), and that Brent basically controlled most situations in their lives with his misbehavior. After Mrs. X completed a series of questionnaires, including the Home Situations Questionnaire (found in Appendix D), inappropriate behavior was noted in several situation types including: while playing with other children, during meals, getting dressed, with visitors, in public places, and at bedtime. Some of Brent's more severe behaviors included hitting and biting other children, actual refusal to dress, resistance during meal time, interrupting with visitors and while on phone, throwing temper tantrums, running off while in shopping centers, and resistance to a regular bedtime. All these behaviors were generally categorized as follows:

Aggressive: Hitting and biting others and temper tantrums

Passive/Aggressive: Resistance to dressing, mealtime, and bedtime

Manipulative: Interrupting

Impulsive: Running off to first distraction

In this case, it was important for Mrs. X to focus on positive behaviors while she also dealt with negative ones. However, some of Brent's negative behaviors could become quite dangerous, so Mrs. X first started to address his aggressive behaviors.

Regarding Brent's **hitting and biting** *(Aggressive Behaviors),* Mrs. X employed the Time Out technique. Brent was a bright child who understood quite well when his mother explained this process to him at his level. She told him what would happen whenever he would hit or bite another child; and she even went through a "dress rehearsal" with him so there would be no surprises to Brent when she began implementing this new procedure in their daily routine. When Brent hit or bit he would be taken to sit in a straight-back chair for four minutes (length of time correlated to his age in years), and a kitchen timer was used to keep time. The chair was placed where Brent could not have access to anything that might be construed as rewarding (TV, etc.). He would be told, "That's a Time Out for hitting (or biting)," and was taken to the chair very quickly. In this way, he got immediate, specific feedback on the reason for the Time Out. Initially he showed some resistance; on a few occasions his mother even had to hold him gently in the Time Out chair until he settled down and completed Time Out. However, within a short time, Brent surprised his mother and basically complied. When Brent completed his Time Out of four minutes, he was asked why he was sent to Time Out. If he could not say, he was told the reason (i.e., because you hit John). No further lecture was delivered as Mrs. X had done in the past for she had learned not to give Brent any type of attention for that misbehavior after the Time Out. In the past, Mrs. X had spanked Brent for such undesirable aggressive behaviors like hitting or biting; she realized from her own experience that spanking was ineffective and perhaps even created more trouble for her and for Brent. She made a conscious decision to eliminate spanking as punishment and to utilize the newly learned effective technique of Time Out for managing these problem aggressive behaviors.

Mrs. X. did not just use Time Out with Brent for his *aggressive behavior*. She also wished to strengthen more appropriate alternative behavior. Thus, whenever Brent was playing cooperatively and sharing his toys with playmates, Mrs. X would go over and put her hand on his shoulder saying, "I really like the way you've been playing with John. How about a little treat?" In the past, whenever Mrs. X had noticed Brent playing cooperatively with another child, she would hesitate to say anything fearing that he might just "start something."

Brent's **temper tantrums** (also *Aggressive Behaviors*) occurred when he "didn't get his way," and were mostly characterized by yelling and thrashing about. To deal effectively with Brent's temper tantrums, Mrs. X decided she would ignore the temper tantrums and felt she could do so with some preparation. First, she would tell herself that she could expect the tantrums to get worse before getting better. Second, once she decided to ignore these types of tantrums, she would be consistent and not give any attention to Brent during these yelling and thrashing-about tantrums. However, she was aware that Brent was quite clever at gaining attention and when he got frustrated at getting no reaction from her, she felt sure that he would "do worse things" to get his mother to "give in to him." Nonetheless, in order that she stay focused on something other than Brent's tantrum, Mrs. X used some of the self-affirmations she had learned (e.g., "I know his behavior is going to get worse; I know he wants me to give in; and what I need to do is to continue to think about me being in control. I need to keep reading this magazine. Actually I know I am not going to get anything out of my reading, but I need to continue concentrating on this magazine."). This self-talk would go on throughout the time of the temper tantrum. Thus, once Mrs. X had prepared herself for the temper tantrums, when one occurred she "simply" (to all appearances!) "weathered the storm." The first time Mrs. X used this technique, Brent became exhausted and, though he had still had a temper tantrum, a different problem behavior was helped: he presented no difficulty at bedtime. Mrs. X noticed that the next few temper tantrums became weaker and shorter, and Brent began having them less and less frequently.

Mrs. X dealt with ***interrupting,*** a *Manipulative Behavior,* basically the same way by using the "ignoring" procedure; however, she also incorporated a Token System, another technique she learned to use. To create opportunities for Brent to learn to better deal with this undesirable interrupting behavior, Mrs. X arranged for a friend or a relative to call her when Brent was around. (These calls were staged such that no actual important conversation took place. Thus Mrs. X could offer to keep ignoring Brent's interrupting while she carried on this "staged call.") Prior to actually carrying out this procedure, however, Mrs. X explained to Brent that it is not proper to interrupt while she is on the phone or while talking to visitors. She further explained that, "When you wait until I'm finished to ask your question, then you will get a chip for your chip bank." (This "Token System" of behavior management will also be used for other behaviors by Mrs. X and will be explained at that point.) For interrupting, Mrs. X decided: (a) to give no reward for Brent's interrupting behavior, so she actively ignored the interrupting; and (b) to reward his appropriate behavior with a chip and verbal praise, "I'm really proud of you—you waited until I was finished talking on the phone to ask your question. Let's put this chip in your chip bank." Obviously, Mrs. X decided that these staged phone calls should be very short (e.g., 30 seconds at first, then up to 60 seconds). Gradually, she also had others call her for varying lengths of time beyond 60 seconds. She found the ignoring technique, combined with a Token System, very effective in helping Brent not to interrupt her anymore. She also found she was pleased with herself for learning this effective technique and being willing to put it into practice and experience smiling success.

Whining during dressing, ***dawdling*** during meals, and ***yelling*** and ***complaining*** at bedtime are all examples of *Passive/Aggressive Behaviors.* Many of these behaviors are also *Manipulative Behaviors* and are quite resistant to change since they do often garner much attention. To deal with these passive/aggressive and manipulative behaviors, Mrs. X decided to employ the Token System again. She first explained and modeled (showed Brent) exactly what she expected him to do, i.e., what the appropriate behaviors were in each given situation. Then she explained the way the Token System would work in these areas. Then she implemented the Token System to deal with these behaviors.

Basically, chips (poker chips or other plastic chips from a school supply house) were used as the tokens. Brent was given a jar, about pint size, and was told that he would get chips (one each) for appropriate behavior during each situation. These tokens were then traded for some privilege. Thus, he received one token for:

❑ *dressing* without whining (he did need some help)

❑ *eating* without dawdling (some leniency was allowed initially)

❑ *going to bed* without complaints by 8 P.M.

Both Mrs. X and Brent would take the earned token to the jar, and Brent would put it in. A trip to a pizzeria cost 10 tokens initially; after a few weeks, the cost was increased to 15 tokens. Brent was able to reach the initial goal with no difficulty; he also continued to progress as the same goal required more tokens.

An example of *Impulsive Behavior* for Brent was **running away** from Mom while shopping. While Mrs. X often explained the danger of running away from her while shopping, this seemed to do little to keep Brent by her side; and screaming, spanking him, or threatening him were not only ineffective, they were extremely frustrating for both her and Brent. Several approaches, new to Mrs. X and Brent, were then used to change this undesirable impulsive behavior. (As with the "staged" phone calls, these "shopping trips" were not for actual shopping but simulated situations in stores used by Mrs. X to help Brent learn to stay by her side.) First, Brent was told that he could have a little prize (cost, about $.50) by staying by his mom during a shopping trip. Basically, this is a "response/cost" procedure where Brent could only lose his prize by running away. His mom would already have bought a $.50 toy car she would take with her. Immediately after the shopping was over (and in conjunction with using this technique, Mrs. X limited her shopping time to brief periods), Brent would receive the car.

In the past, Mrs. X had gone on *extended* shopping trips and thus made it more likely that Brent would "do something" (e.g., run away) to create some excitement and, in effect, get her to leave in disgust. Note that during this behavioral program, though, Mrs. X decided to train Brent initially to exhibit the desired behavior (stay by her side while she shopped) for *short* times (e.g., 10–20 minutes), gradually learning to show this newly learned desirable behavior in increasingly longer time periods, extending her shopping time to 30 minutes and perhaps ultimately to 45 minutes.

Mrs. X also used another level of the Token System, preparing some smaller tokens (e.g., small pieces of brightly colored cardboard) to give Brent as he was at her side. Every other minute or so Mrs. X would give Brent a small cardboard token to put in a kind of pouch or money belt around his waist. Every five tokens he would get could be later traded for one large token. Each time Mrs. X would give Brent a cardboard token she would comment, "I like the way you're staying by my side." She was very careful to be very specific in what she said. Instead of just saying, "You're a good boy," she told him *exactly* what she liked about his appropriate behavior, i.e., that he was abiding by the rule.

After Brent was successful in getting his prize (after shopping), she would ask him, "Okay, Brent, what did you do to get this little car?" If he did not verbalize the answer correctly, Mrs. X would tell him, "You stayed by me while I was shopping." She would also add, "I am very proud of you—you did exactly as I asked. We'll count your tokens when we get home and see how many chips you've earned."

In this case, Brent had the prize up front; he could only lose it. If expectations are not too great, the ADD child responds quite well to this type of system. On the positive side, Brent got "small tokens" that counted toward his larger ones at home. Mrs. X had set up Brent's program so that he continued to be successful and he continued to earn chips and privileges.

For the entire duration of Brent's program and in all behavioral areas, Mrs. X was generally very positive. She gave Brent bonus chips for good behaviors as well as for improvements in his behavior. This means that she didn't wait for him to show "perfect behavior" to get a chip. If he handled something better in the face of frustration or made even gestures of sharing with other children, this was time for verbal praise and a chip. Mrs. X followed the general behavioral principle of "Try to Catch Him Behaving Appropriately."

Mrs. X kept track of Brent's tokens for each behavior listed as well as for his bonus chips. She thus had a good record to show his improvement. When she again completed the Home Situations Questionnaire, she was also able to see clear changes in the severity of behavior problems over time. Brent showed dramatic improvement just within a period of several weeks.

Parents will often ask, "Isn't giving prizes just like bribery?" The answer is no. First, the prize isn't given to your child with a "promise to behave." That never works. It's like you allowing your child to eat dessert and then expect him or her to eat dinner. Second, bribes are most often given to persuade someone to do something illegal or immoral. Here the parent was only asking for better behavior (i.e., a good objective). Third, the parent knows quite well that he or she will not continue to "give prizes" for each appropriate behavior. At some time, the child is weaned from this program. At that point, verbal praise that had previously been paired with the tangible rewards (i.e., prizes) will be sufficient. In the weaning process, the child may be told that he or she may expect a prize some of the time but not every time. A gradual change is then implemented (i.e., every other time, every third time, etc.) until there is a random pattern such that the child then never knows when he or she may get a surprise. (Yes, random reinforcement works well; consider all the people playing slot machines over and over! The winning pattern is random.) In the prior example with Mrs. X and Brent, frustration tolerance was gradually extended. Also, Brent got fewer cardboard tokens and alternately all tangible tokens/rewards were phased out with only verbal praise remaining.

Brent and his mother—and Brent's preschool teachers and peers—are all living calmer, more satisfying lives now. Mrs. X does not miss work so much, she laughs more often, and she's much more productive on the job!

CASE #2: ELEMENTARY SCHOOL-AGED CHILD

Mother's name: Brenda Z; *Father's name:* George Z

Child's name: Josh Z, age 10 years

Brother's name: Jerry Z, age 12 years

During the initial meeting with Mr. and Mrs. Z the counselor noted that both Josh and Jerry fought a great deal with each other as well as with their peers, both around the neighborhood and at school. Josh's problem behaviors seemed the more serious. He had reportedly escaped through the window of his room at night to stay out late with older boys; he was disrespectful, had a quick temper and was very destructive—breaking dishes, lamps, and one time even punching a hole through a wall with his fist. Josh was large for his age and reportedly "quite strong." Very often Josh would try to get his brother blamed for doing some of these destructive acts. At school Josh had recently gotten into a fight and "stabbed another child with a pencil." He generally performed poorly academically, didn't finish his work, and often blurted out answers in school. At times he also became the class clown. Josh was known to have a short attention span and was also quite overactive; he walked around the class and talked excessively. There was a consistent flow of behavior reports sent home; and Josh was often "retained" at recess and got many detentions and suspensions throughout the early grades.

When Mr. and Mrs. Z completed the Home Situations Questionnaire, they noted problem behaviors during play, at mealtimes, while watching TV, in public places, doing chores, doing homework, and in the car. These problem behaviors were itemized and included the following:

1. fighting with sibling

2. fighting with peers

3. name-calling

4. cursing

5. yelling in public places

6. destructive of property

7. failure to do homework

8. failure to do chores

9. creating an uproar in the car

10. disrespectful to adults

Josh did require a combination of medications to address his ADD characteristics as well as his overly aggressive behavior. His parents were well aware of the seriousness of Josh's problems and consideration was given to hospitalization. However, initially, short-term trial on medications with behavioral therapy was decided upon. Should there have been no improvement within three to four weeks, the issue of hospitalization was again to be considered.

Josh showed some significant initial improvements with medication alone. However, many of the aforementioned behaviors continued, albeit in a milder form, or somewhat less frequently in occurrence.

Fighting with Brother, Jerry

Mr. and Mrs. Z agreed that if the *aggressive* acts could be directly observed, then the child who started the aggression would be put in Time Out. The child would quickly be asked to "Go to Time Out for hitting" and a timer was used and set to 10 minutes (close enough to each of their ages). If the initial aggressor (i.e., a parent did not observe the initial part of the fight) could not be determined, then both boys went to Time Out in different places. For Josh, the bathroom seemed to be the best place; for Jerry, in the hallway. When the timer rang Josh or Jerry (or both) could come out and had to state why he was sent to Time Out. When both were punished, it eliminated the kind of "detective work" needed to determine "who started it." In most cases it's impossible for a parent to tell anyway. In the past, Mr. and Mrs. Z often automatically assumed it was Josh, and he would always get the punishment. This often contributed to some jealousy since Josh often concluded that since Jerry very often "got away with things and didn't get punished," Jerry must be the favorite child.

A Home-School Behavioral Program Was Established

Fighting with Peers was monitored by Josh's parents using a daily behavior report (i.e., a Home-School note). Items for the teacher to check were: (1) Class work Completed; (2) Stayed in Seat; (3) Kept Hand/Feet to Self; and (4) Raised Hand Before Speaking. Each item was rated "yes" or "no" for the morning and the afternoon periods. There was also a place on the form for the teacher to indicate any Time Outs or detentions given. At the same time Josh was put on a Point System behavioral program at home to monitor and track those behaviors (from his Home-School note) as well as other additional behaviors including: (5) Doing Homework; (6) Finishing Homework; (7) Doing Chores; (8) Playing Cooperatively. Fines (i.e., loss of points) were assessed for failure to show the appropriate behavior in class and for (a) name-calling and (b) cursing. Yet, the Point System allowed Josh control by being able to earn points for the appropriate and desirable behavior—or choose to lose points (i.e., fines) for exhibiting inappropriate or undesirable behaviors. He was required to earn points each day for daily privileges (e.g., watching TV, using phone, etc.) and could save leftover points for the weekend (in addition to any bonus points he might also earn on the weekend).

Much verbal praise was given for good behaviors as well as for any improvement in a given behavior. Bonus points were given for spontaneous good behavior and for acting differently in a situation than he had in the past (e.g., a situation that might have triggered name-calling and did not was cause for bonus points).

Josh was also taught some unique words he could say whenever he got frustrated and angry, e.g., "Glunk!" Other ways of expressing his anger in non-destructive behaviors (e.g., hitting his pillow) were offered to him as well as other techniques he could use to dissipate his anger (e.g., counting to 10, taking three deep breaths).

Overcorrection/Restitution. These techniques were used to deal with some of Josh's destructive behavior. Since being on medication, Josh was not nearly so aggressive as he had been. Yet, he still tended to act out some anger by slamming doors. Whenever this happened, Josh's father would have Josh go out and come back in the door without slamming it 10 times *(overcorrection)*. He explained this simply as Josh's apparent lack of knowledge about the correct way to enter the house and that what was needed was to simply practice the correct way a number of times. Since this type of behavior was disrespectful and, in the past, had resulted in damage to property, Josh was asked to also pay *restitution* for his actions. In this instance he was asked to perform an extra chore (*not* one from his brother's list) for one week. Failure to perform the extra chore would incur loss of allowance and privileges for one week. Josh rapidly learned to be more aware of how he would enter the house and close the door, and he rarely lost his allowance.

Extra chores were also assigned if Josh was disrespectful to a parent. He would also be asked to practice the appropriate verbalization 20 times (*overcorrection*). Thus, if he told his mother, "Give me a soda!" in a demanding voice, then he would need to practice the appropriate way to ask. Then he would also get the extra chore.

Behavior Penalty. This was used primarily when Josh misbehaved away from home. The penalty was the loss of some privilege that was very desirable for him (i.e., playing Nintendo™). Thus, Josh was told that whenever he teased or annoyed others in the car, or spoke in a "loud mouth" while in public places, he would lose the Nintendo™ game for one day for each incident.

Mr. and Mrs. Z were able to realize, through their learning of these techniques, that in the past, they had been somewhat lax in communicating exactly what the rules and expectations were for their children. After learning behavior management techniques and procedures, they kept the rules simple, few in number, and posted where all could see.

Mr. and Mrs. Z also realized that in the past they had contributed to their children's acquisition of some inappropriate behaviors. Mr. Z openly admitted that he too often cursed and would name-call others. Both Mr. and Mrs. Z admitted that they had also been lax in monitoring TV programs for their children. They were surprised to find that the kids often stayed up and watched late night shows and violent programs on certain channels or the times when Josh would escape to join older boys in their teens, staying up until midnight—all of this occurring after Mr. and Mrs. Z had gone to bed. Appropriate modeling of behavior and coping skills played a major role in Josh's behavior changes.

Last, Mr. and Mrs. Z both became more consistent, handling problem behaviors in the same way. Too often, in the past, Josh could manipulate one parent against the other; now they report, "He hasn't even tried lately."

Of course, Mr. and Mrs. Z have both used "Time In" as much as possible. Here they both go looking for times when Josh is either doing something appropriate or "not doing anything inappropriate." It is at these times that they go over and make physical contact with him. Sometimes it's purely nonverbal contact; at other times, they are very specific in telling him what they like about his behavior and on occasions they simply express their unconditional love. They also use these same techniques in dealing with Jerry as well. Many things have changed: communication has improved, there is greater structure, and far more emphasis on positive behavior. The ratio of positive to negative is at least 10 to 1.

While changes occurred gradually over a period of three to six months, Mr. and Mrs. Z have documented Josh's improvements and are gradually weaning him from some of the more structured behavioral programs. Their entire family has benefitted.

Acknowledgments

Over the many months of work required to finish this manuscript, many individuals contributed—either directly or indirectly—to its production and completion. Without a doubt the most significant contribution was made by Nina Roland, a longtime friend, who not only typed the final manuscript (more than once), but also served as a careful reader, critic, and consultant. It would be difficult for me to think of completing such a project without her assistance. Many thanks also go to my office manager, Peggy Barbeau, for her typing and organizational skills, and to my assistant, Lisa Russell, for her help in information coordination and scheduling. Plaudits to Leo Renaud and son, Bob for special drawings and cartoons. Special thanks go to research assistants Carolyn Hansen, Sheila Robert, and especially Donna Reid for their library research and for their help in setting up the numerous forms, figures and tables in this book. Pertinent comments from Diane Turso and from a consultant reader, Sandra Rief, M.A., have made the technical aspects of writing this book almost easy. And last, I am also most grateful for the exquisite coordination and enthusiastic support from my editor, Susan Kolwicz. Susan has rendered invaluable assistance at every step in the process of creating, revising, and completing this project.

Over the past few years many individuals have significantly influenced the concepts and ideological direction in this book. Certainly, Lynn

Clark, Ph.D., has been a major influence in the area of behavior management; his SOS Program has been an excellent resource for our clinical parenting treatment programs and workshops at the ADD Clinic in Biloxi, Mississippi. I include Dr. Clark's program as a resource reading in this book, and I will continue to recommend it to parents. The works of Gerald Patterson, Ph.D., and Rex Forehand, Ph.D., have had much influence in the behavioral area. Joel Lubar, Ph.D., contributed greatly to my initial orientation to the neurophysiological aspects of ADD; his sophisticated and careful scientific research have been a great source of ideas that continue to directly impact our clinical treatment and research programs.

A very special loving thank you goes to my wife, Alma, who has been a longstanding source of encouragement, offering much nurturing as well as critical comments on the manuscript when needed. Together we have raised our adopted son, Mark, who has ADD (although the concept of ADD was not yet realized at the time we adopted him).

And my last and very special thank you, in fact, goes to our son, Mark. Much of what I have learned about ADD—especially the practical aspects of daily living with ADD—came directly from Mark.

Contents

About the Author   v

Foreword   vii

How This Book Will Help Parents of Children with ADD/ADHD .   xi

How To Use This Book   xvii

Model Behavioral Programs   xxiii

Acknowledgments   xxxvii

1. **Characteristics of Attention Deficit Disorder**   1

Types of ADD: Definitions   3
Other Conditions That May Mimic ADD Symptoms   8
Making a Differential Diagnosis   10
  Background and Developmental History, 10
  Behavior Observations, 12
  Psychological Test Performance, 13
  Rating Scales, 16
Using a Symptomatic Approach   16
Summary of Chapter 1   17

2. Behavioral Determinants **19**

Neurophysiological/Biological Bases 19
   Genetics, 19
   Fetal Alcohol Syndrome, 20
   Neurochemical Factors, 20
   Lead Poisoning, 20
   Food Additives/Allergies, 21
   Other Conditions, 21
"Learning" Additional Problem Behaviors 21
Summary of Chapter 2 24

3. Managing Your Child's ADD Behavior **25**

The Parent-Child Interaction 25
Understanding and Accepting ADD 30
Using the General Behavioral Principles of "A-B-C" 31
Summary of Chapter 3 32

4. Antecedents: What Comes First? **35**

Establishing Rules and Expectations 35
Communicating with Your Child 39
Helping Your Child to Pay Attention 40
Summary of Chapter 4 44

5. Behaviors: A Problem-Oriented Approach **47**

What Is Behavior? 47
Main Areas of Problem Behaviors 51
Summary of Chapter 5 53

6. Consequences: What's Effective and What's Not? **55**

Giving Simple Reinforcement 58
   1. Giving a Positive Consequence: Rewarding, 58
   2. Giving a Negative Consequence: Punishing, 59
   3. Taking Away a Positive Consequence: Punishing, 59
   4. Taking Away a Negative Consequence: Rewarding, 60

Understanding and Using Instrumental Procedures 61
Letting Some Behaviors Become Extinct 62
Using Shaping to Develop New Behaviors 63
Summary of Chapter 6 64

7. Creating Appropriate Behaviors **67**

Problem Areas Facing the Child with ADD/ADHD 67
Modeling Appropriate Behavior 69
Using Differential/Selective Reinforcement 70
Using "Time In" as Well as "Time Out" 70
Summary of Chapter 7 72

8. Removing or Decreasing Inappropriate Behaviors **73**

Selecting Which Behaviors to Change 73
Ignoring the Inappropriate Behavior 74
Managing Behavior with "Time Out" 76
   Outline of Time Out, 78
   Other Forms of Time Out, 79
   Resistance to Time Out, 81
Using Behavior Penalty/Response Cost 81
Being Effective with Grounding 82
Overcorrection: Positive Practice and Restitution 83
Summary of Chapter 8 84

9. Setting Up a Token Economy or a Point System **85**

The Token System 86
The Point System 86
Summary of Chapter 9 89

10. How the Home and School Can Work Together **91**

Creating Contracts 92
Sending School Notes Home to Parents 93
Other Communications between Home and School 95
Transferring Learned Skills from Home to Another Situation . . . 96

Generalization, 96
Transfer of Training, 96
Summary of Chapter 10 97

11. Working with Your Child's Teacher **99**

The Role of the Teacher 100
Suggestions for the Teacher 102
Summary of Chapter 11 104

12. Special Problems for the Child with ADD/ADHD **105**

Dealing with Homework 105
Problems 1, 2, and 3: Assignments, 107
Problem 4: Bringing Materials Needed Home, 108
Problem 5: Taking Hours to Do Minutes of Homework, 108
Problem 6: When and Where to Do Homework, 109
Problem 7: Lying about Homework, 111
Problem 8: Notes from the Teacher, 111
Problem 9: Needing Constant Supervision, 112
Problem 10: Needing Constant Help, 113
Problem 11: Getting Homework Papers Signed, 113
Problem 12: Forgetting Homework at Home, 114
Dealing with Social (Peer and Sibling) Problems 114
Listening, 116
Following instructions, 116
Sharing, 117
Working and Playing Cooperatively, 118
Social Graces, 119
Dealing with Self-Concept and Self-Esteem 120

13. Other Interventions to Use with Your Child **125**

Educational 125
Self-Talk and Self-Instruction, 127
Self-Monitoring, 127
Response Cost, 128
Tape Recorders, 128

Computers, 129
Mnemonic Devices, 129
Speech and Language 130
Pediatric Intervention and Medications 130
Counseling and Other Therapies 134
Individual Therapy, 134
Group Therapy, 134
Family Therapy, 135
Relaxation Training/Stress Management, 135
Activities: Chores/Play 137
Chores, 137
Play Activities, 137
Diet 140
Free Play 141
Family Programs 141
Summary of Chapter 13 143

14. Playing the "Attention Training Game" **145**
What You Need to Play the Game 145
The Parts of the Game 147
Focused Attention (Visual), 147
Focused Attention (Auditory), 149
Sustained Attention (Visual), 149
Sustained Attention (Auditory), 149
Selective Attention (Visual), 150
Selective Attention (Auditory), 150
Alternating Attention (Visual), 151
Alternating Attention (Auditory), 151
Divided Attention (Visual and Auditory), 152
Recording the Child's Performance 153
Summary of Chapter 14 157

15. What Does the Future Hold for the Child with ADD/ADHD . . **159**
Genetic Factors 159
Biological Factors 160

Innovative Therapies 161
   Optimal Arousal Theory, 161
   Biofeedback, 162
   Hypnosis, 163
   Habilitation, 164
   Decision on Alternative Treatments, 166
Will There Ever Be a "Magic Solution"? 167
Summary of Chapter 15 168

16. Final Words for Parents **169**

Suggestions for Parents 170
   Focus on One Problem at a Time, 170
   Have Breaks in Routine Schedule, 170
   Learn Stress Management/Relaxation Techniques, 170
   Daily Affirmations, 171
   Be Assertive, 172
   Join a Support Group, 172
Misconceptions 173
   Misconception 1, 173
   Misconception 2, 173
   Misconception 3, 173
When to Seek Professional Services 174
Summary of Chapter 16 175

References **177**

Appendix A: The ADD Clinic **181**

Appendix B: CH.A.D.D. Fact Sheet on ADD **187**

Appendix C: Information for Teachers **193**

Appendix D: Forms, Charts, and Graphs **203**

Appendix E: Recommended Resources **215**

Appendix F: Glossary **227**

Index **235**

1

Characteristics of Attention Deficit Disorder

onsider a child who is frequently out of his/her seat, running to the teacher, talking out of turn, daydreaming, being easily distracted by whatever happens in or outside of the classroom, fighting with peers and authority over rules and regulations, fidgeting, talking to a classmate, or drumming a pencil on the desk. Such a child may be one of the 3 to 5 percent of school-age children who are described as having Attention Deficit Disorder (ADD).

"What is attention?" may be an appropriate question at this time. When a child is said to have difficulty "paying attention," what does this mean? It sounds like we all know what "paying attention" is all about, when actually, attention is a very complex process that has many components, and any, or perhaps all components, may be implicated in the child's difficulty.

Some of the subtypes of attention have been outlined by neuropsychologists focusing on the remediation of attention disorders. Sohlberg and Mateer (1989) have described several types of attention disorders that would be classified as specific difficulties in "paying attention." The following are adapted from them and include:

1. *Focused Attention*—The most basic form of attention that involves a child's ability to respond to a specific stimulus event (one topic) without a shift in attention.

2. *Sustained Attention*—Reflects a child's ability to maintain attention and persist on task until completion. This would also involve the notion of vigilance and resistance to lapses in attention for an adequate period of time. Further, it is involved in the child's readiness to respond to some stimulus event (i.e., an anticipatory response).

3. *Selective Attention*—Involves a child's maintaining a specific cognitive set in the face of competing distractions. For example, selective attention is involved when the child recognizes that the parent's voice during instructions is the main focus of attention and not others' comments or noises. In the classroom, it is reflected in the child's attention to what the teacher is saying and not others' verbalizations or noises.

4. *Alternating Attention*—Includes the idea of "mental flexibility," as when there is a need to shift attention between tasks that access different modes of information processing or different response patterns. An example would be the student who has to listen to the teacher and take notes at the same time. This situation requires that the child switch from looking at the teacher (processing the information both visually and auditorily) and then transferring it in an abbreviated form through verbal expressive functions in writing. Some continuity of the flow of ideas/words must be maintained so that appropriate concepts, ideas, and facts may be reconstructed in notes.

5. *Divided Attention*—Requires the ability to respond simultaneously to two or more tasks having different demands. This may involve rapid alternation of attention or a somewhat automatic or almost unconscious processing and responsivity on one of the tasks.

A child may have one or more of these difficulties, and there may be different complex neurobiological correlates for each condition. More important, in treatment programs, it is necessary to be as specific as possible in defining and describing the child's problem(s). This will make for more efficient learning and more effective behavioral changes in the child.

A specific attention training program is outlined in Chapter 14. This game-like approach to attention training can be accomplished with a timer and three sets of ordinary playing cards along with a dual cassette recorder.

Types of ADD: Definitions

Basically, there are three main types:

1. ADD with Hyperactivity

2. ADD without Hyperactivity

3. ADD Residual Type, or Undifferentiated ADD

From the 4th edition of the *Diagnostic and Statistical Manual (DSM)* published by the American Psychiatric Association, these definitions have been further modified and are reprinted below:

Diagnostic Criteria for Attention-Deficit/ Hyperactivity Disorder

A. Either (1) or (2):

(1) six (or more) of the following symptoms of **inattention** have persisted for at least 6 months to a degree that is maladaptive and inconsistent with developmental level:

Inattention

(a) often fails to give close attention to details or makes careless mistakes in schoolwork, work, or other activities

(b) often has difficulty sustaining attention in tasks or play activities

(c) often does not seem to listen when spoken to directly

(d) often does not follow through on instructions and fails to finish schoolwork, chores, or duties in the workplace (not due to oppositional behavior or failure to understand instructions)

(e) often has difficulty organizing tasks and activities

(f) often avoids, dislikes, or is reluctant to engage in tasks that require sustained mental effort (such as schoolwork or homework)

(g) often loses things necessary for tasks or activities (e.g., toys, school assignments, pencils, books, or tools)

(h) is often easily distracted by extraneous stimuli

(i) is often forgetful in daily activities

(2) six (or more) of the following symptoms of **hyperactivity-impulsivity** have persisted for at least 6 months to a degree that is maladaptive and inconsistent with developmental level:

Hyperactivity

(a) often fidgets with hands or feet or squirms in seat

(b) often leaves seat in classroom or in other situations in which remaining seated is expected

(c) often runs about or climbs excessively in situations in which remaining seated is expected

(d) often has difficulty playing or engaging in leisure activities quietly

(e) is often "on the go" or often acts as if "driven by a motor"

(f) often talks excessively

Impulsivity

(g) often blurts out answers before questions have been completed

(h) often has difficulty awaiting turn

(i) often interrupts or intrudes on others (e.g., butts into conversations or games)

B. Some hyperactive-impulsive or inattentive symptoms that caused impairment were present before age 7 years.

C. Some impairment from the symptoms is present in two or more settings (e.g., at school [or work] and at home).

D. There must be clear evidence of clinically significant impairment in social, academic, or occupational functioning.

E. The symptoms do not occur exclusively during the course of a Pervasive Developmental Disorder, Schizophrenia, or other Psychotic Disorder and are not better accounted for by another mental disorder (e.g., Mood Disorder, Anxiety Disorder, Dissociative Disorder, or a Personality Disorder).

Code based on type:

314.01 **Attention-Deficit/Hyperactivity Disorder, Combined Type:** if both Criteria A1 and A2 are met for the past 6 months.

314.00 **Attention-Deficit/Hyperactivity Disorder, Predominantly Inattentive Type:** if Criterion A1 is met but Criterion A2 is not met for the past 6 months.

314.01 **Attention-Deficit/Hyperactivity Disorder, Predominantly Hyperactive-Impulsive Type:** if Criterion A2 is met but Criterion A1 is not met for the past 6 months.

Coding note: For individuals (especially adolescents and adults) who currently have symptoms that no longer meet full criteria, "In Partial Remission" should be specified.

Reprinted by permission of American Psychiatric Association: *Diagnostic and Statistical Manual of Mental Disorders, Fourth Edition,* Washington, D.C., American Psychiatric Association, 1994.

When hyperactivity is present, it is difficult to miss such a child as he/she may create much havoc at school and at home. Consequently, this may be the first child to be referred for evaluation and the first to receive help. Without hyperactivity, the child with ADD/ADHD may be misidentified and labeled as "just lazy," withdrawn, "in a dream world," slow, or even "emotionally disturbed."

Recent research evidence indicates that ADD is a physiological disorder characterized by some structural or chemically based neurotransmitter problem in the nervous system. Although the exact underlying cause or causes have not been identified, it appears that this condition is basically inherited, although ADD-like behavior may also be "acquired." In short, structural or physiological differences associated with ADD may be acquired through brain injury, exposure to toxic substances, or as a result of infection with high fevers; these or similar physiological differences may also be inherited. In either case, there seems to be a neurophysiological origin for the behavior and, because it is neurophysiologically based, there is evidence that it will not simply be outgrown with time, unless something happens to change the neurophysiology. In general, this neurophysiological status is characterized by a low level of muscle activity, dry skin, slower brain wave activity across the frontal central regions of the brain, and a tendency to magnify sensory input at the highest level of the brain.

Understanding the neurophysiological characteristics of children with ADD/ADHD allows for a more reasonable explanation of many of their behaviors. Thus, with a low level of arousal (i.e., basically a sleepy state) it is not surprising that many such children are singled out for daydreaming; they are, in fact, simply showing behavior that reflects their physiology. Similarly, when such children are neurophysiologically sleepy, their normal response would be to become more active, motorically, as a form of self-stimulation. Others may use rapid attentional shifts, humming, singing, or other behaviors as a form of self-stimulation. Also, as noted by Lubar (1991) sensory stimuli, like colors or sounds, may not have their normal impact on the nervous system; thus, the child seems to automatically "turn up the gain" on these stimuli, with the result that the nervous system becomes more sensitive. This process would be similar to a tape recorder with voice control. When talking stops, the recorder automatically becomes more sensitive to pick up sounds. When someone speaks after a period of silence, there is often distortion of the voice due to sensory overload. Likewise, this may result in problems when the child suddenly encounters loud sounds or bright lights, such that he/she may show a much more exaggerated "startled response."

Clearly, the child with ADD/ADHD has difficulty in focusing on a specific stimulus, since all stimuli apparently impinge upon his/her senses at once. Such children are unable to effectively "filter out" the background or irrelevant stimuli in order to "focus" on the task at hand. These difficulties generate considerable frustration and tension for the child with ADD and frequently create problems in learning, as well as other behavioral and/or psychosomatic problems. In short, unless tension is released through appropriate channels, there may be an accumulation of stress and, consequently, some internal neurophysiological breakdown (i.e., accompanying stress-related symptoms such as headaches or stomachaches).

The child with ADD/ADHD who develops these stress symptoms, in addition to the other behavioral characteristics associated with this disorder, affects family members, peers, teachers, and others with whom he/she comes into contact. Thus, the child has some specific and powerful influences on parents and teachers. While not all children with ADD/ADHD are alike, some children with the more severe forms (i.e., ADD with Hyperactivity) may actually influence parents, teachers, and other authority figures as to which disciplinary techniques will be attempted. Frequently, parents will comment, "I've tried everything and nothing seems to work." Many admit feeling quite guilty for getting so angry and perhaps using severe physical punishment; some have even stated that, "I just about abused him and he goes back to doing the same thing." At this point, many such parents admit feeling quite helpless and perhaps totally responsible for causing the overall situation, while others seem to blame themselves but only for being unable to manage their child's behavior. Similarly, many teachers admit to feeling quite helpless in dealing with these difficult behaviors.

Basically, both parents and teachers need to understand that many of the behaviors of the child are neurophysiologically determined and, as such, cannot easily be changed. While stimulant medication may change the neurophysiology temporarily, withdrawal of the medication will result in a dramatic return of many of the original characteristics. What seems to work best at the present time is a combination of neurophysiological control, through use of appropriate medication(s), combined with behavior management. At times, there may be nothing that works to completely control ADD behavior, so it is important to recognize and accept this fact. However, use of specific behavior management techniques may greatly help in managing these difficult behaviors both at home and in the classroom.

Other Conditions That May Mimic ADD Symptoms

In determining whether a child has ADD, it is essential to consider other possible diagnostic conditions whose symptoms may mimic those of ADD. Specifically, we may consider *anxiety disorders, depression,* and *conduct disorders* for a comparison of symptoms with those of ADD disorders. For example, in one-fourth to one-third of children with ADD, at least one episode of major depression has been reported during childhood, and anxiety is reported to be as high as 25 percent in ADD children. Also, about one-fourth of those children with ADD have a learning disability. Of those children with dyslexia (a specific reading disability), one-third have ADD. Figure 1-1 compares disorder-specific and overlapping symptoms of ADD, anxiety, depression, and conduct disorder groups. The accompanying chart classifies some of the core symptoms for those particular disorders. (This symptom group is not meant to be exhaustive; it simply provides some comparison and differentiation of the above-named disorders.)

One important factor to consider is that some of the symptoms may be basic or primary characteristics related directly to the neurophysiology of the disorder. Other symptoms may be secondary or tertiary symptoms, representing reactions to the primary characteristics or learned behaviors associated with them. For example, the child who is physiologically impulsive may have difficulty with social activities, such as playing games, because he/she may use poor judgment in games, violate rules and

Figure 1-1.

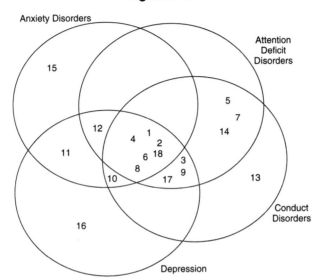

	Symptomatic Behavioral Characteristic	Attention Deficit	Anxiety Disorder	Depression	Conduct Disorder
1	Poor Concentration	X	X	X	X
2	Restless	X	X	?	X
3	Fails to Complete Tasks	X		X	X
4	Day Dreams	X	X	X	X
5	Impulsive	X			X
6	Poor Sleep	X	X	X	X
7	Aggressive	?		?	X
8	Mood Disturbance	X	X	X	X
9	Poor Self Concept	X		X	X
10	Quiet and Withdrawn	?		X	
11	Guilt Over Transgressions		X	X	
12	Memory Problems	X	X	X	
13	Stealing/Lying				X
14	Poor Social Skills	X			X
15	Fearful/Avoidance	?	X	?	
16	Crying	?	?	X	
17	Sensation Seeking (High Risk)	X		?	X
18	Difficulty Focusing on Task	X	?	?	?

Key: X = Symptom Usually Present
    ? = Symptom Possible
    Blank = Symptom Not Usually Present

thereby be unaccepted by his/her peers. Other children may have had poor interpersonal experiences that may have caused them to be physically aggressive towards their peers and, in an indirect manner, to use poor judgment or to violate rules. Children with ADD and conduct disorders or oppositional disorders may show some of the same behaviors, but for different reasons.

Making A Differential Diagnosis

While parents do not need great detail regarding assessment procedures, they should be aware that because of obvious overlap of symptoms at a behavioral level, several sources of information must be considered when a diagnosis is made. The following are important areas to explore in formulating a diagnostic impression:

Background and Developmental History

For some time, ADD was considered a problem that was first seen in the early years and later outgrown; now, it is generally agreed that (inherited) ADD continues throughout life for most people. While ADD is primarily an inherited condition, ADD-like behavior can also be acquired (e.g., head injury), presenting a pattern quite similar to that exhibited when the condition is inherited. Family medical history, including psychiatric conditions on both sides of the family, is clearly very important to consider along with the child's medical history. A child whose parent had ADD could have experienced the cumulative effects of lead poisoning, and thus have "a dual etiology" for the disorder. A history of ear infections, especially with high fevers, may also be a contributing factor. Other possible significant medical conditions for the child include asthma, thyroid dysfunction, hypoglycemia, sleep apnea, encephalitis (brain infection), pinworms, mild brain damage (head trauma), and seizure disorders.

Although the ADD pattern persists throughout life, it may change in the way it is manifested from infancy to adulthood as adapted from Goldstein & Goldstein (1990):

❑ **Preschool** ADD children are impulsive, non-compliant, and may be described as "fearless in the face of danger." Often there are associated speech and language problems, and parents report that normal punishment and rewards seem to be ineffective with this child.

❑ In **middle childhood,** generally between the ages of 6 to 12, many of these children begin to have difficulty completing tasks and exhibit the characteristic inconsistency in work, completing work one day but not the next. The child begins to have difficulty in social situations, seems emotionally immature, and is most often rejected by peers because of his/her inability to cope with rule-governed behavior.

❑ By **adolescence** the child's hyperactivity (if it *was* present) typically subsides, and problems with attention and impulsivity often remain. By this time the child may have had a history of failures in academic performance as well as marked difficulties in his/her social relations. Many of these teenagers may then tend to associate with peers who have similar problems; this often results in escalation of risk-taking behavior. They are certainly more subject to peer pressures regarding the use of alcohol or other addictive substances.

❑ In **adulthood** many symptoms continue; there is a generally higher incidence of problems relating to achievement and vocational/work issues. Psychological problems and marital difficulties are more frequent and about one-fourth may even show antisocial characteristics; about half become alcoholics.

There are several important predictors of adolescent/adult outcomes as has been noted by Goldstein & Goldstein (1990):

a. *Intelligence*—In general, the more intellectual resources, the better the chance for a positive outcome.

b. *Socioeconomic Status (SES)*—The higher the SES of the family, the more likely the person with ADD will follow through with treatment.

c. *Socialization*—The child's ability to develop and maintain social relationships appears quite important.

   d. *Activity Level*—The ADD child with hyperactivity represents a more severe form of ADD that will, at times, result in a poorer outcome.

   e. *Aggression*—This is a factor that is difficult to modify and may place the ADD child at greater risk for alcoholic and/or antisocial behavior.

   f. *Family Mental Health*—This is clearly an important predictor because when the family is dysfunctional, the chance of a poor outcome is higher.

However, studies have found that the single *best* predictor of a positive outcome was having a supportive adult (a parent, a teacher, friend, or counselor) during the early years of development. This adult could therefore act as a buffer to the child's difficulties. Conversely, the single most important predictor for a negative outcome was the presence of early signs of aggression in the child's behavior. One important point needs to be emphasized. Outcomes are not etched in stone at the time of birth for the ADD child. There are many factors that determine the eventual outcome, including unknown or unexplainable changes as well as specific treatment interventions. Thus, in some cases, there is a kind of spontaneous remission. Studies and clinical reports also show that those ADD children who receive both medication (when indicated) *and* a comprehensive behavioral intervention program fared best in eventual outcome as young adults.

Behavior Observations

At times, children with ADD will present an enigma for parents. For example, a child who is frequently running around a classroom, unable to sit still, will sit quietly in a doctor's office or another unfamiliar or novel situation. "Inconsistency" thus appears to be the most "consistent characteristic" of ADD. In natural situations, it is important to recognize whether the child is able to maintain focus on a task or whether he/she appears to attend every sound and distraction. Actually, the term "Attention Deficit" is a misnomer as these ADD children attend to all stimuli "equally." Their problem is one of filtering out background "noise" from important information. This condition presents many difficulties for the ADD child. Thus, the central problem is a deficiency in their ability to selectively focus and maintain their attention.

Psychological Test Performance

There is no one specific test for diagnosing ADD; yet recently there has been a published test entitled "Attention Deficit/Hyperactivity Disorder Test." This test is helpful in gathering and organizing background information from the parents (similar to that obtained from a history) and is based solely on the *DSM* IV criteria; it does not, however, consider the child's performance on various tasks. It should not be assumed, because of its title, that this one test may be used as a sole test for diagnosing ADD. Clinical observation and results of the child's performance on specific tests (which measure verbal, nonverbal, visual motor, fine motor, gross motor, memory, and attentional skills) are also essential for the psychologist in describing the pattern of behaviors that the child presents and in evaluating and forming a diagnosis. Those children who are mentally retarded may have difficulty with attention and concentration; however, ADD is a condition that exists in children of average or above-average intelligence. Some computerized tests of attention are available, providing scores that can be compared with children of the same age (i.e., norms). This can provide some useful information, but certainly should not be used exclusively to diagnose ADD. Many of these computer tests have several components. For example, the Gordon Diagnostic System (1987) consists of three distinct tasks. The *first* measures self-control and is entitled the Delay Task. For this task, the child is told he can press a large blue button as quickly or as slowly as he wishes. He is told that if he presses too fast he will not earn points; but at the right pace he earns a point, and a light comes on each time he presses the button. This provides a description, over a timed interval, of how the child is able to pace himself when he is in control of the task. The *second* task is entitled the Vigilance Task and measures the child's ability to pick out a sequence of two numbers that are repeated periodically during the timed interval. On this task, the clinician is able to determine how well the child is able to accurately pick out the sequences and thus assess any attentional lapses. The clinician is also able to determine how impulsive the child may be by the number of errors he makes during the task. This is especially reflected by the child's rapid pressing of the button when he sees the first number in the sequence without waiting to see if it is followed by the second number. A *third* and similar task is labeled the Distractibility Task. On this task, the child again must pick out the identified sequence (e.g., a five followed by a three), but now there are numbers flashing randomly on either side of the center screen. This is a very complex, high-arousal task that is quite difficult even for adults and may provide important information primarily for older ADD children. Other assessments of attentional behavior have become available more recently and include: (a) "Tests of Variables of Attention" (TOVA) and (b) "Intermediate Visual and Auditory Test" (IVA). Although limited research is available for each of these tests, since they are of recent origin, they may provide greater detail of attentional processes and especially the IVA which has both visual and auditory attentional measures.

One very important aspect of the psychological evaluation is to determine whether the child presents evidence of a learning disability. According to the revised definition of a learning disability by the National Joint Committee for Learning Disability in 1981, "Learning disability is a generic term that refers to a heterogeneous group of disorders manifested by significant difficulties in the learning and use of listening, speaking, reading, writing, reasoning, or mathematical abilities. These disorders are intrinsic to the individual and presumed to be due to a central nervous system dysfunction. Even though a learning disability may occur at the same time with other handicapping conditions (e.g., sensory impairment, mental retardation, social cultural differences, insufficient or inappropriate instruction, psychogenic factors), it is not the direct result of those conditions or influences." In 1987, the report to Congress included "social skills" under the area of significant difficulty.

Simply stated, a learning disability exists when a child fails to learn despite average or above-average abilities. Consequently, there must be a significant difference between the child's ability (assessed by intelligence tests) and his/her academic achievement (assessed by standardized achievement tests). The criteria for this difference, which may vary from state to state, is generally accepted to be at least 15 points, and more typically 20 points, in difference between the child's ability test score and his/her academic achievement in: (a) oral expression, (b) listening comprehension, (c) written expression, (d) reading (decoding), (e) reading (comprehension), (f) math calculation, and (g) math reasoning.

It has been estimated that approximately 10 percent of the population of the United States has a learning disability. Recent reports have also suggested that about 10 percent of these persons also have ADD. However, other reports have indicated that the overlap may be greater and may range from 33 percent up to 80 percent. Like ADD, learning disabilities (LD) also appear to have a neurophysiological basis; yet, unlike ADD, there is no good evidence that medication will aid those children who present only with a learning disability. Basically, learning disabilities reflect deficiencies in information processing, rather than an inability to selectively focus and maintain attention.

Verbal-language dysfunction in the left hemisphere is found in a specific reading disability (dyslexia) and/or spelling disability. Right-brain dysfunction may be reflected in drawing skills that involve visual-motor and visual-spatial components. Math disability may involve greater dysfunction of the right brain versus left brain in young children; in older children, math, too, may become more verbal as the child encounters verbal math problems, and thus difficulty may be manifested by those who present greater dysfunction within the left side of the brain. Neurodevelopmental lags in specific areas of the brain may therefore be associated with either verbal or nonverbal difficulties, or both. Children with right-brain dysfunction may perform adequately in school, while still experiencing problems in math, exhibiting some motor incoordination, or handwriting difficulties. For the child with left-brain dysfunction, school is harder because most academic subjects require that the child be able to read and to comprehend what he/she reads. Those children who experience problems in both left- and right-hemisphere functions may become most severely impaired and many of these students may eventually drop out of school. These types of learning disabilities may become the central focus when evidence for ADD is lacking **or** may become one area of an overall treatment program where ADD and LD co-exist.

Rating Scales

Both parent and teacher rating scales exist. However, the most critical and revealing information may be obtained from the child's teacher, who may be in the best position to rate the child as she/he has more information on behavior at various developmental levels and can compare a particular child to others in the class. These ratings are quite helpful, not only in the diagnostic process, but may also be quite useful in the monitoring phase where the child's progress is noted during various treatment modalities. ADD appears to be a condition that is clearly dependent upon situational factors and expectations in the classroom. As demands increase for the child to "sit quietly at his desk" and "stay on task" to complete assignments, more ADD symptoms may appear for the identified child with ADD. Rules and regulations, as well as demands in the classroom, may bring out ADD symptoms that might have been dismissed in the home situation with comments such as "kids will be kids" or "he's all boy!"

Once all of the above information is obtained, a formal diagnosis may be made by the psychologist and treatment goals established for the child and his/her family. The emphasis must be on the entire family as ADD is not an isolated condition; *all* family members are affected by it.

Using A Symptomatic Approach

The ADD pattern may vary significantly from one child to another. However, when you consider the unique set of genetic factors, internal and external environmental circumstances, and the learning experiences for each child, this is not unexpected. Thus, treatment approaches are often multi-modal involving parents, teachers, physicians, and psychologists, as well as other professionals. Often, it is the psychologist who will coordinate the treatment program and establish the target goals. These target goals of treatment ultimately focus on specific behaviors to be modified or established. These specific behaviors (e.g., impulse control, improved cooperation with peers, staying on task, completing work, controlling aggressive behavior—to name a few) will form the basis of a symptomatic approach to treatment.

SUMMARY OF CHAPTER 1

Most people have no idea of the complexity of the process of "Attention" as it is used in a medical or behavioral sense. Basically, there are five main classes or types of Attention: Focused, Sustained, Selective, Alternating, and Divided attention. According to the DSM IV Manual (the accepted standard diagnostic manual for doctors), there are three basic subtypes of attention disorders:

❑ ADHD, Combined Type

❑ ADHD, Predominately Inattentive type

❑ ADHD, Predominately Hyperactive-Impulsive Type

The physiologically based problem, Attention Deficit Disorder, is primarily inherited, yet some forms of ADD appear to be acquired (for example, through injury to the brain). Nevertheless, the main difficulty for the person suffering from ADD involves difficulty in focusing and not being able to filter out irrelevant stimuli; and this concentration difficulty appears to be associated with a low-arousal state. Since some other disorders—for example, underlying anxiety, aggression, or conduct disorders—often mimic ADD in symptomatology, a trained and experienced professional should make a differential diagnosis. This evaluation process requires analysis of the child's background, developmental history, behavioral observations, psychological test performance, and rating scales completed by the teacher and/or parent. There are many variations of the ADD pattern, and treatment is most effective when it addresses ADD's specific symptoms.

2

Behavioral Determinants

Neurophysiological/Biological Bases

The ADD behavioral pattern appears to be determined by a number of conditions that contribute to the neurophysiology of behavior and the kinds of reactions or learning experiences the child encounters. This is more easily seen in Figure 2-1.

At present, there are only a few ways to modify the neurophysiological factors. Medication appears to be the primary one. Possibly biofeedback, genetic engineering, or some as-yet-undiscovered procedure may be alternatives that will modify our approach to the child with ADD in the future. However, at present, medication may "temporarily" change ADD behavior. The emphasis is on "temporary" because when medications are withdrawn, the behavior returns to a pre-medication level. A brief review of some of the factors that affect behaviors from a neurophysiological level include the following.

Genetics

Research has shown there is a higher rate of ADD in those families where one or both parents have had similar problems.

Figure 2-1.

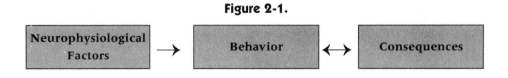

Fetal Alcohol Syndrome

Women who consume alcohol during pregnancy run a higher risk of having a child with ADD, as well as other learning and behavioral disturbances.

Neurochemical Factors

While there is no direct evidence at present, such factors are implicated by the reaction children show upon administration of specific medications. Although no structural abnormalities have been found in gross anatomical studies, there have been suggestions of differences in nerve cell functions in certain brain regions that may relate to ADD behaviors. One study by Zametkin (1990) has reported differences in arousal levels of adult ADD subjects in the way glucose (sugar) is metabolized in more frontal central regions of the brain. Similar computerized EEG studies of brain wave patterns have reported greater slow-wave activity in the same region of the brain supporting a generally low level of arousal or "sleepy state" that is slow to activate.

Unpublished studies by Dr. Grad Flick on a small sample of ten children have also indicated that disorganization of brain wave activity in the more central frontal regions of the brain become more organized and stabilized with the administration of a stimulant medication. Further research with larger samples will, however, be needed before more definitive conclusions can be drawn.

Lead Poisoning

This factor seems to vary with elevated blood levels found in different geographic areas, but can account for a small percentage of ADD symptoms.

Food Additives/Allergies

Originally proposed by Dr. Benjamin Feingold in 1975, these factors were once thought to account for all ADD symptoms. It was believed that through special diets, these ADD behaviors could be controlled. Recent evidence, however, has indicated that only about 5 percent of all ADD children may show a reaction to food additives and dyes. There is some evidence that carbohydrates may be modified by greater protein intake and their ADD effect may thus be lessened.

Other Conditions

An overactive thyroid may produce hyperactive behavior. Also, some seizure disorders may result in periodic attentional problems. Secondary reactions to other medications may give rise to attentional and behavioral problems, especially for children on some asthma medications, such as Theophylline.

With allergies and respiratory problems in general, difficulty in breathing may cause drowsiness. Medications used to treat these problems may open up air passages but may also interfere with attention and concentration. Even some of the over-the-counter medications may cause the child to become drowsy or even agitated and thus exhibit poor concentration and increased activity.

Since many children with ADD have a history of chronic ear infections, their hearing may be affected. Although the child may pass the brief auditory screening test administered in most schools, subtle hearing problems may exist; these subtle hearing defects may be ruled out by a more comprehensive audiological examination.

"Learning" Additional Problem Behaviors

Although ADD behavior appears to be neurophysiologically determined, the consequence of that behavior often results in additional learned components. For example, the child may be told many times to keep away from Dad's tool box. However, upon entering the garage and seeing the tool box, the child immediately becomes interested in the tool box and without thinking of the rule (stay out of Dad's tool box), he gets into it and gets "in trouble" again. When Dad discovers the child has broken the rule again, Dad gives him a spanking. There is a physical-emotional response (pain) from the spanking now associated with this behavior (i.e., getting into the tool box). This does not, however, serve to keep the child out of the tool box as he might do the same thing the very next day. Behavior similar to that illustrated with the tool box behavior becomes extremely frustrating for parents as the child does not seem to learn from his/her experiences. Even though many of these children could state the rule, they simply cannot stop their impulsive behavior. Depending upon their reaction to this behavior, authority figures come to be viewed as being quite mean and punitive. Should this sequence be repeated many times, this component (i.e. punitive response) may become a learned perception and may alter how the authority figure is viewed. This state of affairs may become increasingly worse and further affect the ADD child's

BY THE TIME I THINK ABOUT WHAT
I SHOULDN'T DO—I'VE ALREADY DONE IT!

behavior and relations with many other authority figures. In short, it becomes a generalized perception.

The second example might involve a child in school who impulsively blurts out answers instead of raising her hand to speak. Sometimes comments will be made such as, "Joanie, why can't you ever learn? What's the matter with you?" In time, these reactions may generate thoughts such as, "I must be really stupid—I can't learn to raise my hand before I speak." Thus, over time, a child's self-concept may be affected.

The child showing ADD behavior will often be reacted to or treated differently than other children. Initially, his/her behavior may be dealt with using common techniques. A simple request to stop or change the behavior, ignoring the behavior, or physically punishing it, may simply result in exacerbation of the behavior. This may occur because greater attention may actually reinforce the behavior. Also, physical punishment may provide greater stimulation and cause the child to seek out high-risk or high-arousal situations. Ignoring behavior will certainly result in frustration. For a child with low frustration tolerance, as is true of most children with ADD, this may result in a rapid increase of the inappropriate behavior. Should the child receive attention for this behavior:

❏ he/she will persist for a longer time as the child never knows when attention will come and when the parent will give in

❏ the behavior is reinforced at a higher level of intensity

Thus, not only will the child engage in the behavior for a longer period of time, he/she may also appear to exhibit a more intense form of that behavior.

In short, while the ADD *behaviors* are *neurophysiologically driven*, the *reactions* the child receives will determine the *learned component*. Understanding the nature of ADD behaviors will make a difference in how you treat the child. For example, the parent who sees the child's repeated breaking of a rule as a personal act of defiance may react quite punitively towards the child, using physical punishment. The parent who understands that the child responds on impulse may be less angry and may simply take a privilege away for breaking a rule. As you can imagine, these different reactions will generate quite different perceptions of adults and also teach the child very different ways of dealing with problems. In most all cases involving children with ADD, it is possible to manage the ADD behavior utilizing techniques of behavior modification. These are based on principles of learned behavior. It is certainly possible to alter the child's view of the world, of authority figures, and of himself/herself by giving more appropriate reactions to his/her behavior.

SUMMARY OF CHAPTER 2

ADD has a neurophysiological basis with its etiology primarily in genetic factors. Specific tests of nervous system functioning reveal that there are differences in the brains of those with ADD and that these differences occur in the more frontal-central regions. However, this "difference" does not imply "brain damage." ADD-like behavior can also be created by things like lead poisoning and other environmental factors that affect the nervous system. Often, too, in either instance, there is also a learned component to ADD behavior; but, for the most part, the extent of this learned component depends upon how others have reacted to and interacted with the child. On many occasions in social or school settings, the child may have received negative reactions from siblings and peers and even from teachers and adult friends and relatives; such negative responses can contribute to a poor self-concept and perhaps a generalized perception of others as being "rejecting," "critical," and "mean."

3
Managing Your Child's ADD Behavior

I n order that parents obtain a fundamental understanding of how to manage ADD behavior, there must be a general understanding of the nature of the parent-child interaction process, as well as an understanding and an acceptance of ADD.

The Parent-Child Interaction

Some early research studies in clinical psychology once suggested that more aggressive children tended to have parents who were more punitive, more negative and less affectionate. There was clearly a correlation, but these studies erroneously concluded that aggressive children are that way because of the punitive style of their parents. Likewise, in early clinical practice, many clinicians, when presented with a child for evaluation, would tend to look for what the parents may have done wrong or failed to do in order to account for the child's problems. Then, and even today, many parents are often blamed and held responsible by others for their child's problems. It is not unusual to hear parents report that, "His teachers say I just need to be more firm with him," or relatives state, "My mother tells me I spoil her—she thinks I should not let her get away with all the things she does." Parents also tend to blame themselves when they say, "I know it must be something I've done. My child is not like others in the neighborhood." Such comments frequently lead parents to feel guilty, inadequate and depressed, with low self-esteem where their children are concerned.

Some of these early beliefs reflected the inaccurate notion that there was a *unidirectional* pattern in the parent-child interaction.

This belief placed the responsibility of the child's behavior solely on the parent. Inappropriate behavior was thus believed to be a reflection of inadequate parenting.

Today, we realize that a *bi-directional* view of the parent-child interaction is more accurate.

In this model, the *child* may have just as much an effect upon what discipline the parent uses as does the parent. Interactions are thus reciprocal. Within this model, which was originally proposed by Dr. Russell Barkley (1981), we can at any point in time view the outcome of the interaction as a function of the **constitutional, genetic, emotional, environmental,** and **learning factors** that abide in *each* person, parent, and child. This makes the nature of each interaction more complex and more difficult to understand. For example, it has already been noted that parents of children with ADD are more likely to show adult characteristics of ADD. Consequently, when the child acts impulsively, there may be a tendency for the parent to react impulsively with discipline, or just the opposite may occur if the parent is aware of these impulsive tendencies (i.e., he or she may take "too much time" to react or not react at all). In either case, the child may not benefit. There may be many factors outside of the parent-child interaction that may affect this interaction as has been noted by Barkley (1981). On the parent side, **financial, marital, stress,** and **health problems** may affect how the parent functions. ADD adults are,

for example, more prone to stress-related/emotional problems. Such difficulties may modify the parent's threshold. All parents are aware that
when stressed or drained, they may be less tolerant of a child's behavior
and this may affect their reaction to the behavior. On the child's side,
school problems, peer problems, health, and **stress problems** may
also affect their behavior in the parent-child interaction. For example,
the child who has experienced a fight in school or who was criticized in
class because of his/her behavior may come home with a heightened
level of suppressed anger (i.e., chip on the shoulder) that may be more
easily displaced within the parent-child interaction.

At times, some parents fail to take appropriate action in confronting
their child's behavior due to the following factors that have been outlined
by Lynn Clark, Ph.D., in his book *SOS* (1985) and used here with his permission. Dr. Clark discusses several types of parents who find it difficult
to discipline:

1. *The hopeless parent* believes the child is unable to change his/her behavior. Often this type of parent may have started out ignoring the
   child's behavior before going to more restrictive commands and commands with greater negative affect. With continued failure to achieve
   control, such a parent may have resorted to physical discipline which
   has also failed. Not knowing what else to do, the parent may simply
   have acquiesced to the child's demands and behavior, ultimately lead-
   ing to a state of "learned helplessness." Such a parent can thus note
   the child's inappropriate behavior while commenting inwardly or
   outwardly, "I don't know what to do—nothing seems to work."

2. *The non-confronting parent* may hold the belief that the child will
   not love the parent if he or she confronts the behavior. Often, such
   decisions may center around the parent's own early feelings of being
   unloved or unappreciated.

3. *The low energy parent* may have some physical or emotional problem that "drains him/her of energy." These parents are preoccupied
   with their own problems and do not appear to have sufficient resources to confront misbehavior.

4. ***The guilty parent*** may experience much self-blame for the child's problems and this may prevent the parent from responding. A parent who believes he or she is already responsible for the child's misbehavior may be reluctant to "make the problems worse."

5. ***The angry parent*** may fear losing control of anger that may hurt the child. Often such decisions relate to the parent's own experiences as he or she may comment, "My father really beat me, and I don't want to do that to my child." Unfortunately, some inadequate means of control may be attempted (e.g., shouting) that may do little but give attention and reinforcement to the child's behavior.

6. ***The hindered parent*** may be so affected by what others say about the parent that he or she feels inadequate and lacks confidence in his or her own parenting skills. Many of these parents comment that spouses, friends, or relatives often tell them things like, "You let that kid run all over you. I would never stand for that."

7. ***The troubled parent*** may have personal problems that affect his or her marital relationship or work activity to the point where the parent is unable to devote sufficient attention to the child's problem behavior. Often such parents are inconsistent in how they handle problem behaviors, resulting in confusion on the child's part and lack of learning. Unfortunately, many of the child's problem behaviors may have a direct impact on the marital relationship and the parent's work activity.

Reprinted with permission: "Reasons Parents Don't Discipline" from *SOS! Help for Parents* by Lynn Clark, PhD., 1996, Parents Press.

Spouses often comment that so much time is spent with the child that there is little time for themselves or each other. Other parents note that, "I'm just about ready to lose my job because I have to go to school so often because of my child's behavior."

According to research by Drs. Russell Barkley and Charles Cunningham (1980), mothers of children with ADD tend to act in more negative and direct ways and to be less responsive to their children's good behavior in general. However, when children improve their behavior when taking medications or through other interventions, the mothers became less directive in reducing their commands, and appeared capable of being just as responsive in a positive way as mothers of "normal" children.

Understanding and Accepting ADD

Understanding the nature of ADD behavior is critical for the parent to deal effectively with it. First, it is important to understand that the basic behavior is driven by this child's neurophysiology. This can alleviate much guilt and fault finding, self- and other-blame that many parents look to in their early attempts to deal with ADD behavior. Second, it is essential to understand that the most consistent finding about ADD behavior is its *inconsistency.* Thus, the child's good days and bad days, which may be so puzzling to both teachers and parents, may become more readily accepted. It is not at all unusual for parents to comment that, "His teacher said he did all of his work yesterday, but none today. If he did it one day, she knows he can do it." This inconsistency frequently sets children up for unreasonable expectations because of parents' and teachers' lack of understanding of the child's inconsistent work or behavioral pattern. The child's neurophysiology changes from one day to the next and may be affected by his/her stress events, food and drink intake, sleep patterns, environmental changes, and by both prescribed and over-the-counter medications. Whatever affects the child's neurophysiology also affects his/her behavior.

It is of paramount importance for the parent to learn to distinguish which behaviors are a function of the ADD and related conditions, and which behaviors are not. If a directive is given to a child (e.g., "Pick up your toys and put them in the closet"), and the child fails to do it, you may simply ask the child to repeat to you what you asked him/her to do. If the child is able to repeat the request, this is an example of outright *non-compliance,* **not** *inattention.* Many parents have been told their child is "just a normal child" or "don't worry; the child will grow out of that stage." Others comment that, "Well, the father said he was just like that when *he* was a child, and he'd get a beating every day." Parents are often confused by what others tell them and as a result sometimes deny that their child has a problem. This is indeed unfortunate, as the longer the problem goes untreated, the more difficult it is to deal with it. Older children and adolescents with ADD frequently have many additional problems to deal with including poor self-concept, a long history of failure in school, depression, and, at times, "acting out" of aggressive behavior. Ultimately, this may result in the child dropping out of school or necessitating some type of residential placement to impose limits and control behavior. Early understanding and acceptance of ADD will clearly have a greater effect on the success of treatment. It is critical to know that, at this time, there is no "cure" for ADD. It is a condition that can, however, be managed once it is recognized, understood, and accepted.

Using the General Behavioral Principles of "A-B-C"

If parents have a general background of basic principles of behavior, they will be in a better position to deal with behavior problems, even when faced with the so-called "difficult to manage behavior" of the child with ADD. The basic principles are as simple as A-B-C. Figure 3-1 outlines the sequence used in later discussions.

For appropriate and effective behavior management, it is essential to have a good understanding of these three components. (Chapters 4, 5, and 6 will each deal in detail with one of these three components.) Some behavior may occur capriciously without any apparent cue or trigger. While appropriate consequences are necessary for behavior originating

Figure 3-1.

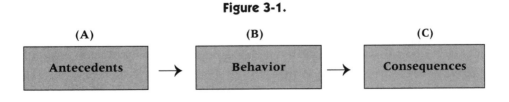

(A)		(B)		(C)
Antecedents	→	**Behavior**	→	**Consequences**

Figure 3-2.

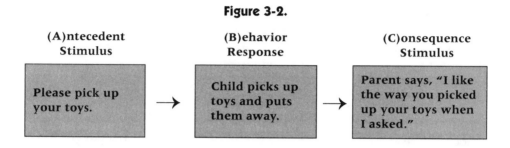

(A)ntecedent Stimulus	(B)ehavior Response	(C)onsequence Stimulus
Please pick up your toys.	Child picks up toys and puts them away.	Parent says, "I like the way you picked up your toys when I asked."

without a stimulus cause, it is equally important to understand how to bring specific behaviors under the control of a specific stimulus (e.g., a verbal request). Once this happens, a learned behavior has been introduced. Ideally, the sequence might go like that shown in Figure 3-2.

As you can see, when this sequence occurs, the sequence may continue with another response from the child, e.g., the child feels good or happy (B), internal response with outward smile, which becomes a stimulus (A) for the parent who also responds (B) with a good feeling and a smile. Even without a technical analysis of this sequence, you can quickly see that more occurs than just a *learned response* to the request. Both child and parent experience good feelings from the interaction. This is in marked contrast to a sequence where a child may experience pain, and the parent may feel anger and frustration over the child's failure to comply. Using the basic behavioral principles in the A-B-C format can lead to enhancement of the parent-child interactions and, over time, to a more positive emotional bond between the parent and child.

SUMMARY OF CHAPTER 3

An important component to understand about ADD is the area of parent-child interactions. We have known "forever" that parents greatly influence their children, and today we realize that kids—including and maybe especially ADD kids—also influence their parents. Particularly when parents are unaware of and uneducated about ADD as a real disorder—and not just a sign of a "bad kid"—parents' reactions and interactions with their child can most certainly be affected, albeit unknowingly to the parent, by the child's presenting (mis)behavior. Parent and child each bring a unique set of factors (genetics, physical, social, and emotional) to their interactions.

You, as parent, must understand ADD behavior and accept it, realizing that ADD is a neurophysiological problem, and that inconsistency in the child's performance is but a recognizable—and sometimes aggravating—outward sign of this disorder. It is, however, important to recognize which behaviors are physiologically based and which essentially represent non-compliance.

An overview of General Behavioral Principles involves three important components: Antecedents, Behavior, and Consequences.

4

Antecedents: What Comes First?

Any successful behavior management program must be based on a good foundation, which requires clear communications and clear-cut rules and expectations. For example, commands or directions given to the child must be clear and concise, and there must be a way to verify that the child understands the message that was sent. If the goal is to foster more appropriate behavior, then it is important that the child clearly understand what rules apply in specific situations and what behavior is expected. Rules and expectations form the most basic part of the foundation for a successful behavioral program.

Establishing Rules and Expectations

Rules are found everywhere. We cannot drive a car, work, or even play games without rules. Yet, in some families, there may be few, if any, rules and they are almost always *implied,* rarely stated or written down. Now sometimes rules will come up during periods of misbehavior. For example, when a child is jumping up and down on the sofa with dirty shoes, a parent may yell, "You know you're not supposed to jump on the furniture. Get off!" The child may comply and smile while getting off, but the incident may be quickly forgotten only to recur within minutes, hours, or days. Other times, a child may be told before going to the shopping mall, "Now, I'll expect you to behave yourself while I'm shopping." The child may comply by shaking his/her head "yes," and the parent unknowingly thinks he or she has a binding contract, only to find that the child misbehaves in every store to the point that the parent has to leave the shopping mall. The parent is now embarrassed, frustrated, and angry, expressing these feelings by pulling the child along, commenting loudly, "I can't take you anyplace—you're such an embarrassment!" Now, in all probability, the child really didn't want to go to the shopping mall and eventually got what he/she wanted; what the parent got was emotionally upset. It is also good to note that the parent's expectations were not clear; what does "behave yourself" mean?

The point is, as parents, you need to establish rules in various situations to let the child know what behavior is appropriate or not appropriate in these situations. What are these situations where rules are needed?

❏ Situations Requiring Rule-Governed Behavior

Awakening	Visiting	Eating
Talking	Dressing	Homework
Bed time	Watching TV	Chores
Playing	Riding in the car	Expressing anger
Being home on time		Greeting others

For example: Consider the child before who was playing on the sofa, jumping up and down. A rule may be stated: "It is appropriate to sit on the sofa; it is inappropriate to jump on the sofa."

Families will differ with regard to which rules they select to formally state or write down and post. Some parents may say, "Well, our furniture is old. I don't really mind our little ones jumping up and down on it." So, what guidelines should there be to establish a set of rules? One guideline might be whether the child would be welcomed to do that activity at a friend's house or if that activity would be appropriate and accepted in the school classroom or lunchroom. Another criterion might be the age of the child. While jumping on a sofa may not be totally inappropriate for a toddler without shoes, it may be considered universally inappropriate for a twelve-year-old just home from football practice. What is being discussed here is the notion of boundaries, or limits, for the child.

Seriously consider the number of rules you set. A child who has fifteen rules to remember will no doubt have more trouble than one who has only two or three. Rules may also change with the age of the child and with the child's limitations. A good starting point would be to write down no more than ten rules, and then select the most important two or three. From this overall list of rules, you may decide which rule is the most important to tackle first.

"Did you 'member to say 'Thank you' and 'I had a nice time'?"

THE FAMILY CIRCUS reprinted with special permission of King Features Syndicate.

❏ Example of Rules for Children

1. Remain at the table while eating.

2. Keep hands to self when angry.

3. Wait turn to talk. Don't interrupt.

4. Remain "quiet." Keep hands to self in car.

5. Keep feet on floor and off furniture.

Rules should be written in large print, and they should be reviewed periodically. At some point, when the child is able to correctly list or state all the rules, you may arrange a special treat as a reward. The message here should be "it pays to know the rules." However, be aware that with some children, especially children with ADD, merely knowing the rules is not always a guarantee for success. Some inappropriate behavior may continue even though a rule can be stated. This should not deter the parent from setting up the rules and periodically reviewing them. In fact, the more structure that can be provided for the child, the better the success with the behavior management program.

Some of the things we expect a child to do may not necessarily involve a rule, but may simply describe which appropriate behavior(s) will be monitored. Different from rules, our *expectations* may involve several components that describe a series of behaviors we expect of the child. For example, we might tell a child, "Now, this is what I expect of you while we are at the zoo. First, I want you to sit in your seat (with seat belts on) to and from the zoo (not climbing on the seats). Second, I want you to hold my hand while we are walking through the zoo (not run away from me), and third, I want you to keep your hands away from the cages (we can't feed the animals)." These expectations will vary with the age of the child and with the child's ability to comprehend and retain what you say. In addition to a review of these expectations, we may also rehearse the expectations by having the child show you how he or she will sit in the car, hold your hand, and keep his/her hands by his/her side, only raising them to just wave to the animals. By rehearsing, you are allowing the child to process the information you give using visual and auditory cues, along with kinesthetic (movement) cues from actually going through the motions of what is expected.

Rules and expectations provide a good structure for the behavior that is to be exhibited. There needs to be good communication between parent and child for the information to be processed. If the child does not get a clear message, he/she cannot make an appropriate response; the child can't "read your mind." While it may seem as though some children may possess an extrasensory dimension, it is best to leave nothing to chance; you simply must express your requests directly and clearly in your communication with the child.

Communicating with Your Child

This may actually be the most crucial aspect of the entire behavioral sequence for children with ADD. Being distractible, many of these children may get only parts of communications and therefore seem to respond inappropriately. For example, if we say to the child, "Get your shoes and put them in the closet," the child may hear "Go get your shoes in the closet." When the child brings you a pair of shoes, you may wonder what is going on. Many children with ADD receive undue criticism and are shamed for such behavior by comments such as, "Don't be an idiot (or a clown). Do what I said!" The child often, in confusion, says, "Huh?"

There are a few basic steps needed to make sure you have the child's attention:

1. Move close to the child and get eye contact. You may gently hold his/her head or shoulders to do this, again depending on the child's age. Too often, directions are given from across the room, making it unlikely that the child will hear all that you say.

2. Speak clearly and distinctly in a normal tone of voice. Most children with ADD are quite sensitive audiologically. They, in fact, may hear sounds that others may ordinarily block or ignore. You don't need to yell; and, actually, yelling may be aversive for the child.

3. Present the command or directive in a simple, concise manner emphasizing what you wish the child "to do." For example: "Pick your clothes up off the floor and put them in the clothes hamper." Avoid giving negative commands (i.e., what you don't want).

4. Verify that the child has heard what you have said by simply asking him/her to repeat what you just said. If the child is able to repeat it, say, "That's exactly right. Now do it." If the child cannot repeat it, give the request again using steps 1 through 3, and again ask the child to repeat it (step 4). If the request is still too complex, you may break it down further into part A (Pick up your clothes) and part B (Put them in the hamper). Each component may be supervised. Thus, "pick up your clothes" (the child gets as many as possible), then, "put them in the hamper" (bring the child to the hamper to put the clothes in). Then the two steps are repeated until the task is complete. Normally, however, it will only require a single statement for each such task.

Helping Your Child to Pay Attention

Parents and teachers say "pay attention" many times with the average child and many more times with the ADD child. What does "pay attention" really mean? (Refer again to Chapter 1.) While many people inherently seem to "know" what is communicated, how can this be explained to the child?

As indicated in the Calvin and Hobbes cartoon, it is sometimes obvious when a child is not paying attention by the position he/she assumes. The child's "body language" gives him/her away, despite the child's attempt to "look good" for the teacher or parent. While it is possible to use some type of physiological monitor to determine when the child is attending (in order to reinforce it), this would clearly be impractical in the home or classroom. There are several ways a parent or teacher could get some estimate; one is to simply ask the child; another is to have the child rate his/her attention on some attention-measuring scale. One such rating

CALVIN AND HOBBES reprinted by permission of Universal Press Syndicate.

device, labeled "The Attention Meter," is provided in Figure 4-1. A similar procedure has been described in detail by Garber, Garber, and Spizman (1990) in their book *If Your Child Is Hyperactive, Inattentive, Impulsive, Distractible.* (No attempt will be made here to explain their procedure. The interested reader is referred to their chapter on "Stretching Attention Span" for details.) The purpose of the procedure outlined here is simply to promote greater *awareness* of the concept of "paying attention" and related issues of distractibility; no attempt will be made here to encourage

Figure 4-1. Attention Meter

Goals   Seconds

10″	20″	30″	40″	50″	60″

(For Stories One Minute of Less)

Goals   Minutes

1′ 10″	1′ 20″	1′ 30″	1′ 40″	1′ 50″	1′ 60″

(For Stories Up To Two Minutes)

Goals   How Well Did You Attend?

1	2	3	4	5	6	7	8	9	10

the child to increase attention span over time. In fact, the most critical measure in this process is how well the child has processed information and been able to answer questions.

Employing the "Attention Meter," the child is given a story to read or to listen to on tape. Remember that children who have difficulty reading will tend to become distracted and will have more trouble answering questions about the story. If there are obvious reading problems, only use the tape version for this task. Using a stopwatch, begin timing when the child starts; temporarily stop the watch each time the child gets off task (i.e., looks around, begins playing with a piece of string, or some other behavior that might affect his/her ability to "concentrate" on the task) and then re-start it when he/she returns to the task. The stopwatch will then show the accumulated time for the child's attention to the story. Selected stories, initially, should be very short (i.e., one to two minutes). Have a few questions (i.e., two to five) available for the child when using stories one to two minutes in length. For each story read or listened to estimate a goal of how long the attention span will be. Encourage the child to set a reasonable goal (e.g., at least 40 seconds on a 1-minute story, or 1 minute and 30 seconds on a 2-minute story). When the goal is set low enough, the success will be optimized. Suggest to the child that goals may be increased with each success. It is also useful to estimate a rating of how well the child thinks he/she can do with regard to his/her attention to the story before (on a 10-point scale) and then again after the story is read (on a 10-point scale). Subsequently, the actual time is recorded. The chart in Figure 4-2 will be useful in monitoring awareness of attention.

At the far right of this chart is a place to indicate how many questions a child was able to answer (e.g., ?/2 for short story, or ?/5 for the longer stories). This will perhaps be the most useful information as the child can certainly be reinforced for improvement in the percentage of correct answers over time. Attention span per se would be much harder to estimate from the child's performance.

A third method is to model the behavior you wish to establish. This alternative procedure, in general, will be covered in greater detail in Chapter 7. In this situation a parent can demonstrate the notion of "paying attention" versus getting "off task" to the child. (See Figure 4-3.) For

Figure 4-2.

Date	Story Read, on Tape	Goal M/S	Actual M/S	Rated *B* Goal	Rated *A* Actual	No. of Questions Answered

("Goal" and "Actual" are to be expressed in minutes and seconds (M/S), "Rated *B* Goal" means the goal before the process; "Rated *A* Actual" means the actual time. These ratings should reflect how close the child actually came compared to the goal he/she set.)

example, a story might be recorded on tape so that the total story time can be determined; the parent could then demonstrate attending by first listening and then periodically engaging in other behavior, e.g., playing with a pencil, looking around the room, etc. It will be the child's task to judge when the parent is attending or not attending. The accuracy of the child's perceptions may be determined by using the stopwatch to time the parent's time "on task" and then calculating the parent's time "off task" by subtracting the recorded time "on task" from the total time of the story (i.e., minutes as indicated).

The child may then reverse roles and it will be the parent's turn to see how much the child is on or off task. Again, this type of exercise with parent and child would be more beneficial in promoting greater *awareness*

Figure 4-3.

Date	Story	Minutes	Paid Attn/Time "On Task"	Did Not Pay Attn/Time "Off Task"

of when the child is attending (on-task) and not-attending (off-task) rather than having the effect of expanding attentional processes directly. Finally, a more direct form of attention training, the Attention Training Game, will be discussed in Chapter 14.

Simply telling a child to pay attention or stay on task does not appear to be effective. If it were, parents and teachers would not need to say that as often as they do. Sometimes, adding a nonverbal component to the attention process may make it more exciting or game-like for the ADD child. For example, when Johnny appears to be "daydreaming" during homework or class work, a parent or teacher might have a prearranged cue to get the child back on task and attending. The child may be told that, "When I tug on my ear that will mean I want you to listen to what's being said." This nonverbal cue may also avoid some embarrassment and self-esteem problems for the child who may get comments to "pay attention" many times during the day. Questions such as, "Now what is it that everyone needs to be doing at this time?" also avoid focusing on one child and stimulate all children to question themselves.

Cues may be provided for rule-governed behavior in many other ways. In addition to posters, notes can be placed in strategic places; a wrist alarm watch with daily reminders can be used; and, there is a nonverbal tactile cue (similar to that of a beeper) that can be set to vibrate at a certain time (the MotivAider®, which will be discussed in more detail in Chapter 14). This device was invented by Dr. Steve Levinson in 1980 and produced by Behavioral Dynamics, Inc., since 1988.

Remember, *antecedent* stimuli are crucial for obtaining appropriate behavior. When the child knows what to do, he/she has the opportunity to do it. Let's move on to Chapter 5 where the focus will be on *behavior.*

SUMMARY OF CHAPTER 4

There are two important components to the behavioral principle of Antecedents: (1) the development of rules and expectations, and (2) communication. Simply stated, specific rules and expectations must be developed by the parent(s), and you must clearly communicate them—

preferably in writing as well as verbally—to your child. Both components are required.

Critical to the child's response is the concept of "paying attention." Attention is very complex, and several training methods are suggested for the child to use to improve his or her attention. Alternatively, you, the parent, may also provide cues for the child in order to initiate or elicit some specific behavior. Either way, it is established that when your child knows clearly what is expected of him or her, only then does he or she have the opportunity to do it.

5

Behaviors: A Problem-Oriented Approach

What Is Behavior?

Once you have more clearly specified "antecedent events" by communicating instructions, requests, or expectations for the ADD child, you will have the basic foundation in place for your behavioral program and can turn your attention to the next component—behavior. What is behavior? Very simply, behavior is what the child does. It is *observable, countable,* and *changeable.* Behavior is *not* what the child doesn't do, i.e., not doing work is not a behavior. "Playing with a pencil" while not doing work might be "the behavior" that is in question. Thus, you will want to keep your focus on what the child is doing and work with this. It is also important to note here that not all children with ADD are alike. The fact that your child has ADD does not specify what problems he/she may have. Thus, you need to differentiate between the *label* of ADD, which is useful for diagnostic purposes and insurance claims, and, more importantly, specify what problems the child presents and work with these behaviors. This approach is "problem oriented."

Behavior can be classified as appropriate or inappropriate; desirable or undesirable. It is often useful to make a list of each category. For example, list one group of behaviors you might describe as "appropriate and desirable." Then make a second list of your child's behaviors that would be described as "inappropriate or undesirable."

Figure 5-1 shows a chart that may be helpful in putting together these lists.

Interestingly, parents often find it much easier to list the undesirable, inappropriate behavior, especially when the child has ADD. Since the perception may be that there is more of the "undesirable behavior" than the

Figure 5-1.   Child Behavior List

Undesirable Behavior— Inappropriate Behavior	Desirable Behavior— Appropriate Behavior
1. _____	1. _____
2. _____	2. _____
3. _____	3. _____
4. _____	4. _____
5. _____	5. _____
6. _____	6. _____
7. _____	7. _____
8. _____	8. _____
9. _____	9. _____
10. _____	10. _____
11. _____	11. _____
12. _____	12. _____
13. _____	13. _____
14. _____	14. _____
15. _____	15. _____
16. _____	16. _____
17. _____	17. _____
18. _____	18. _____
19. _____	19. _____
20. _____	20. _____
21. _____	21. _____
22. _____	22. _____

"desirable behavior," the "undesirable behavior" may be remembered more easily and more vividly. This is unfortunate, but it is reality. Unless you consciously direct attention to the "desirable behavior," it is often overlooked. Generally, "desirable behavior" may be weaker and seen less often, compared to "undesirable behavior" in the child with ADD. Since these "desirable behaviors" are seen less frequently, they are easily overlooked. In contrast, "undesirable behaviors" occur more often and get far greater attention from parents; thus, they are more easily identified. A few of the behaviors in each category are listed in Figure 5-2.

There are many more behaviors that could be listed, but each of these two groups of behaviors will give some sample of the child's social behavior, respect for authority, emotional responses, and attention to commands or requests. For the sample behaviors listed, there are alternative "desirable" behaviors for each "undesirable" behavior. Similar sets of appropriate and inappropriate behaviors could be listed for other contexts (e.g., school and classroom).

In clinical practice, when parents are asked to state the problem behavior their child exhibits, parents often respond vaguely, such as "It's her attitude" or "He's just lazy" or "She's just out of control." The parent should then be asked to clarify, "Well, what do you mean she has a bad attitude?" With some elaboration, the parent may state that the child just "whines and whines when it's time to do homework." More specific

Figure 5-2. Examples of "Desirable" versus "Undesirable" Behaviors

Desirable Behaviors	Undesirable Behaviors
Waits turn to talk	Interrupts others
Helps siblings with tasks	Fights with siblings
Says "Good Morning"	Snubs others
Cares for toys	Destroys toys
Strokes/cuddles pets	Hurts pets
Listens to parents	Talks back to parents
Carries out tasks	Ignores commands

information provides clues to the behavior problem. Most often, the child is showing some type of inappropriate behavior or may not have developed the appropriate behavior for the situation.

Problem behaviors may occur in the following situations:

Home

1. Sibling relations

2. Peer relations

3. Parent relations

School

1. Classroom
   - ❏ Academic work
   - ❏ Peer relations

2. Cafeteria
   - ❏ Eating behavior
   - ❏ Peer relations

3. Grounds
   - ❏ Relationship to objects
   - ❏ Peer relations

4. Bus/Transportation
   - ❏ Safety issues
   - ❏ Peer relations

Outside the Home or School

1. Sibling relations

2. Peer relations

3. Parent relations

4. Safety issues

5. Eating

6. Moral issues

Main Areas of Problem Behaviors

Problem behaviors generally fall into one of four basic areas:

1. Relationship with parents

2. Relationship with siblings

3. Relationship with peers

4. Personal areas pertaining to:
- ❏ Safety
- ❏ Morals
- ❏ Habits (eating, elimination, hygiene, appearance, and dress)
- ❏ Emotional control and expression

For the most part, behavior problems occur in relationships with other people. The most common ones, of course, occur within the parent-child relationship, and the most frequently cited ones in this category would be noncompliance, sassing, and acting-out anger. Within sibling relationships, fighting (mostly over toys and position) is the primary behavior problem. With peers, it is again fighting and failure to "play by the rules" in games and other situations.

Many specific problem behaviors of the child with ADD occur in "personal" areas. There are, of course, problems with compliance and abiding by rules; there are difficulties in all relationships. However, some behaviors are unique. In the area of safety, for example, many children engage in behaviors that are quite risky. These behaviors might include jumping from atop the garage, trying to catch a knife thrown in the air, or holding onto a car to get up to speed while on inline skates. Many of these so-called "high risk" behaviors are dangerous, but do give much stimulation to a generally low arousal level in the nervous system. So, they are sought after by many, but certainly not all, children. In a recent report on TV in a major city it was noted that there had been an increase in the frequency of "surfing" by many young adolescents. Dangerous activities, such as riding on top of a commuter train, riding on the top of elevators, and riding on the top of moving cars, have all increased dramatically as these young persons claim "boredom" being responsible. These activities are all variants of what is called "surfing." Many of these adolescents have died or been maimed as a result of these activities.

In the same way, some "morally inappropriate behavior," such as stealing, represents a high-risk behavior that increases arousal as would lying. In short, there is some degree of excitement in being able to commit these acts and "get away with it." Inappropriate habits centering around eating, elimination, hygiene, appearance, and dress may correlate with the neurological focus in the frontal area of the brain documented in research with children with ADD. With a neurological focus on the more anterior or frontal surface of the brain, ADD children may have more difficulty in these areas of moral behavior. Such behaviors are not totally unlike those of an adult who has experienced brain injury in the frontal areas of the brain and shows some deterioration in specific personality characteristics or who may appear to be generally lethargic and apathetic. Thus, the child may present similar problems from a failure of this area of the brain to develop normally. Similarly, emotional controls are often lacking and, with a low level of frustration tolerance, the child may act out anger inappropriately and impulsively in temper outbursts. Initially, mood changes may be rapid and dramatic, with depression alternating with acting out of anger.

Whatever the category of behavior, it is clear that in order to change it, the behavior must be adequately described, observed, and monitored. The problem is inappropriate behavior; to remove or minimize the problem, you must direct attention to changing the inappropriate behavior. Behavior in which the child is deficient, e.g., where there is a developmental delay or an aspect of neurological immaturity, will be dealt with in a later chapter. In these cases where the appropriate behaviors are absent, there will be attempts made to foster the development of the appropriate skill or behavior. The focus in this case will be adding a "new behavior" instead of changing an "old behavior." Regardless of whether we need to change an old (inappropriate) behavior or develop a new (appropriate) behavior, the consequences that follow behaviors are critically important. Thus, we must now turn our attention to a discussion of the kinds of *consequences* that are available and which ones we must use to change or to develop behaviors.

SUMMARY OF CHAPTER 5

Behavior is defined simply as "what the child does." For our purposes, classifications of behavior are "appropriate" and "inappropriate." Most behavior problems occur in relationships with others (i.e., parents, siblings, teachers, and peers); and some inappropriate behaviors are more serious and may involve dangerous acts, violation of morals, specific habits, or issues of emotional control. To change an inappropriate behavior of your child, that specific inappropriate behavior must first be described, observed, and monitored. (This process of describing, observing, and monitoring also applies in the development of a new appropriate behavior, which oftentimes is an alternative to a given inappropriate behavior.) Regardless of whether a behavior is appropriate or inappropriate, though, the Consequences of any behavior make up the third critical component of the ABC sequence.

6

Consequences: What's Effective and What's Not?

Having discussed *antecedents* and *behavior*, the final main component of the behavioral program sequence, *consequences*, must be considered. At this point, most parents reading this book already know what has *not* seemed to bring about more desirable behavior with their child. This is a little misleading because some of the techniques previously used by the parents *might have worked if they had been properly implemented*. A few words of explanation are obviously in order.

First, many parents state that punishment doesn't work—they've tried it. Well, clearly, *physical* punishment does not benefit the child, but there are *other forms* of punishment that ***do*** *work if used properly and consistently*. What typically happens, though, is that because of the high frequency of inappropriate behavior, correspondingly more punishment is administered in general. There seems to be a tendency for the parent to resort to more restrictive and punitive forms of punishment as well. A child in this situation might best be described as being on a deprivation schedule. Many such children lose so many privileges for so long that

CLOSE TO HOME   JOHN McPHERSON

CLOSE TO HOME reprinted with permission of Universal Press Syndicate.

"punishment" has become a prime source of "attention." Some parents comment that they actually spend more time in punishing situations than in situations that are associated with fun and pleasure. When this imbalance develops and negative attention becomes the prime source of attention, the child may actually resort to an even greater number of inappropriate behaviors simply because there is more attention, albeit negative, associated with inappropriate behaviors. Misbehaving to gain negative attention is not something wished for by the child or by the parent; it simply develops through an escalation of the cycle of inappropriate behaviors and the resulting negative attention that causes more inappropriate behavior and so on. It is clearly not a devious plan by the child who simply craves attention.

Second, many parents talk of using appropriate forms of punishment, for example, "time out," but due to inadequate understanding and training in the procedure, they may inadvertently cause more inappropriate behavior. ("Time Out" will be addressed in another chapter.) Third, many parents say that punishment is ineffective with their child because "he said so." The child may, in fact, state "go ahead and punish me; I'm going to keep doing the same thing. You can't stop me." When parents believe the child and give up on a technique (in this example, punishment), they may simply reinforce the child's *manipulation* of them. Basically, it's not important what the child *says* about whether the punishment works or not, it is what he/she *does!* Change in behavior will, therefore, be the guideline regarding when to modify a technique, not what the child says. Remember the old cliché, "Actions *do* speak louder than words."

The procedures outlined here and in the following four chapters are based on research-tested principles of learning. You will see how new behaviors are learned and developed when they do not already exist to be strengthened (i.e., reinforced) or weakened (i.e., punished). In short, some behaviors will not be found in the child's behavioral repertoire, so they must be established.

By definition, a *reward* is anything that increases a child's specific behavior that preceded it and motivates him/her to continue to respond with increasingly more varied behavior that may be shaped, or to maintain a certain level of a specific behavior that has already been established. A *punishment*, on the other hand, is anything that decreases a child's specific behavior that preceded it and lessens his/her tendency to continue that behavior. In this discussion of consequences, the emphasis is placed on *rewarding* appropriate behavior and *punishing* inappropriate behavior. However, at times, a parent may unknowingly do just the opposite. Since this reversal of the intended use of reward and punishment may adversely affect the child and may actually result in an increase of misbehavior, the following additional clarification is provided.

1. **Rewarding inappropriate behavior**—When a parent accidentally attends to and gives in to the child's whining, this "inappropriate behavior" is strengthened. Simply lecturing the child or stating "it is not nice to whine" will result in more whining.

2. **Punishing appropriate behavior**—As odd as this may seem, parents will, at times, punish a child with negative comments. For example, if a child just cleans up her room without being asked, a parent may say, "Well, you finally did something right. Now, I've got some more jobs for you." It is so important to avoid this kind of backhanded compliment. When such comments are made, they will result in less of the appropriate behavior being shown in the future.

Giving Simple Reinforcement

When a behavior is followed by some consequence that is either positive or negative in nature, the behavior may be strengthened or weakened, respectively. Consider the administration of the following four types of consequences:

1. Giving a Positive Consequence: Rewarding

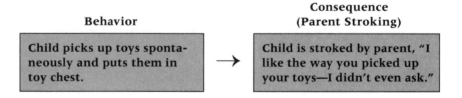

Behavior	Consequence (Parent Stroking)
Child picks up toys spontaneously and puts them in toy chest.	→	Child is stroked by parent, "I like the way you picked up your toys—I didn't even ask."

The child feels good when stroked by the parent, and this positive consequence will most likely result in an increase in compliant behavior if the consequence (i.e., parental stroking) is consistently applied and all other things remain equal.

2. Giving a Negative Consequence: Punishing

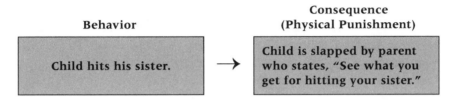

Behavior

Consequence
(Physical Punishment)

Child hits his sister. → Child is slapped by parent who states, "See what you get for hitting your sister."

The child feels pain and may consequently develop several perceptions of the situation:

❏ The child gets the idea that he should not hit his sister.

❏ Adults are mean. They hit you and cause you pain.

❏ Confusion—parent tells me not to hit my sister, yet parent hits me.

❏ I only know what not to do; I really don't know what I should do.

3. Taking Away a Positive Consequence: Punishing

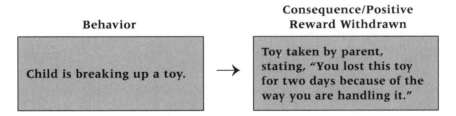

Behavior

Consequence/Positive
Reward Withdrawn

Child is breaking up a toy. → Toy taken by parent, stating, "You lost this toy for two days because of the way you are handling it."

The child is caught breaking a toy, so the parent takes away the toy. If the toy was of some interest to the child (i.e., a positive consequence), its loss would be unpleasant, but mildly so, and the child would wish to get back the toy. It is important here that the child knows the specific reason why the toy is being taken away.

4. Taking Away a Negative Consequence: Rewarding

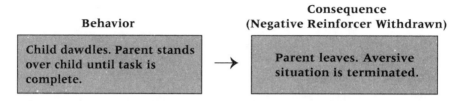

Behavior	Consequence (Negative Reinforcer Withdrawn)
Child dawdles. Parent stands over child until task is complete.	Parent leaves. Aversive situation is terminated.

The child is acting in a manner not conducive to the completion of a chore or task—it could even be a homework assignment. By remaining with the child (i.e., a negative consequence), the parent acts as a mildly aversive or mildly unpleasant stimulus. The child should get a clear message here—complete the work and I will not bother you. It is imperative that the parent remain until the chore is completed. Should the parent leave, the child may begin work, but not complete it, since one of the hallmark features of ADD is that the child may become distracted and will "get off task," resulting in his/her starting but not finishing his/her work or chores. This procedure of removing a negative consequence, because it requires so much of the parent's time, may have only limited usefulness. It is, of course, the easiest to backfire on the parent, especially if the child has become good at manipulating the parent. In this case, the child may simply prefer to maintain the parent's presence through "dawdling" or "helpless" behaviors, rather than finish the work and have the parent leave.

Several general comments are appropriate at this point. First, the number of positive consequences should be far greater than the number of negative consequences. Some say at least five positive for every negative; others suggest ten positive to each negative. Clearly, the positive consequences need to outnumber the negative ones by a far greater ratio during the beginning stages of behavior change.

Second, praise needs to be very specific. Say exactly what you liked about what the child did and avoid the general "good boy" or "good girl" type of statement. It may take some time to get comfortable with this procedure and it will require continued awareness on the part of the parent.

Third, one way to track good behavior and note how it increases is to keep an "appropriate behavior diary." This takes time and effort but the results will be worth it. Many parents otherwise may simply not be aware of their child's appropriate behaviors, as so much attention has been focused on "inappropriate behavior." It is also important here to note even slight improvements, as dramatic changes will not occur that often. Focus on small changes and comment on them saying, "That's one for the book."

Fourth, when a child exhibits an appropriate behavior, the parent can not only specify which behavior he or she liked; he or she can also implant the idea of what feeling should be associated with it. For example, "You should feel very good about the way you helped your little brother clean his room."

Last, parents must be attentive to their child's behavior **and** respond quickly to it. For appropriate behaviors, parents should reward with praise and physical contact (touching the shoulder or back); parents should avoid the mistake of punishing appropriate behavior with negative comments or actions. For inappropriate behavior, mild punishment (time-out/behavior penalty) is due but not physical punishment (spanking). Parents also need to avoid rewarding inappropriate behavior; this happens when they attend to and threaten the child by lecturing or scolding instead of immediately following through with a punishment for the "inappropriate behavior."

Understanding and Using Instrumental Procedures

These are essentially named instrumental procedures as the child's behavior may become *instrumental* in achieving a desirable consequence. This procedure is best known in common sense parenting as "Grandma's Rule," i.e., a child getting his/her dessert after eating the main portion of the meal. This communicates to the child what behavior of his/hers will be instrumental in getting a dessert (a reward). The dessert then becomes a reinforcement or reward for the behavior that led up to it, namely finishing the meal. There are many variations of this procedure applicable to many situations and problems. Some examples are given in Figure 6-1.

Notice that all of these examples are stated in a positive framework. However, many parents may use this in reverse when they say, "If you

Figure 6-1.

First you _____ ,	then you may _____ .
. . . do homework	. . . watch TV
. . . take out the trash	. . . have a treat
. . . clean your room	. . . go out to play

don't clean your room, you won't be able to go out to play." Without getting into a discussion of semantics, it can be flatly stated that **positive statements** are more effective. It is far better to discuss what you **do** want the child to do than what you **don't** want him/her to do. Also, use of the negative approach, beginning with "If you don't . . . ," implies doubt regarding whether or not the child will do what you ask. This is in contrast to stating, "When you do this, you can do that." There is no expression of doubt whether or not the task will be done, only a question of "when." This puts the burden of completing the task solely upon the child. He/she then determines when the most pleasant consequences will occur by his/her "decision" to perform the task. Within this framework, you are thus giving the child responsibility to make his/her own decisions and to understand that he/she is in control of his/her destiny, "at least insofar as the immediate consequences go."

Letting Some Behaviors Become Extinct

Behavior that is undesirable, but does no harm to the child or others, may be best subjected to extinction. Simply stated, when a behavior continues to recur without some form of reinforcement or reward, it becomes progressively weaker until it reaches a point where it will eventually stop. One such behavior that is often used as an example is temper tantrums. Many times such behavior is "purely a show." It often continues because it gets some pay off, i.e., the child gets attention, eventually gets what he/she wants, or noticeably "drives the parents crazy" (a form of retaliation by the child).

One of the classic studies on extinction was published by Dr. Carl Williams (1959). He reported that the identified child had become accustomed to staying up late and getting extra attention because of a short-term illness. Following the illness, the child expected the parents to continue to allow him to stay up late, as well as to give him extra attention at bedtime, making requests in a very demanding manner. When a decision was made to withdraw this attention and to set his bedtime at a specific hour, the child became visibly upset and began to scream and cry. On the first night this occurred, there was extensive crying for a period over several hours. The second night, the child simply went to sleep very quickly—presumably out of exhaustion. However, the crying and screaming continued the third night, but for a lesser amount of time. Over a matter of a few nights, extinction occurred with the crying and screaming behavior dropping down to zero. This also reportedly occurred with no visible emotional scars to the child. Subsequently, no significant fearful, depressive, or aggressive behavior surfaced. Setting firm limits, more desirable behaviors were rewarded and given much more emotional support.

Using Shaping to Develop New Behaviors

Sometimes a behavior does not exist. Here the child may be developmentally delayed in a specific area or the behavior may have been slow to develop because of some physical impairment that prevented the child from making certain types of responses. Shaping may then be utilized to foster the development of new behaviors. Technically, shaping is a procedure where successive approximations to the desired response (behavior) are reinforced (rewarded). Shaping occurs normally in all children; it is used most often in learning basic developmental skills. For example, a child who is learning to talk may say "wa wa" for water. This may initially bring water to her, but over a period of time, the parent expects more and, when the child emits a verbalization that is a closer approximation to "water," she will not only get water, but also more praise.

Often, it is necessary to pronounce the appropriate word for the child so that "modeling" may be used in conjunction with the technique

of shaping. Following the modeling of a word, the child may spontaneously pronounce the word better, and this "new behavior" can be rewarded not only with the desired water, but also with the comment,
"That was much better, the way you said water." Closer and closer approximations to the desired pronunciation may then be encouraged.

This procedure requires much time and patience and the ability to
pay close attention to subtle changes in the child's behavior. It can be
used over a period of time to establish completely new behaviors along
with sensitivity and consideration given to the child's developmental
readiness to acquire these new behaviors.

A second example might involve a social skill often found deficient
in some ADD children, namely "sharing and cooperating" in social play.
Many children with ADD may impulsively grab toys from their siblings or
peers. Demonstration of "taking turns" playing with a toy may therefore
be needed, with reinforcement (reward) contingent upon appropriate
imitation of the behavior that is modeled (i.e., taking turns). Problems
involving social skills will be covered in detail in a later chapter.

SUMMARY OF CHAPTER 6

Figure 6-2 gives you a list of do's and don'ts for reinforcing appropriate
behaviors.

Figure 6-2. Summary of Do's and Don'ts

❏ DO's	❏ DON'Ts
DO provide a consequence (punishment) for inappropriate behavior.	*DON'T* just threaten to use some consequence (punishment).
DO reward appropriate behavior.	*DON'T* punish appropriate behavior.
DO punish inappropriate behavior.	*DON'T* reward inappropriate behavior.
DO reward immediately.	*DON'T* ignore appropriate behavior.
DO punish immediately.	*DON'T* ignore really inappropriate behavior.
DO use mild punishment for inappropriate behavior.	*DON'T* use physical punishment for aggressive behavior.
DO reward with social praise and touch.	*DON'T* use physical punishment for ADD.
DO tell child what you want.	*DON'T* tell child what you don't want.
DO build on small changes.	*DON'T* expect major changes in behavior.
DO be specific about *behaviors* that are liked.	*DON'T* use "good boy/good girl."
DO model behavior you wish to establish.	*DON'T* wait for important behavior to appear.
DO use "Grandma's Rule" positively.	*DON'T* reverse "Grandma's Rule."
DO withdraw attention to some inappropriate behavior.	*DON'T* attend to behavior undergoing extinction.
DO focus on *behavior.*	*DON'T* focus on the *child.*

7

Creating Appropriate Behaviors

A s has been previously noted, the first step in changing a behavior is to have a specific description of the inappropriate behavior and some idea of which appropriate behaviors may be available to take its place. However, not all appropriate behaviors are established in the child's behavior repertoire and readily available. Some appropriate behavior may be occasionally emitted and observed and must be considered weak; others may not have been established at all. So, before we can begin to focus on creating appropriate behavior, we need to know in which behavioral areas the child may be deficient, and then identify those behaviors that are needed to replace any inappropriate behavior.

Problem Areas Facing the Child with ADD/ADHD

Children with ADD have multiple problems that will affect many areas of their life. Characteristic ADD behaviors of most concern are those associated with the child's primary problems. (See Figure 7-1.)

Figure 7-1.

Primary Problem	Characteristic ADD Behaviors	Alternative More Appropriate Behaviors
Attentional Problems/ Distractibility	short attention span rapidly shifting attention gets off task forgets to do tasks	sustained attention focus on one thing stays on task remembers to do tasks
Impulsivity	acts too quickly acts before thinking	delays response(s) thinks before acting
Hyperactivity	is overactive; moves around exhibits excess vocal motor activity	sits still remains quiet
Social Problems	ignores peers, siblings exhibits anger to peers, siblings hogs toys	greets peers, siblings plays appropriately with peers, siblings shares toys
Aggressiveness, Oppositional Behavior	acts out anger is defiant to authority; says, "No!"	controls anger expression is respectful of authority; says, "Yes, sir," "Yes, ma'am."

In dealing with the child, you must first know which behaviors need to be established. Many parents will note many differences among their child and other children of the same age. Some parents note that the child with ADD appears to be behaviorally very much like a younger child, i.e., he/she appears immature. To some degree this is true and has been borne out by research.

Since the characteristic behavior of the child with ADD has primary neurophysiological determinants, it is not easily changed with regard to attention, hyperactivity and impulsivity. However, this does not mean the parent should give up when thinking of creating more appropriate behaviors. There have been many success stories regarding behavioral changes of ADD characteristics. Most times these changes have occurred over a period of time and because they are formed more slowly (in contrast to the changes that are effected by some medicines), *these behavior changes* are not so readily noticed. These changes of ADD behavior through behavioral techniques are much more subtle. There have also been cases where children discover for themselves without direct intervention what works to achieve better self-control or to focus their attention better, and many have become quite successful as adults. A few of the more successful persons who reportedly had ADD include Thomas Edison, Ben Franklin, Ernest Hemingway, and Winston Churchill; there are many more.

For every inappropriate behavior, there is an alternative and opposite appropriate behavior. For example, one of the many problems with sustained attention is that the child may become distracted and get "off task." If "off task" is inappropriate, then the opposite would be "on task." If "reacting too quickly" is inappropriate regarding impulsive behavior, then "delaying response" would be appropriate. The critical factor is to delay responding until some point is reached where the child has sufficient information to make an appropriate response. This comparison would also apply to other behaviors shown in Figure 7-1. For each inappropriate behavior, focus on developing the opposite appropriate behavior. However, in many cases, the question is: How can we go about working with behavior that does not exist?

Modeling Appropriate Behavior

Modeling a behavior may be the first step in creating and developing alternative appropriate behaviors. Many children learn through imitation; it is one of the most basic forms of learning beginning in early childhood. A young child learns to imitate words to pronounce them better; the toddler imitates older children in their activities; and the adolescent imitates the young adult. Sometimes, this imitation may create additional parental stress over the child mimicking inappropriate, undesirable behavior.

Often in the classroom, a teacher may put a student who has poor work habits next to a good student so that he/she may imitate the more appropriate work habits (e.g., staying on task, raising hand to answer, sitting still, etc.). Or, if a child has problems sharing and cooperating, he/she may have to be shown how to act appropriately in this regard. In modeling, the first step is to exhibit the appropriate behavior; the next step is to have the child "do it"—which may be the more difficult part. Occasionally, a child will spontaneously imitate a behavior; more often, it is necessary to encourage and prompt the child to try the behavior.

Using Differential/Selective Reinforcement

Once the behavior has been modeled and the child has either spontaneously shown it, or he/she has shown the behavior at the urging of the parent or teacher, it is then necessary to reinforce that behavior. At this stage, the newly emitted behavior is very weak and, unless there is some reward, the behavior in question may not reappear for a while.

Initially, when the more appropriate alternative behavior is shown, the parent needs to reinforce it with social praise and perhaps some tangible reward (especially if the child is young). Over a period of time, social reinforcement will be most effective. Periodically, some tangible reward should be given again, especially if the child is young (preschool age). Initially, it is important to be *very selective* in giving more attention to this "new behavior." Over time, it will be necessary to reinforce the behavior *differentially,* depending on how well the child shows that behavior.

It is now important to clarify what is meant by *differential reinforcement.* At first, the behavior may not be exactly what is ultimately desired, but it is a starting point. Since behavior will tend to vary over time, the child will exhibit more desirable variations. Those variations that come closer and closer to what is ultimately desired can be selectively attended to and reinforced with comments, such as "You did much better at sharing with your brother." This general procedure would work just as well with the example of "sharing" as it would for "talking."

Using "Time In" as Well as "Time Out"

A relatively new concept called "time in" fits into this framework of developing appropriate behavior. The concept was first alluded to by Dr. Edward

Christophersen in his book *Little People: Guidelines for Common Sense Child Rearing* (1988). It has also been emphasized in workshops presented by Dr. Joseph Olmi (1993).

Basically, it is useful because it stands in contrast to a punishment procedure called "time out." "Time in" refers to an approach whereby the parent states the behavior he or she likes in the child and makes physical contact with the child, putting his or her hand on the child's shoulder. Instead of withdrawing attention and physical contact with the child, these verbal and physical strokes are given freely. In neurolinguistic terms, it is likened to an "anchor." In this context, the "stroke" (putting the hand on the shoulder) provides an anchor for the child when he/she is behaving appropriately. Reportedly, high levels of self-esteem and self-confidence are the direct result of such warm physical contact with the child. With increasing age, and especially in the case of the ADD child where there is typically an increase of inappropriate "difficult" behaviors, there is a corresponding tendency for parents to distance themselves from the child. Thus, for the child, there may be little physical contact except when disciplined. While this may not be true of all children, it is certainly the case for most of those who present with excessive aggressive behavior. Thus, "time in" is particularly suited to the child with ADD and counteracts the excessive negative attention that so often occurs.

Three important points are made by Christophersen (1988):

1. Keep your child close to you so that the "time in" procedure may be possible.

2. Make frequent one- or two-second physical contacts (touching) with the child at any time other than when he/she is engaged in an inappropriate behavior. On a daily basis, this count of physical contacts (touching) should be anywhere between 50 to 100 times (according to Dr. Olmi, 1993).

3. During times when the child is engaged in isolated play, go over and stroke the child without interrupting his/her activity. This procedure helps the parent to increase attention to the child and to literally "catch the child while he/she is being good."

While some children may initially get "off task" when strokes (praise and physical contact) are given, this tendency towards distraction may simply reflect the deficiency of strokes that the child has had for appropriate behavior. In short, the more serious the ADD behavior, the more negative strokes (and consequently the fewer positive strokes) the child will have received. In such cases, the positive strokes may certainly be a "distraction," but one that may simply require a bit more time for the child to adjust. Over a period of time, the child will most likely show a more adaptive and normalized response to such praise and physical contacts.

SUMMARY OF CHAPTER 7

Sometimes desired appropriate behaviors simply are not in the child's behavioral repertoire, and it becomes necessary to create such appropriate behaviors. Behavioral interventions can effect real changes in the ADD child, but such changes occur slowly and generally with quite subtle improvements over time. While creating desired appropriate behavior is oftentimes difficult to accomplish, the results of your patience and efforts can be quite rewarding for you, the parent, and the new behavior of lifelong use for the child. "Modeling" helps develop these types of created new behaviors.

First, just show your child what you wish for him or her to do, and then patiently and consistently encourage imitation of that modeled behavior. Second, you, as parent, can be very selective in reinforcing certain behavior. Rewarding improvements is an excellent way to "shape" various behaviors. The "Time In" concept focuses on positive attention to the child while he or she is "either doing the appropriate thing" or "at least not doing anything that is inappropriate." "Time In" offers you an excellent balance for the often more frequent negative attention given inappropriate behaviors.

8

Removing or Decreasing Inappropriate Behaviors

B ehavior that is inappropriate is clearly unwanted. How to effectively and nondestructively get rid of this unwanted behavior clearly presents a challenge. It is a given that if the behavior is followed by a negative consequence, that behavior will become weaker. One quickly learns to avoid the hot stove after touching it once or twice. However, some children have nervous systems that are lacking specific pain fibers so that information (i.e., negative consequences) about the hot stove may not be present. As you can easily see, such a condition in a child can be very dangerous and the child cannot learn if he/she gets no accurate feedback. When a nervous system is deficient or different in providing information to the child about whether a behavior is appropriate or not, a parent (or significant other) can supply that feedback information to the child.

Selecting Which Behaviors to Change

Which behavior to diminish or eradicate is usually not that difficult to decide. Most parents agree that behavior(s) dangerous to the child or others (e.g., aggressive behavior or "high risk" behavior) should come first on the list. Behavior that is annoying to parents, teachers, and others may be a close second. This latter group may include temper tantrums, annoying noises, gestures and actions, verbal comments such as name calling, whining, back talk, and general noncompliance.

Ignoring the Inappropriate Behavior

One of the simplest techniques to change behavior is to withdraw attention from that behavior. Attention is a critical factor in the developmental history of establishing the behavior in question, as well as playing a major role in maintaining it. Don't be misled; your attention as a parent is extremely powerful, and your child will seek it. As previously noted, your child may get much attention, but for the *in*appropriate behaviors that continue to make them more likely to occur. Some parents say, "I give my child a lot of attention for her appropriate behavior." This may well be true, but if the attention is given to both desirable and undesirable behaviors, nothing changes in the balance of the two. (See Figure 8-1.)

Figure 8-1.

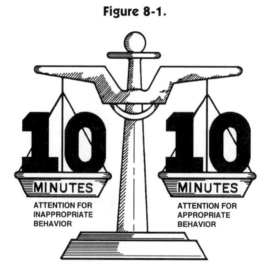

In order to shift attention in the positive direction, parents and others must ignore the inappropriate behavior and attend to the opposite, alternate appropriate behavior. For example, if parents decide to ignore *whining*, they must attend more to when the child *talks normally* in those situations where he had previously whined. If a child whined in the past when he didn't get what he wanted but now "talks" to the parent about when or how to get the desired thing, this is an improvement and should be noted by giving special praise, a treat, and, of course, physical contact. Naturally, when the child asks for something in an appropriate manner, he is more likely to get it. However, if the parent does not wish for the child to have this (appropriately) requested thing, the parent can still reinforce the child for the *manner* in which he asked for that thing. The parent may then elect to let the child know when he *can* have the requested thing.

Ignoring a behavior is not easy. First, the parent must be prepared for what is to happen when a behavior is ignored. Once the specific undesirable behavior is selected to be ignored, the parent must literally talk to him- or herself about the child's reaction. For example, the parent might say, "I know that when I withdraw my attention, Jerry is going to be frustrated and angry, and his whining will be more intense. I'll have to continue to talk to myself so that I don't make the mistake of giving in and paying attention to him."

Second, "I know that once I choose to ignore a behavior, I'll have to *continue ignoring* it until it is under control. If I attend to Jerry while he is engaged in more intense whining, I will simply reinforce it at a higher level, and I'll also be rewarding him for being persistent. This will only serve to establish the behavior even stronger and I'll have an even more difficult time getting rid of it." Keep talking to yourself in a positive way to prevent yourself from falling back into paying attention to the inappropriate behavior. Remember, the child is quite experienced in getting attention from you, and you are quite accustomed to giving it. Change will not be easy.

Third, once you are successful at waiting out the child, it will be important for you to reward *yourself* for your ability to change the way you react to your child's behavior. Thus, say to yourself, "Good. I did a good job of controlling myself and the situation." Also, say to yourself, "I am in control!" These forms of self-talk are important for the parent of a child with ADD because one or both parents may have had a background of ADD problems with difficulty controlling anger and reacting impulsively. It is important for the parent to realize that these cognitive self-talk strategies can play a critical role in dealing with the child's behaviors including his whining, as well as his comments and criticisms.

Managing Behavior with "Time Out"

This procedure has almost ubiquitous status in behavior management. Simply put, "time out" is probably the most talked about, discussed, and broadly interpreted behavioral procedure. It is like the previous principle of ignoring, in that with time out, there is an attempt to remove all forms of reward or reinforcement that may be associated with the child's behavior. Here we are talking about removing the child for a short period of time from all situations where stimuli might reinforce her behavior, like being asked to "sit in the corner."

For example: A child hits his sister. As a result, he is told, "No hitting; go to time out now." The child is told to go to a room that is boring (often the bathroom), and a kitchen timer is set outside the door for several minutes. (The usual criteria is one minute for each year of chronological age. Also, no more than ten words and ten seconds should be used to get the child in time out [according to Dr. Lynn Clark, 1985].) This is important so as to provide an immediate consequence for the behavior. Now, during the time the child is in time out, *no one* should make contact with, talk to, or play with the child. The child is not allowed TV, a toy, or a game to play with while in time out. When the timer rings, the child is made aware that he can come out and resume his activity. However, immediately upon coming out of time out, the child is asked the reason he was sent to time out. If the child can correctly state the reason, he is reinforced with "That's right." If the child can't say, he is given the answer and then allowed to resume his activities. This time out procedure follows closely the steps recommended by Clark (1985).

The following are guidelines for time out:

1. Inform the child about which behaviors will qualify for time out. Specify *acting-out behaviors* as noted in the following Target Behaviors adapted from Dr. Clark's (1985) list:

Hitting others, threats to hit	Throwing objects at others
Temper tantrums	Mistreating, hurting pets
Hostile teasing	Obnoxious, loud crying
Sassy talk, back talk	Slapping
Angry screaming	Pinching
Toy grabbing	Scratching
Toy throwing	Dangerous acts
Destroying toys	Cursing
Kicking others	Pushing others (hard)
Biting, threats to bite	Damaging property
Hair pulling	Mocking parents
Choking others	Loud complaining, demanding
Spitting, threats to spit	Name calling
Persistent interrupting:	Making faces at others
—Adult conversation	Disobeying a command to
—After a warning	stop a misbehavior

Use time out only for behaviors that would be classified/labeled acting-out or aggressive-type behaviors. Whining, pouting, fearful, seclusive, timid, irritable, and grumpy behavior would not be appropriate for time out. Also, it is important to note that failing to perform some chore or forgetting something would not be appropriate for this procedure.

2. Do a "dress rehearsal" for time out. For example, tell the child, "For some time now we have had some hassles over name-calling. This is not much fun for me or for you." Tell the child what you expect of her and say what will happen should she "name call." Direct the child in this little performance. For example, say, "Now, let's suppose you have just name-called. 'Time out for name-calling' is 10 minutes." After the child goes to time out, click the timer to ring the bell. When she comes out, ask her, "O.K. Why did you go to time

out?" If the child can say the reason for being sent to time out, say, "Good, that's exactly right." If not, tell her the reason. This dress rehearsal for time out is very important so that each person knows what his/her responsibility is in the procedure.

Outline of Time Out

Select one acting-out behavior or general noncompliance for the focus or "target" behavior. For example, "hitting a sibling."

Target Behavior. Hitting a sibling

Place for Time Out. Use a place where the child will not get attention from others. Also, try to clean the place of any objects that may be dangerous or may elicit interest. Usually a bathroom, hallway, or corner will be adequate. You should not lock a door on the child or place him in a closet or anyplace where he might become fearful. The door of the bathroom should be left partly open so that the child can hear the timer.

How Much Time in Time Out? The usual criteria is one minute for each year of age (according to Clark [1985]). When there are a number of children in the family for which time out is used, a set number of minutes may be used, e.g., 5 minutes. The time spent in time out should generally not exceed 12 minutes.

How to Measure Time. Use a kitchen timer. The timer removes the parent from the control position. The timer is objective and doesn't forget how long the child has been in the room. The timer can't be manipulated to get out sooner and the timer provides structure for the child. Note that this latter point is in direct contrast to statements parents often make: "You can come out of your room when you decide you can behave." How does one decide when she is ready? Most children would decide immediately. Now, if the child could go through the set of criteria and come up with several solutions to her problem behavior, this may be an alternative to time out and a topic to be discussed in a later chapter. In the beginning stages of the behavior modification program, however, a specific time out should be used.

While in Time Out. Many parents make the mistake of lecturing the child while he is in time out. This simply makes time out ineffective as the child is now getting "attention" for being in time out. When the parent is talking to and looking at him in time out, the child is being rewarded for what he has done. Many threats may be made by the child placed in time out, such as "This doesn't work, you know—I'm not going to stop"; crying or saying, "Something hurts"; or, the ever popular pleading to go to the bathroom (this would not be a problem if the bathroom is used as the time out space). These should all be ignored unless physical danger is clearly present. Should the child act out and become destructive during time out, there must be reparation. The child must clean up any mess he makes and/or reimburse the parent for any damages. Resistance to go or stay in time out will be addressed shortly.

After Time Out. After the child comes out, the only thing the parent should do is ask, "Why were you sent to time out?" as suggested by Clark (1985). If answered correctly, let the child go her way, saying "That's right." If not, tell the child the reason and let the child go her way. Parents need not get the child to promise never to do that behavior again or to sit through a lecture on the "Perils of Hitting Your Sister." This is certainly not the time to do this and maybe there shouldn't be a need for it at all. When a disproportionate amount of attention is given for any behavior, it sends up a red flag to the child: "This is what will really get my parent upset. This is the button to push to really stir up some excitement."

Other Forms of Time Out

Here are additional ways to use the time-out procedure to deal with specific problems, as also suggested by Clark (1985).

Time Out for Toys. When a child is misusing a toy or acting out in a destructive way with the toy, the toy itself can be put into a time out as you say, "It's not right to break your toys. It goes in time out." The toy can then be taken out after a short period of time. For a toy that is used every day, a short period of 15 minutes may be sufficient. Other time outs may range from one day to three days, again depending upon the frequency of use of the toy or interest in the toy and, of course, the age of the child. Obviously, there is a judgment involved here, but the time specified is not that critical, only that it is reasonable and not excessive. In addition, you can always reward good behavior following an infraction with "time off" so that the child might get the toy back sooner. Time off should not, however, be used for any time out of a toy for less than one hour. The concept of "time off for good behavior" may be used when a toy or privilege is removed for more than one hour.

Time Out for Two.   When siblings fight, it would be rare to find only one at fault. It is therefore customary to time out both children using either an *average of their ages* or some pre-set time, such as 5 minutes. This procedure avoids the usual question, "Who started it?" The answer usually received is a unanimous response from both children, "She did," as they point their fingers at each other. It is so important to deal with problems as soon as possible; when time is taken to "try to get to the bottom of the fight," the effectiveness of the punishment (time out) is lost. Also, the parent usually gets so confused that he or she may drop the incident and both kids win by avoiding punishment; however, the parent loses. The guideline is simple: Punish both with time out, saying, "Both of you have a time out for fighting." This denotes physical fighting as an inappropriate way of solving problems.

When both children come out of time out, in addition to asking why they were sent to time out, the parent may inquire, "Now, can you think of any other way you could have solved your problem?" Both Siblings are competing for a "good answer" and to develop concepts of problem solving that do not involve physical fighting. This now becomes a learning situation where you can foster the development of cognitions that will hopefully be able to mediate aggressive behaviors in the future. This is a variant of the technique of "thinking before acting" and a means of controlling impulses.

Time Out for the Young Child.   For children less than two years of age, the same procedure is used; however, instead of sending the child to a bathroom or hall, an upright chair is used, as recommended by Clark (1985).

Resistance to Time Out

A simple solution to a child's resistance to time out is to add additional minutes to time out. If a young child attempts to leave his time out chair, simply stand behind the child and hold him in the chair. Obviously, this procedure would be appropriate for young children only and should not require any excessive force that may injure the child. However, other than saying that when the child calms down and the timer bell rings he can come out, no other statement of "lecturing" or "scolding" should be given. Also, it is clear that you should not look at the child; this is the reason for standing *behind* the chair. Should the child get additional attention or be able to manipulate you into "giving in," you will be faced with an even more difficult and resistant behavior pattern. For the older child you may add one minute to time out for each instance of resistance (also recommended by Clark [1985]), but should not exceed more than five extra minutes. If resistance continues, you may use a *behavior penalty*, where something is taken away from the child. This procedure is discussed in the following section.

Using Behavior Penalty/Response Cost

The last procedure discussed in this chapter is a behavior penalty, sometimes termed *response cost*. This procedure involves taking a privilege away from the child for a short period of time. For example, the penalty for leaving your homework assignment book in school is no TV, or if the child forgets her books, there may be a loss of TV for that night. If a child wishes to *avoid* a homework project, she cannot do it this way, for the privilege of watching TV is not restored until the homework book is brought home with the assignments initialed by the teacher as complete or not complete. This avoids the decision by the child to give up TV for one night for not having to do an unpleasant homework assignment. The assignment must be made up; until this is done, TV privileges are not restored. Be aware, however, that there may be many reasons why homework assignments may be unpleasant and the child would want to avoid one. For example:

❏ They may have too much work (for them).

❏ The child may have a writing problem that makes it difficult to complete long written projects.

❏ The child may also have a learning disability, making it difficult to do math, spelling, or reading homework.

The behavior penalty has some advantages over time out in some situations. When you are outside the home situation, it may be difficult to employ time out. A behavior penalty can be used while riding in a car, in a shopping mall, or visiting a friend's home. It is quick to administer. You must be sure to follow through with the behavior penalty at the first opportunity. If the child gets many behavior penalties, but does not have to serve them, he will quickly realize that he is dealing with a parent who does not mean what he or she says. The parent's words are empty and therefore useless. For the parent who is inconsistent, confusion reigns and learning any basic rules of behavior becomes quite difficult for the child.

Being Effective with Grounding

Perhaps universally known and extremely overused is the technique of *grounding* a pre-teen or teen to the house for days or even weeks. Despite its lack of effectiveness for most teens with ADD, grounding continues to be relied upon by many parents. One of the central problems with this procedure is that the parent must also be grounded to supervise the child.

However, two factors that may improve its effectiveness are: (1) Length of grounding—a weekend or week should be the maximum sentence; and

(2) instead of just having the child "hang around the house," select three extra chores for the child to perform. Once these are completed, the grounding may cease. There are, of course, no privileges (TV, telephone, etc.) allowed during the period of grounding.

Overcorrection: Positive Practice and Restitution

This infrequently cited procedure was originally introduced by Drs. Azrin and Foxx (1977) to deal with toilet training and later was applied to other problems. Basically, there are two stages to this procedure. First, the child is asked to practice a new behavior many times just after having committed the offensive opposite behavior. For example, the child might walk into the kitchen and in a demanding tone of voice address his mother, "Get me a soda!" To teach the child the proper way to ask, the

"All those basketball guys
must've been naughty 'cause
they're all havin' to take
a 'timeout.'"

FAMILY CIRCUS reprinted with special permission
of King Features Syndicate.

mother may have him go out and walk back in to ask, "Mother, may I have a soda?" and then repeat this whole sequence *ten times.* The child is told that in order to establish this more appropriate behavior, he must practice it; thus, the first step is called *positive practice.*

Second, because of the aggressive/demanding tone of voice that was grossly disrespectful to his mother, he is asked to pay *restitution.* The child may then have to perform some added chore or do something special for his mother (e.g., vacuum the whole house or at least a part of it). At this time, the child may repeat his request, "Mother, may I have a soda?" The child will then receive his request. While sometimes difficult to use, this procedure can result in rapid change of even some very resistant behaviors.

SUMMARY OF CHAPTER 8

To remove or decrease inappropriate behavior, a parent may ignore certain behaviors that may be annoying, while using Time Out or Behavior Penalty with those behaviors that may be more difficult to manage and may perhaps involve an aggressive component. It is imperative that you, the parent, be well prepared to handle these difficult behaviors and know what to do when resistance or other complications are encountered. Grounding is one other alternative procedure and is often used with older children and teens. Overcorrection involves the use of positive practice, i.e., repeating the "desired behavior" several times and the restitution that involves a payback for the inappropriate behavior through the child's performance of additional chores.

9

Setting Up a Token Economy or a Point System

he most effective and ultimately successful programs involve a combination of procedures. For example, we have already discussed how punishment alone, even though mild, is never effective by itself. The reason is simple—it just does not tell the child what to do, only what *not* to do! It is imperative that, as parents, you think not only of removing the unacceptable behavior, but also of fostering, developing, and maintaining acceptable and desirable behavior. Here again, you need to think of problem behavior versus alternative good behavior. While punishment is directed to the unacceptable behaviors, you must be developing more appropriate alternative acceptable behaviors through modeling and then subsequent reinforcement. Such programs can be worked out informally or can be set up in a formal manner to address both inappropriate and appropriate behavior, as exemplified in the Token System and the Point System.

The Token System

This system is employed mostly for younger children under 6 years of age as it involves the use of some type of physical token, for example, plastic poker chips, carnival tickets, or colored tokens from a school supply house. When the desired behavior is shown, a token may be given to the child to put in a clear, pint- or quart-size jar. In this way, the young child can see the tokens filling up the jar and know how close he may be to getting the reward (i.e., when the jar is full). The reward may be a trip to a fast-food restaurant, or to the zoo, or whatever else might motivate that child. The behavior specified must be clear to the child (your expectation) and he should receive the token immediately after completing the behavior.

For example, if the desired behavior is the child picking up his toys, then the child must know where to put them. Direct cues or instructions may be given at first, but if the situation is one where the child would routinely put the toys away after playing with them for that day, then only an indirect cue may be needed. The parent may then say, "What do you need to do with your toys now?" This allows the child to develop the thought, "Oh, it's time to put the toys away." Perhaps the child doesn't actually say that to himself, but some type of verbal mediation occurs. This makes the child more responsible for his behavior as he is not simply responding to the parent's request.

What many children do is depend on their parents to give them a signal as to when some behavior must occur. Over time, this behavior, when shown routinely, may appear to become more spontaneous and may be reinforced accordingly. At this time, the parent can say, "Great, you thought of putting your toys away all by yourself; I'm so proud of how you're taking care of that." Later, the word *responsibility* can be introduced as "I'm so proud of how responsible you're becoming. You're really being more grown up."

The Point System

The point system focuses not only on appropriate behavior but also on inappropriate behavior, especially for older children (9 to 12 years of age).

For younger children (6 to 8 years of age), only appropriate behavior may be used in the system, i.e., an entirely positive approach. However, these are only guidelines; a bright 7-year-old may be able to deal with both appropriate and inappropriate behaviors in his/her system.

See Figure 9-1. First, a list of *appropriate behaviors* is developed. These are the behaviors you wish to see more frequently from the child (e.g., brushing teeth, cleaning room, finishing homework, etc.). These are the behaviors that will *earn points* for the child. The *inappropriate behaviors,* also specifically listed, are the ones where the child *loses points* (i.e., he/she is fined). These behaviors include fighting, sassing, name-calling, temper outbursts, etc. Points are kept on a daily basis. With accumulated points, the child will earn privileges (such as TV time, riding a bike, getting a special treat, etc.). See Figure 9-1 for point assignments.

At any time during the day, the child may have access to privileges assuming that she has sufficient points for that privilege. This also assumes that the child has had no serious infraction of general rules. If a serious misbehavior has occurred, there can be a temporary suspension of all privileges, including these on the behavior chart. Points used are subtracted from net points (i.e., points earned minus fines), and the remainder at the end of the day goes into a weekend savings. So each day is a new start. Points do not carry over from the day before. In this way, the child is continually motivated to earn points and avoid fines. Weekend privileges will depend on the child planning ahead to save enough for the weekend. For the child with difficulty in foresight, this becomes a good learning experience.

These programs must be set up carefully and with one criteria—*they must be successful!* If the program is not successful, it must be analyzed to see what the problem is. Then, it can be revised so that it will work. It makes no sense at all to set up a program in which the child will fail because we make it too difficult for him. *Success builds on success.* Failure experiences do nothing but devastate the child's already weak and fragile self-concept. Children with ADD in particular have a high rate of failure in school behavior programs because these programs are set up for the general, normal student; the student with ADD rarely gets the weekend prize and, over time, becomes discouraged, frustrated, angry, and depressed. These children have difficulty completing school work and they

Figure 9-1. Home-School Behavior Chart

Behavior List	Points	Monday	Tuesday	Wednesday	Thursday	Friday	Saturday	Sunday
Total Points								
Points Used/Fines								
Net Points/Day								

Fines List	Points	Monday	Tuesday	Wednesday	Thursday	Friday	Saturday	Sunday
Totals								

Note: For behaviors, assign 1 point each; For fines, assign 2 points each; Keep points for privileges low (e.g. 2–10 points each).

rarely, if ever, get the little prize for a week's work. So, when a program fails, it's not the child who has failed. It is *our failure* to set up the program so that the child can be successful.

SUMMARY OF CHAPTER 9

The most effective and ultimately most successful programs involve a combination of procedures that address both inappropriate and appropriate behaviors. The "Token System" may be most effective for young children in developing appropriate behavior. This system can be combined with other techniques that address the inappropriate behaviors. The "Point System," however, may address either appropriate behaviors only or both appropriate and inappropriate behaviors. When a parent sets up a program such as this, it is crucial for the program to be successful. If you design such a program to be so difficult that the child fails, nothing will be accomplished. Let your child be your guide in establishing programs that will work and give benefit to the child.

10
How the Home and School Can Work Together

W hen parents wish to obtain more rapid behavior changes, or to effect more behavior changes across different situations, it is necessary to extend behavioral programs beyond the home/family situation into other areas. This type of extended program is especially important for the child with ADD. Learning a particular behavior is easier when there are more learning opportunities and when the learning occurs across various situations. The learning is then generalized to an even greater variety of situations. Thus, setting up programs that involve the child's school teachers, day care or after care centers, or recreational centers may have far-reaching effects.

Since the child with ADD has so many behavior problems elicited in the school setting, it is very important to try to involve the child's teachers in a program. This inclusion of teachers may be as simple as checking to see if homework assignments have been copied correctly or turned in. More complex programs may require that the teacher rate the child in several areas, such as class work, behavior, and homework. Some teachers may resist doing any elaborate ratings on a daily basis or even to check homework assignments; however, a parent can certainly request the teacher's assistance in these programs and perhaps work out some compromise. If not a complete rating, then perhaps a simple check of homework assignments at the end of each period can be done. While teachers may sometimes resist completing a rating or checklist, often they may not be aware of how much time may be spent in dealing with the child's problem behavior through other means. For example, talking with the child, parent meetings, discussions in teacher staff meetings, etc., may all require additional time for this one identified child. Thus, it may be advantageous for the teacher to participate in the behavior program if the teacher's time can actually be saved. (This is discussed in greater detail in Chapter 11.)

Creating Contracts

One procedure parents can use in both home and school situations is the *behavioral contract*. While most appropriate for older students and adolescents (ages 10 to 15), it may be used for some brighter younger children as young as 8 years of age. This procedure is really just a variation of "Grandma's Rule" (see Chapter 6). It involves something you wish or expect and something the child wishes to have. It is an agreement between parent and child that is put into writing. A sample form is given in Figure 10-1.

Figure 10-1.

I, _____ (name of the child), agree to

_____ (perform task expected by parent/teacher). In

return, I would like _____ (to have some wished-for

reward).I therefore agree to the contract specified above.

_____   _____

(Parent's Signature)   (Child's Signature)

Perhaps the parent wishes to have the child "take out the garbage on Mondays." In return, the parent agrees to allow the child to "use the home computer for a game for one hour." Often when we use such an example, critics will say, "Well, that's something the child should be doing anyway (referring to taking out the garbage). We shouldn't have to give the child anything." First, there are certainly some tasks that children find distasteful, as do adults. Such tasks may be a little less distasteful if something pleasant is earned. Second, it may be difficult to establish a routine habit with certain activities that are essential, but not intrinsically motivating. To reward such behavior helps the child develop habits that affect organization and neatness. Third, most children, and adults as well, do not wish to perform "work activity" unless compensated for it. One need not use money as a reward, unless the activity in question is one normally included in the child's routine chores.

Sending School Notes Home to Parents

A school note is a form of communication between the teacher and parent. School notes can be incorporated into formal or informal behavior programs. For example, a report is used to show the child's work and behavior during class.

This type of report gives the parent some idea of how well the child did (e.g., staying on task) during class. If the child did well, he/she may have finished his/her work for most assignments, and we could have added another thing for the teacher to check. This type of report also gives some idea about the child's behavior during class. The sample rating sheet shown in Figure 10-2 doesn't specify what behavior the child may have shown or not shown, but again, it does give *some* information; and it is quick and easy for the teacher to use. A very detailed rating sheet could be used if the situation warrants that and if the teacher will use it. Some examples of variations of this form is found in Appendix D. In brief, the rating form is flexible and amenable to change in accordance with the child's needs and the degree to which the teacher is willing to participate in the behavioral program.

Figure 10-2. Sample School Note Rating Sheet

Pupil:			Date:	
Teacher:			Class:	
Circle Appropriate # to Indicate Child's Work and Behavior				
Ratings:	**Excellent** **3**	**Good** **2**	**Fair** **1**	**Poor** **0**
Morning: Classwork *on task*	3	2	1	0
Classroom behavior	3	2	1	0
Afternoon: Classwork *on task*	3	2	1	0
Classroom behavior	3	2	1	0

When the child brings the rating sheet home each day, the information is transferred by the parent to a larger home sheet (i.e., the Home-School Behavior Chart) where points may be given. (Refer to Figure 9-1 in Chapter 9.) To keep it easy, the point values (0, 1, 2, 3) are already on the rating sheet. The better the behavior, the more points. We could also simply multiply by some factor such as 2, to make the difference between an excellent rating and a poor rating even greater (i.e., 6 points versus 0 points instead of 3 points versus 0 points). These behavior ratings could then be part of a list of behaviors at home, as well as at school, that may be put on the Home-School Behavior Chart.

It must be clearly emphasized that it is most beneficial for parents and teachers to keep behavior programs as simple as possible to encourage continued participation. The more complex the system, the more difficult it is to implement it with success. Teachers should have a good understanding of what needs to be accomplished with the ratings and why this behavioral program is important.

An "end of the week" rating sheet may also be considered in lieu of the daily sheet or after two weeks of using the daily sheet. This once-weekly general rating may be used until the program is terminated. A good guideline for termination may be when the goals of the program are accomplished. Of course, the main goal would be general improvement. The parent may elect to terminate the program after about four to six weeks with demonstrable improvement in behavior and/or academic performance. Or, if there is some doubt, the program may be continued until the end of the general (9-week) grading period. This would allow for greater change and also provide some estimate of the consistency of that change. The parent may then elect to give a provisional termination to the program and to utilize some form of behavioral contract to achieve continued motivation—or to simply agree to reestablish the program should the child falter in his/her performance in school.

Other Communications between Home and School

Sometimes it simply cannot be worked out that a school program can be established along with the home program. In such cases, it will be important to arrange a weekly conference (either in person or by phone) with the child's teachers. This would best be done at the end of the week. A judgment, not so good as more objective criteria, can then be made as to whether the child had an excellent, good, fair, or poor week regarding work and behavior. Some positive consequences can then be arranged to reward the child for: (a) continued improvement; or (b) maintaining an excellent, good, or fair status. This is quite subjective, so much leniency must be used.

Specifically, a parent might ask a teacher two questions:

1. How would you describe the child's class work this past week?
   Excellent — Good — Fair — Poor

2. How would you describe the child's behavior this past week?
   Excellent — Good — Fair — Poor

There can be a preset number of points for each rating so that the child can combine his/her points at home and at school to obtain privileges. Basically, the same rating system can be used:

Excellent = 3 points

Good = 2 points

Fair = 1 point

Poor = 0 points

Transferring Learned Skills from Home to Another Situation

As previously noted, one of the main reasons behavioral programs in the home are extended to the school setting is to obtain faster learning so that the child shows appropriate behaviors over different situations. This results in more generalized and stronger behavior.

Generalization

Generalization procedures may take different forms depending on how specific the parents' focus on the behaviors. For example, it is not uncommon for grandparents to be involved in the child's program. Parents may explain the goals of the program as well as any rules involved. One parent may say, "Dad, you know that playing exciting games with Jeff is not going to help him settle down for bedtime. We've found that about one hour before bedtime it's best to have some quiet time, reading or just relaxing. Wrestling or tickling or exciting games or TV shows just get him wound up." Then the parent may ask the grandfather, "Would you be willing to work with us to give him the same experience before bedtime? It will help him learn much faster."

Transfer of Training

Transfer of training is to practice role playing or modeling of a behavior before going into the real-world situation. The situation in which practice occurs should be as similar to the original situation as possible and ultimately practice needs to be held in that original identified situation. Parents have often asked, "Will my child ever be able to sit with us for religious services?" The answer first depends on whether the appropriate behaviors are able to be shown in the home situation. If you can gradually increase the child's ability to behave appropriately, then at some point you can make the training situation (home) more like the identified situation (church, synagogue, or other place of worship). For example, this can be done using a tape-recorded church service. When the child demonstrates appropriate behavior at home with the (taped) auditory cues of the church service, she is ready for the next level. Subsequently, the type of recorded church service may be used in the actual church when no service is in progress. Using the empty church, combined with the auditory cues from the taped service, will be the closest approximation you can get to the actual service. Once the child is able to handle this new level of training, she can then be brought to church with a reasonable time goal to meet. In other words, you should not expect the child to be able to stay in her seat for the entire service. Should misbehavior return, you can simply take the child out of the church. However, it's important to state how long the child was able to stay in church and set a goal to beat for the next time.

You might keep a record on a sheet with goals and sub-goals clearly indicated. A common example used in fund-raising involves a thermometer with marks going up the tube and the ultimate goal at the top. Each time the child reaches the next level, there is cause for some reward. If the church service is 60 minutes, for example, you might mark off the tube in twelve 5-minute segments. Each additional 5-minute goal achieved would then be colored in with a red marker and the reward clearly stated. Obviously, the more difficult (i.e., longer time in seat), the more valuable the reward. During the actual service, the child should also be quietly praised (patting the shoulder or leg and saying, "You're doing a good job of sitting quietly"). Sitting at the back of the church would be most appropriate for this learning to occur.

SUMMARY OF CHAPTER 10

To facilitate behavior changes in general and specifically to modify inappropriate behavior in school, extensions of the Home Behavior Program may be used. First, a Behavioral Contract may be written to establish and clarify agreements between the parent and child. In exchange for more appropriate behavior (which is clearly explained) from the child, specific privileges will be granted by the parent to the child. School notes should improve communication between the school and home and could well become part of an overall behavioral program. In lieu of such a formal communication program, though, you, the parent, may converse with the teacher directly in person or by phone. Last, some specific training may take place in the home situation that should have a direct influence on the type and frequency of similar behaviors in the school setting, resulting in more of the desired behavior(s) in the school environment. This latter procedure utilizes the concept of "generalization" (transfer of learned skills from one environment—the home—to another—the school).

11

Working with Your Child's Teacher

The teacher of a child with ADD can have a tremendous impact upon the child and, in fact, can make a great difference in the ultimate kind of life this child may lead. Studies and anecdotal clinical reports indicate that for the child with ADD who is successful as an adult, the single most important factor is often a teacher who understood the nature of ADD and was willing to adjust the child's academic program to accommodate his/her difficulties. We think nothing of providing special ramps for wheelchair students, allowing crutches on the school grounds, or even providing oral readers for students who have temporary visual problems. All of these allowances are designed to compensate for the child's handicap; it is assumed that when the child no longer needs the crutches or other special assistance, he/she will give them up and go back to a normal routine. However, some children have permanent disabilities and may need special assistance throughout their lives.

We must keep these same accommodations in mind when dealing with the child who has this disorder. First, teachers who are not familiar with ADD should receive the handout on ADD found in Appendix B. Second, parents need to be persistent to get the needs of the child with ADD met. Every child is entitled to an education and the school must, by law, meet the needs of the child with ADD. There are many possible suggestions for the teacher, which are listed in Appendix C.

The Role of the Teacher

Usually, the opinions of the teacher are first obtained by a psychologist or medical doctor during the evaluation process. This information may be obtained by the psychologist who conducts the psychological evaluation or by the medical doctor who may consider whether medication is appropriate for the child. Teachers are asked for their input on various rating scales and questionnaires to help assess ADD characteristics. Most all of these rating scales by themselves have limited value; however, when used in conjunction with other psychological test data and background information, they provide a very important piece of the puzzle, and many of the ADD patterns do indeed present a puzzle. The most difficult part of the evaluation for the clinical psychologist is to differentiate among various other conditions and ADD. The teacher is in a very unique position to provide certain critical data, as the child with ADD may often manifest the most significant ADD characteristics in the classroom setting. This classroom setting, by its very nature and demands, tends to elicit more ADD behavior than most other situations. Therefore, the first role of the teacher is that of *assisting* in the diagnostic process. However, the teacher does not, and should not, diagnose ADD; the clinical psychologist and/or medical specialist (i.e., pediatrician, neurologist, or psychiatrist) determines the diagnosis. It is therefore inappropriate for the teacher to tell the parent, "Your child has ADD. He needs to be on medicine!" What this teacher can say is that, "Your child is having some problems in the classroom that prevent him from completing his work. He has a short attention span, is distractible, disorganized, and often gets into trouble by blurting out answers. I think he has normal or perhaps even above-average abilities, but he's surely not able to fully utilize them. I believe a psychological evaluation and consultation with your pediatrician would be in order." Teachers may thus share their concerns with parents and, should a learning disability be suspected, refer the child to the school team of specialists for assistance in planning how to best help the child. This may mean that an individualized education program (IEP) will be written addressing the child's needs or a special education referral for psychoeducational assessment be made along with recommendations for outside referral to ADD specialists (psychological and medical).

Note that the teacher should refer the child for a psychological evaluation *and* a medical consultation. The teacher, together with the school nurse, may also mention that some medical conditions could account for these behaviors. This covers all possible aspects of the diagnostic process.

It is important to note that teachers are not qualified to state that the child "should be on medicine" or, if on medicine, to "get her on a higher dose." However, the teacher is perhaps best qualified to monitor the child's reactions to medicine, and give this feedback to the medical doctor or psychologist.

A note about teachers and medication: Many teachers seem to think that if a child is on medication for ADD, then nothing else needs to be done. It is important they know that even though medications may make it more likely that a child will stay "on task," there are many occasions when the child will not be on medication. Also, many behaviors are not influenced by the medications. Teachers should also be aware that some medications may help the child, but are useful only to a point; additional medication may actually interfere with learning. Thus, academic performance may be compromised at a dose level that is most effective in controlling unacceptable behavior. Lighter doses have therefore been generally more effective when combined with behavioral programs (Carlson et al., 1992). Sometimes less than a full dose of medication may be used. Research has also shown that more medication is not always better (Pelham et al., 1985) and that, clearly, the dual approach of medications and behavior modification works as a very powerful combined program. Furthermore, research has consistently shown better outcomes when the child has had both a medication regime and a behavior modification approach (Pelham & Murphy, 1986). It is also important to note that the child may rarely rely on medications indefinitely; having a learning component to improve "on task" behavior will thus be beneficial when the medication regime is terminated. It is possible, in some cases, to reduce or "wean" the child from medications with the assistance of the behavioral program. It is generally agreed that the less medications used, the better for the child. While most medications for ADD are safe, there is always some risk with any medication, and side effects should also be considered. Risk factors and side effects should, in fact, always be considered when designing the "dual-approach" treatment program. In some cases where children cannot take a certain medication because of a conflicting medication or simply because of a prior adverse reaction to the ADD medication, comprehensive behavior programs are essential.

Typically, the pediatrician evaluating for ADD will send out rating forms to both teachers and parents and should include a list of possible side effects when the child is placed on medication. In this way, the pediatrician may get feedback on what is happening with the child who is on a specific medication. A list of medications with some side effects that could be of concern is included in Figure 13-1 in Chapter 13.

Suggestions for the Teacher

There have been many long lists of suggestions to aid teachers in dealing with ADD behaviors in the classroom; a sample list is found in Appendix C. Some of the most frequently cited suggestions for teachers are:

1. **Preferential Seating:** This does not necessarily mean the child sits in the front; rather, the child sits next to a good student (as a model).

2. **Use a Small Tape Recorder:** This can help the child who might have a writing problem (as many do) get assignments or other information recorded for later transcription. The recorder allows the child to write the assigned task under less pressure.

3. **Use the "Premack Principle":** Have the child do the more unpleasant or difficult work first, then follow with easier work. The

easier work will act to reinforce the prior, more difficult work, and make it seem less aversive.

4. **Use a Self-Monitoring Procedure:** Here the teacher may have the child put a mark on the page whenever he/she was "on task" in response to a cue. This cue, or beep, is usually provided by a small tape recorder and presented via headphones. A tape with a beep randomly delivered over an approximate interval of 45 seconds may be used. A commercially available program by Dr. Harvey C. Parker (1991) is available from the ADD warehouse and listed in Appendix E under Recommended Books, Suppliers, etc.

5. **Use the Response Cost Procedure for Work Activity:** A small 3 × 5 card is taped to the child's desk. Periodically, while walking around the room, the teacher notes which students are off task and marks their cards. Each child could start with, for example, 50 points; each mark would subtract 5 points. If the child has 25 points remaining, he/she can have free time, go to the computer, etc. Here the child has all the points needed and can only lose them. This procedure appears to be highly motivating for the child with ADD.

There are many other suggestions for teachers to use when working with the child who has this disorder, and there are many other types of problems to be addressed, both academic and behavioral. Focusing on positive behavior and creating good feelings would seem to be the most important general suggestions for the teacher, parent, or anyone else who works with the child. Embarrassment from critical comments made in front of the whole class does nothing to help the child and only degrades the child and the teacher who uses it. Anyone who has worked with or lived with the child who has ADD knows the frustrations that parents and teachers feel. Yet, most all ADD children are emotionally as well as neurologically sensitive.

One compensatory adjustment that some children with ADD develop as a defense is "clowning behavior." They elicit laughs, which are rewarded, and this technique directs attention away from their own inadequacies and deficiencies. Much of the clowning behavior occurs without full awareness or conscious volition. Some of our best comedians started this way, as they would often boast or attest to on late-night TV talk shows. However, the fortunate few who are successful with clowning behavior stand in marked contrast to the tragic many who fail with humor, dropping out of school, and developing even more deviant behavior that may ultimately lead to delinquency and perhaps to more serious criminal behavior. Most all parents are aware of the significant correlations between dropping out of school and later delinquent behavior.

To reiterate, focusing on positive behavior and creating good feelings (through positive strokes) would seem to be the most important general suggestions for the teacher working with the child who has ADD. Teachers who are supportive, caring, and knowledgeable can help the child avoid such devastating consequences of school failure and being a dropout. For a successful outcome, teamwork is required. The parents, teacher, psychologist, pediatrician, and social worker must work together in separate, but sometimes overlapping roles, to assist the ADD child in compensating for his/her biological deficiencies in behavior.

SUMMARY OF CHAPTER 11

The teacher plays a very important role in the success or failure of the child with ADD in school and perhaps even in life. Anecdotal reports indicate that one of the most critical predictors of the ADD child's outcome as an adult is that special teacher or other significant person from his or her school days. Such a special teacher would understand the ADD behavior of the child, express care, and take extra time and be willing to modify classroom procedures to enhance that child's probability of success.

This teacher may play one of several significant roles. First, teacher input is typically essential in formulating a diagnostic impression and in recommending referral of the child for other evaluations. Second, the teacher may be quite helpful in monitoring the child's behavior to determine whether medications and/or behavioral programs are effective; and third, some teachers actively participate in the ADD child's behavioral programs.

12

Special Problems for the Child with ADD/ADHD

hree of the most significant special problem areas for the child with ADD are *homework, social relationships* (including peer and sibling problems), and *self-concept/self-esteem.* While these areas of difficulty are not unique to these children, they occur so frequently that they would best have special emphasis. Using a basic behavioral approach, specific suggestions and guidelines will help to alleviate these problems.

Dealing with Homework

During all my years of clinical practice, almost every parent has voiced complaints centering around homework. For some, it is a battleground; for others, a source of constant irritation. Many parents wish to avoid homework issues just as much as their child. Of course, the problems with homework begin at school and continue until the child returns the homework to school the next day. Here are twelve of the most common homework related problems:

1. Fails to write down assignments.

2. Writes the wrong assignments.

3. Forgets the assignment book.

4. Forgets materials needed.

5. Takes hours to do minutes of homework.

6. Hassles about when and where to do homework.

7. Lies about having done it.

8. Fails to bring notes home concerning homework.

9. Needs constant supervision with homework.

10. Needs constant help with homework.

"Zordon just called and said all
Power Rangers should be
doing their homework."

FAMILY CIRCUS reprinted with special permission of
King Features Syndicate.

11. Forgets to get homework papers signed.

12. Forgets homework at home.

Perhaps other issues could be added to this list, but parents are well aware of these and other problems that often make them feel that they are back in school. Many parents work closely with their child each day and, out of frustration and perhaps guilt, sometimes assume responsibility for their child's homework.

Using a behavioral approach, each homework problem area listed above will be discussed, along with suggestions for coping with each problem.

Problems 1, 2, and 3: Assignments

Using a homework assignment book devoted to assignments would solve these three problems. An example of the homework assignment sheet is found in Appendix D. Several sheets can be put in a brightly colored binder clearly marked Homework Assignment Book.

Anytime a child has homework in the subject indicated, he/she will write the assignment and the teacher will initial it. Should there be an error, it will be corrected before the child leaves school. The assignment book always goes home, whether or not the child has homework. So, if there is no homework, the assignment book still is expected at home. There must be repeated emphasis upon establishing a routine so the child will develop the habit of bringing the assignment book home. If the book is left at school, *all privileges* that the child would normally receive are suspended for that day *and until* the child has caught up all the work (when applicable). However, when the child complies on each problem area, points may be earned and recorded on a chart. Whatever homework issues are relevant for your child may be listed on the Home-School Behavior Chart so that the appropriate behavior may be encouraged and reinforced. For example, a specific child may forget materials needed, or fail to write the assignment correctly, or even forget to bring the assignment book home. Despite the built-in corrections for such problems, there will be a more rapid adaptation to the homework routine when the child's compliant behavior is rewarded.

Problem 4: Bringing Materials Needed Home

Again, when the child fails to bring home needed materials, *all privileges* are suspended until the child is officially caught up. If this happens on a weekend, there will be no weekend privileges. To determine this on Friday, it will be necessary for the parent to look at the assignment sheet and see if all materials are available to complete the assignments.

Problem 5: Taking Hours to Do Minutes of Homework

This is a very common complaint of parents of children with ADD. First, it will be necessary for the parent to look over the amount of homework assigned. If it appears that an excessive amount of homework is given compared to his/her peers, in general, a consultation with the teacher may be in order. Second, it will help the child to break up long assignments into smaller groups of work, thereby creating interim goals the child realizes he/she can accomplish. Thus, when 20 math problems are broken down into four groups of five problems, the seemingly impossible assignment becomes manageable and attainable. Short breaks between the segments of the assignment may become reward times. Thus, if a child usually gets four cookies for a snack, he/she could have one cookie after completing each group of five problems. Gradually increase the work segments so that eventually the child is able to tolerate longer strings of work activity.

A second but different approach to this problem is to challenge the child by saying, "You know, it sure would be interesting to see how long it takes you to complete these 20 problems. Let's time it." Very often, when a child is being monitored, he/she will work more quickly. If this procedure gets a good response, the child can be rewarded with social praise, such as, "I really am impressed; you normally take so long, but you finished in just 30 minutes." The only equipment needed to carry out this procedure is an inexpensive sports-type stopwatch.

Last, a self-monitoring system can be employed. The child wears headphones and listens for a periodic beep that occurs approximately every 30 to 60 seconds. As soon as the beep is heard, the child then marks a sheet for each beep to indicate whether he/she was on or off task. Depending on the length of each task, a child may mark the sheet 10 to 20 times. (A commercially available tape [H. Parker, 1991] is available through the ADD Warehouse and is listed in Appendix E.) While this procedure sounds distracting, it has worked well with many children and has helped to reduce off-task behavior as well as distractions. Perhaps having the headphones on may also reduce auditory distractions in the child's homework/study environment. (The next problem will focus more on the ideal conditions under which homework should be done. Many of the following topics are covered in detail in a book entitled *Winning the Homework War* by Kathleen Anesko and Fredric Levine [New York: Simon & Schuster, 1987].)

Problem 6: When and Where to Do Homework

Basically homework is a habit and like any other habit needs to be developed as such. In order for the child to learn more appropriate homework behavior, he/she will need to have a set routine and to practice in the same way. Several things must be considered; the most important factors are place and time.

Where to Do Homework. Where a child does his/her homework is important. The child should not do it where he/she would be subjected to constant distractions. Remember, homework conditions need to be similar to conditions in school so that the work habits learned at home will be more likely to generalize and transfer to the classroom. This is not unlike practicing lines for a play at rehearsal so that you can transfer this learning to the stage where you will perform. If conditions are similar, there will be generally good transfer; when conditions are dissimilar, transfer may be poor. A child really needs a relatively quiet place, preferably a desk, in which to work. Sitting at the kitchen table where others are passing by, talking, etc., is not conducive to good work. However, some recent research has indicated that the place does not have to be totally quiet. This is fortunate as our ultimate target for generalization of work skills, the classroom, is often found to be "somewhat noisy" on occasions. This will be discussed further in another chapter.

When to Do Homework. Many students sometimes simply model parental lifestyles, trying to fit homework into their busy schedule whenever they can. Parents can be effective models for their children in this regard when they demonstrate how to prioritize and schedule their own work and leisure activities. More than any lecture, this can serve as a model for scheduling important activities so that specific goals are met. Homework needs to be scheduled at generally the same time each day. However, some special events may require occasional reorganization; maintaining some flexibility in the schedule should not be a problem.

Parents often ask, "Should my child do homework when he or she first comes home?" Such an individual determination needs to be worked out with the child. Play activities after school may be very important for the child's social development, so he/she may elect to play, then eat, and then do homework after supper. Many say, "Well, my favorite TV programs come on after supper." Again, scheduling decisions should be made by the parent in consultation with the child. Homework is *scheduled* at a *regular time,* either after school or after supper, depending upon what works best for the individual child. What should not be sacrificed is homework time. This should be viewed as almost "sacred," an important idea to communicate to the child. Although the amount of time scheduled is arbitrary and basically dependent on the child's teacher, a general recommendation is for at least one-half hour through 1st grade, one hour throughout the elementary grades, and at least two hours per night for upper level grades through high school.

Using something called the Premack Principle, you might suggest that homework be done prior to something that is fun or at least prior to something that is more enjoyable, i.e., play, TV, computer time, or even another homework subject area that is more desirable and interesting. The first task will thus become more palatable and may be completed with fewer hassles over time. It is also suggested that homework time be used for some educational purpose, even when there is no homework assigned. An educational game, reading time, review of some prior work, or even preparation for an upcoming test or project are all possible alternatives. Such use of the scheduled time block continues reinforcement and thus strengthens the habit routine.

Problem 7: Lying about Homework

If this problem persists, a parent can implement the homework assignment sheet (see Appendix D) previously discussed. When there is a homework assignment sheet initialed by the teacher, the parent knows what work needs to be done. Then, if the child says, "Yes, but I did it at school or on the bus," the parent can verify that the work was completed by the teacher's initials on the homework assignment sheet or a note from the teacher stating that homework was completed in school. Unless one or the other is presented, *all privileges* are suspended. This means that even though a child might not do his homework right after getting home, he must show the parent what he has to do along with any work he has completed at school.

Problem 8: Notes from the Teacher

On the sample homework assignment sheet found in Appendix D, there is a place for the teacher to check if there is an additional note regarding homework. There might be a progress report or a behavioral note that needs to be sent to the parent in an official form. Consequently, there is a place to indicate that a separate note will accompany the homework assignment sheet. If the homework assignment sheet is kept in a folder with pockets, sending home progress notes, discipline reports, or other communications should not be a problem. Otherwise, there is room on the homework sheet for written comments that may take the place of a formal note. Notes should be treated the same as materials that need to be brought home, i.e., *all privileges* suspended until the note is received.

Problem 9: Needing Constant Supervision

Few parents may be willing to sit by the child while she works and perhaps no one should do it. According to authors Kathleen Anesko and Fredric Levine, parents should act as consultants to their children regarding homework, that is, available on-site but not always with the child. Help the child when you can, but don't do the work.

Many parents ask, "Should I check on my child to see if he is working?" The answer is yes, if this can be done in an unobtrusive manner. Monitor the child in such a way as to not significantly interrupt his work because sometimes the child will get off task when interrupted. Perhaps the best way to deal with this is to tell the child that you will quietly check to see if he is working or not, and that you will mark a card when

"You misunderstand. I'm a homework consultant, not a homework subcontractor."

FAMILY CIRCUS reprinted with special permission of King Features Syndicate.

he is working. A sample Homework Check Card is found in Appendix D and it can be used as a weekly card. Ten checks are possible each night for a theoretical total of 50 during the week (weekend homework through Thursday). Occasions when the child is off task will be subtracted from on-task totals. On Friday, the net total can be given and, assuming there are no other outstanding problems (e.g., incomplete assignments, missing notes, etc.), the child can be eligible for a special reward with a minimum of 30 points. Since the child would not know when he would be checked, random observation should keep the child on task for longer periods. Questions for assistance will not count as being off task.

Problem 10: Needing Constant Help

Many parents find they can best help the child by getting him/her started on an assignment. Thus, showing the child how to approach a task or reviewing with the child some homework problem may be all that is needed. Within the general behavioral format outlined, the child should get the message that the homework is his/her primary responsibility. Sometimes a child will complain of writing and have much difficulty with written assignments, experiencing a problem in fine-motor coordination termed "dysgraphia." Some of these children could profit from the use of a computer, where smooth fine-motor coordination is not required. ADD children generally seem to prefer the use of a computer because of its stimulating graphics, which can make many assignments easier. Much of this should be discussed with the child's teacher. Ability to use a computer will help the child throughout his/her lifetime of learning and working.

Problem 11: Getting Homework Papers Signed

Again, the use of the homework assignment book allows for the teacher to check where and when parents are required to sign homework papers. Failure to bring homework or other test papers home may also result in the suspension of *all privileges.*

Figure 12-1.   Summary of Parent's Basic Homework Rules for Their Child

> 1. Have a specific time for the child to do it.
> 2. Have a specific place for the child to do it.
> 3. Reward partial work when subdivided; then for completion of work.
> 4. Monitor and reward on-task behavior.
> 5. Be a homework consultant for the child.

Problem 12: Forgetting Homework at Home

At times a child will complete his/her homework, then simply leave it at home. This is an *organizational* problem, not a memory problem. On the homework assignment sheet, there is a place to check when homework is completed and put in the appropriate subject folder. All completed homework should be checked by the parent and initialed when complete. Thus, if the child forgets the homework, but brings the homework assignment book to school, the teacher knows that the homework was completed and inspected by the parent.

Figure 12-1 gives a summary of the basic homework rules for the child with ADD.

Dealing with Social
(Peer and Sibling) Problems

Fitting into our society has become a most important issue, even for young children. A wish to be accepted by the group and be liked by others is important, even in the early grades of elementary school. Peer pressures begin to exert quite strong influence for children as early as kindergarten. Decades ago, such social issues were not really critical until the adolescent years; with the increasing frequency of violence in our society, however, there is even more emphasis on getting along and being accepted. It is not uncommon today to hear of children killing other children, or even killing their parents. Solving problems through the use of aggression is often modeled on television programs and in movies in an ever-spiraling attempt to see who can depict the most gory scenes or use the most violence and inappropriate language that stays just within the crudest of acceptable limits. Many of these TV programs and movies do have an effect, as violence is often made to look glamorous or even humorous. There was once a "comedian" who set fire to a chair on a national talk show; he got laughs. Other late TV shows, often watched by even young children, may depict aggression and disrespect, along with much inappropriate language, nonverbal gestures, and activities. The influence of TV is widespread and it may therefore have a greater impact upon the child. Compared with movies, TV is also regulated much less by the parents. In fact, many parents may be surprised to learn what type of TV shows their child may watch when not supervised. What can you do?

You must be responsible in monitoring what your children watch. It *does* make a difference. When inappropriate, aggressive or high-risk behavior is modeled by so-called TV or movie stars, this makes it more difficult to deal with children's social behavior problems, and especially those of the child with ADD. Remember, one of the major sources of learning is through imitation.

What, then, are the major social problems of the child and what can we do about them? Basically, we can group problems with social skills into five categories:

1. Listening

2. Following instructions

3. Sharing

4. Working/playing cooperatively

5. Social graces

Let's focus on developing and maintaining each one within the home context, where parents can structure activities that contain all of the elements critical to the establishment of the various social skills listed.

Listening

Listening is a most critical skill and certainly a problem for many children with ADD. With more severe forms of ADD, listening may be a problem when the children are focusing on listening in a two-person conversation. Milder forms of ADD may certainly present problems in the classroom, but there may be no problem on a one-to-one basis. It would therefore benefit the ADD child to practice listening skill exercises in a two-person format. Daily short practice sessions no longer than five minutes are suggested. A good procedure to use is reading, as many parents already read to their children. Select a short story and, before beginning to read, be sure to have the child's attention with his/her eye contact. Once the short story is read, ask the child to retell the story in his/her own words. If the child can do this, he/she is rewarded with social praise and physical contact. If the child has difficulty, the procedure is repeated using shorter paragraphs or individual sentences. Again, this is followed with the request to explain what has been read. The most basic exercise and variation would be to use individual words for this child to repeat. However, the parent must go to the level where the child can achieve success and then gradually proceed to more difficult tasks.

Following Instructions

When practicing this exercise, give no more than three requests at a time. If the child succeeds, reward him/her; if not, go to two requests or one request at a time. Requests should be simple and have some social relevance. Most children with ADD have trouble complying with more than two requests, but many can handle three requests, so that still would be a good starting point for this exercise.

An example may be setting the table for dinner. The sequence may be given and initially reviewed (modeled) in the following form: First, put the placemat down; second, get the silverware (knife, fork, and spoon) and put them down on the placemat in their correct position; third, get glasses for drinks and plates for food. Reward the correct following of instructions, especially if the correct sequence is performed. Give feedback, *not criticism* and repeat the procedure at another time. The feedback in this example would simply involve showing the child the correct way to set the table. Learning by imitation is again quite important, so be sure to show the child what you wish to be done.

Sharing

At times, there is so much sibling rivalry that there may be a major problem with this issue, especially when one child in the family has ADD while a sibling does not. Often the child with ADD will get the impression that he/she is the favorite child, since so much time and attention is devoted to him/her. On the other hand, the child with ADD may in some way be less desirable than a sibling and therefore feels a need to take things away from the other child as compensation. Often, such conflict with siblings and peers over sharing various toys, seating in the car, being first in line, and so forth, may serve to make life difficult for the parent; perhaps at no time has the parent ever expressed a wish for the children to develop a better approach to sharing. Although this idea may have been expressed in the form of a complaint, in all likelihood, it was not directly expressed in a statement such as, "This is what I expect you to do."

One problem situation may involve sharing a toy or sharing TV time with a sibling. Parents are even surprised to find that when duplicate toys are bought, the child with ADD will find some slight imperfection to indicate that his/her toy is less desirable than the toy given to a sibling; consequently, the child still wishes to play with the other child's toy. To deal with this problem, after indicating that more sharing is needed, it is first necessary to model appropriate sharing behavior. After modeling, ask both children to imitate what you have shown them. For example, you play with the toy and then give it to one of the children. If each child is able to demonstrate correct sharing, then ask each child if he/she thinks there will still be a problem with sharing. If either one says "Yes," it is important to hear what the child has to say ("Well, what can you do about that?") and note his/her possible solutions to that problem. Have each child give a solution to the problem until a solution is reached that is adequate and acceptable to both children. This form of problem solving puts the responsibility on the child to ultimately resolve his/her difficulties with sharing. The longer the children spend hassling over the solution, the less time there is for play with their games and toys. If a toy is in question, conflict and fighting can result in the toy going into "time out" until an agreeable solution is reached.

Selecting TV programs presents another possible sibling problem whose solution may depend on your initial intervention. For example, you may state, "You watch your program this week and your brother will watch his next week." If fairness is disputed, flip a coin to see who gets first choice. If your initial solution at intervention is not accepted, then ask for other ideas; however, neither one's TV program can be watched until the conflict is resolved.

A unique device now commercially available is called TV Allowance™. Each child has a code number so that you can track TV times and programs for each child. With this device, you can easily provide extra time for cooperative behavior around TV time, while subtracting time for hassles over TV programs.

Working and Playing Cooperatively

This has always been a major problem for children with ADD. Many of the suggestions on sharing also apply here. As in sharing, when you observe cooperative behavior, it is important to reinforce it through social praise plus physical contact, as well as with some other rewards. You can say to the children, "You know that it has sometimes been difficult for you two to play together or work together without fighting. I'm going to be looking for times when you two get along in play or work without fighting. When I see this, I'll let you know, but I'll also put a mark on this Behavior Check Card (sample also found in Appendix D). When you reach ten marks, we will have a celebration by going somewhere that you both like."

Neither child will know when the parent will be observing, so this kind of random check results in far greater consistency in exhibiting appropriate cooperative behavior. If necessary, modeling cooperative behavior for various games (playing by rules) or working activity (dividing up the work) may be needed prior to this procedure. As the children get better and their point totals increase, you can set higher goals (e.g., 20, 30, 40, or 50 points) to get the payoff.

Social Graces

These are the niceties you would like to develop in your children: greeting others, saying thank you, introducing others, giving and receiving compliments, offering to help, being sensitive to what others are feeling, and apologizing. Daily hygiene may also be included here.

A "Social Graces Checklist" (sample found in the Appendix D) may be used to reward the child and to communicate what is important and acceptable social behavior. You may, for instance, tell the child that you will be looking for these various social graces and trying to "catch her when she's good." It is important that you define each of these social graces behaviorally so the child knows exactly what you will be looking for during each week. You may also tell the child that he/she will get a mark (point) each time he/she shows one of these behaviors in a natural circumstance (you would not accept the child simply saying "hello" to someone many times just to get points). Each reward would thus be specific in a social situation or involving a certain person in a social relationship. A list of these may be made into a poster to be displayed in some conspicuous place. Practice sessions can be set up to review any of these behaviors in which the child may be deficient. Many times, a child with ADD may not be aware of certain behaviors that are shown infrequently. Over a period of one week, you can then list the child's most frequent and least frequent social graces.

The emphasis should not be on deficiencies, as most ADD children already feel "deficient" in one or more ways. Keeping a positive focus, you should point out behaviors that the child is currently showing, and that other ones (low in frequency) will need some work to further develop them. Again, modeling and imitation may be used initially. Feedback on the appropriateness of the child's behavior will be most useful.

Figure 12-2 summarizes the points you need to remember regarding social problems.

**Figure 12-2. Summary of Important Points for Parents
                Regarding Social Problems**

---

1. Monitor and supervise what movies and TV shows your child watches, as well as to regulate their exposure to other violent or inappropriate material.

2. Practice appropriate social behaviors such as listening, following instructions, sharing, and working or playing cooperatively with others; and utilize modeling to demonstrate these behaviors when necessary. Reinforce appropriate behavior with praise, feedback and touch, as well as points or tokens.

3. Assess the need to work on social graces and work on developing those social skills in which the child is lacking. Again, use modeling with imitation initially, when necessary, followed by strengthening and maintaining these behaviors through the reward systems discussed.

Dealing with Self-Concept and Self-Esteem

Basically, the way in which a child perceives himself/herself comprises his/her self-concept. For any individual child, with or without ADD, there may be many views of the "self." For example, one child may be good at socializing with others, poor in math skills, and good at soccer. However, the ADD child's difficulties in the classroom may be almost overwhelming, diminishing his/her realizations of his/her positive attributes, and thus causing the child to make comments such as, "I'm stupid" or "I'm really weird."

As in the cartoon, it's important for the child to make the distinction between the behavior and the person. The importance of internal dialogue or self-talk is critical. For example, a child might be criticized for not doing his/her chores when the parent says, "You didn't put out the garbage." The child who equates this with, "I don't help; I'm no good" must learn to change this self-talk to more appropriate comments such as, "That's correct, I didn't put out the garbage; I need to do this now" or "I'll need to put up a reminder for myself to do it next time." In this way

"You may have done some bad things, but that doesn't necessarily make you a bad dog." (Illustration used with permission from Frank Cotham.)

the child can conclude, "I am OK, my behavior needs to change (improve)."

Many books have focused on a person's internal dialogue or visual imagery in both negative and positive themes. A child with ADD may be subjected to more teasing or name-calling such as, "You're a retard" or "You're a sissy; you can't even throw a ball." These statements create powerful effects on the child, often resulting in anger and/or depression.

The child may say, "So many kids say I'm a retard—it must be true" or "Kids say I'm a sissy and don't include me in their games—it must be true." Parents who hear their child relate such thoughts to them often find that simply telling the child, "You're not retarded" or "You're not a sissy" often does not completely comfort them. What is needed is a technique to replace the negative statements and images with more positive ones.

One useful procedure involves the assumption that our experiences are recorded in the brain much like that of a videotape recording. Most children today are familiar with video recorders; consequently, the child can imagine rewinding his/her videotape of the unpleasant experiences and recording a different ending. In the example of other kids commenting "You're a retard," the child might end the tape by saying, "My abilities are good and I make good grades to show it." With regard to the other comment regarding acting like a sissy, the child might say, "I can play like any other kid." The child may be encouraged to literally orchestrate a "new script" for his/her videotape and to replay it as often as needed.

A child's self-esteem is also related to how he/she feels about himself/herself. It is a generalized feeling that has been formed over the accumulation of a variety of life's experiences. Very often this feeling is based not only on what the child perceives, but also on the expectations others may have about the child.

Consequently, when children are told, "I know you can do this work, you completed it yesterday," the child's inconsistent work set him/her up for a failure to meet the expectations of others (parents and teachers) and thereby create a negative weight on the self-esteem scale. The more experiences the child has that are characterized as failures and disappointments, the more negative or lower will be the child's self-esteem. Since the child may encounter failure and disappointment in many areas of his/her life other than in the academic area, there is a general tendency for that child to develop not only a poor self-image (i.e., poor self-concept), but also many negative feelings (i.e., low self-esteem).

It is imperative that you, as well as relatives, teachers and others who have frequent contact with the child, focus and emphasize on what the child does well. Remember that it takes at least five, and perhaps up

Figure 12-3.   Summary of Important Points on Self-Concept and Self-Esteem

1. Self-concept is defined as the way(s) in which a child views himself or herself.
2. Distinguish between *behavior* and the *child.* What the child *does* is not equated with the child as a person.
3. A child's self-esteem is determined by how he or she feels about himself or herself. It is accumulative and changes with life experiences over time.
4. Both self-concept and self-esteem can be modified and consequently enhanced.

to ten, positive comments to counteract one negative one. The child is constantly subjected to potential negative comments either from himself/herself or from others. You therefore need to be aware of this and redirect the child's focus on more positive characteristics while working to change the more negative behavioral features.

Figure 12-3 gives a summary of the points for enhancing an ADD child's self-concept and self-esteem.

13

Other Interventions to Use with Your Child

Success in both academic and social-emotional areas of life for the child with ADD may depend on a multidisciplinary treatment approach. Some children may need very little assistance; others may need daily help in many areas of their life over a long period of time. The most effective programs for the child are ones in which each problem behavior is addressed by their respective disciplines providing interventions based on educational techniques, speech and language therapy, medical treatment and medications, counseling, behavioral training, along with daily activities structured by parents. In this chapter, a number of these interventions will be discussed. Some of the most creative interventions have been reported by parents.

Educational

Since this book is intended primarily for parents of children with ADD, those interested in detailed discussions on educational interventions will

CLOSE TO HOME   JOHN McPHERSON

**"We finally got smart and had
speed bumps installed."**

CLOSE TO HOME reprinted with permission of Universal
Press Syndicate.

find these references at the end of the book. However, you must realize
that the more learning trials provided for your child across a wide range
of situations, the greater the generalization of what the child has learned.
Here, our focus will be on those educational interventions that you, as
parents, can use to help your child transfer these learned skills into the
classroom.

In general, all children, including those with ADD, learn better when
they are *actively* involved in a task, as opposed to their assuming a *passive*
role. In short, you may help your child but don't *spoon feed* him/her in

learning as the child will certainly not experience this in the real world of the classroom or later in the real-world work environment. More specifically, work with your child as his/her teacher would in the classroom. This will thus facilitate his/her use of skills learned at home and in class.

Self-Talk and Self-Instruction

When you help your child with homework, you may model this procedure of "thinking out loud" using self-talk—verbalizing each logical step needed to solve a problem or to complete a task. Basically, the child not only learns that it is okay to talk to himself/herself while working, he/she also learns a process, asking questions of what the next step is, and telling himself/herself, "What I need to do next is . . ." Having such a dialogue appears to help the child who otherwise tends to rush through homework. The self-talk technique is especially useful in doing math problems and while writing.

Self-Monitoring

This procedure has been previously discussed in Chapter 12. The use of a tape recorder with headphones may assist the child in reducing distractions. However, with this procedure, the child listens to a tape (continuous loop) with beeps. The child then records whenever he/she is "on task" or "off task" when a beep sounds. Using this procedure at home as well as in class may be a very powerful tool to help the child stay on task more often. While there is no specific age cut off, this type of self-monitoring may work best with older children (probably 10 years or older).

An electronic device called the MotivAider®, invented in the early 1980s by Dr. Steve Levinson, is also available; it can cue the child to engage in some specific appropriate behavior. It looks like a beeper and is worn on the belt or carried in the pocket; the device can be set to deliver a 2-second vibration that may occur from once a minute to once every several hours. The cue (the vibration) is directly associated with a special "private message" the child will know. For example, the child may be told that when she feels a cue, that is a signal to "pay attention" or "get back to work if you are off task" or perhaps something more general as to just "check to see if you are doing what you are supposed to be doing!" Once the child improves, the device may be set to vibrate less frequently and may eventually be phased out. The MotivAider® (Levinson et al., 1995) appears to be a unique device that is appealing to children and "relieves teachers or parents of the need to nag."

Response Cost

Another procedure also discussed in more detail in Chapter 12 is the response cost. Here, the child may lose points from a total of 50 for getting off task. The homework monitoring sheet (or Homework Check Card) is used for this procedure. If there are sufficient points at the end of the week, there is some positive consequence.

Tape Recorders

Small tape recorders can be useful in school and at home. At home, the child may use one to record spelling words. It provides an additional sense modality (auditory) through which learning can occur. Thus, the child can write the words (kinesthetic mode of learning), visualize them (visual mode of learning), and hear them spelled out in his/her own voice (auditory sense modality of learning). This procedure may develop internal auditory cues that will be very useful when the child has a spelling test. As most spelling tests are dictated, associating the sound of the words with their visual and kinesthetic cues would certainly benefit the child. It is also a procedure that allows the child to practice writing and learning words in the same manner he/she will be tested.

Since many children with ADD have handwriting problems, they may find the tape recorder useful in recording stories and paragraphs that they are assigned to make up and write. This procedure of saying and reading words thus reduces the pressure of writing (which may slow down cognitive thought processes), frees the more relaxed creative right-brain thinking, and enables story construction to be more interesting.

This technique, however, depends entirely on acceptance and approval of the use of the tape recorder by the child's teacher.

Another use of the tape recorder would be to have the parent (preferably in the father's voice as this has been shown to be more effective) record instructions or motivational comments or organizational plans, as well as cues for breaks (this use of the tape recorder would be in lieu of a timer to cue the child). All statements recorded should, of course, be in a positive framework and should not sound like drill-sergeant orders.

Computers

Kids appear more motivated when using computer programs to learn skills and tend to stay on task for longer periods of time according to research findings by Mary J. Ford, et al. (1993). A computer program called "Kid Works 2" produced by Davidson and Associates (see the References) allows the child to combine text and pictures to tell a story. The fascination of a computer that talks will certainly hold the child's interest. Children could, for example, type in reminders for rules or projects and have the computer tell them to carry out the instructions. It's like having a powerful parental ally on your side to back up your requests.

Mnemonic Devices

Memory aids have been very helpful for children with learning disabilities and can be used for children with ADD. For example, children may be taught to use visual images, rhymes, and songs to associate specific lists on chains of information. Another specific mnemonic procedure is termed the "write-say" method. This simply involves having the child *write* and therefore *see* misspelled words several times while spelling them *aloud.* In this procedure visual, auditory, and kinesthetic modes of learning are involved. Such multi-modal approaches have been quite effective not only for spelling, but also in learning multiplication tables in math.

Small electronic devices may also be used by the child to record important information in class for later replay at home. The only constraint is that such devices have limited capacity except for some of the more expensive ones.

Speech and Language

A small minority of children with ADD, and particularly those *without* hyperactivity, may exhibit speech and language problems, yet may not present such compelling behavior as to result in early evaluation. Many of these children are quiet; a high proportion are female. It is in the psychological evaluation where subtle and not so subtle speech and language problems are detected. At home, parents can help by utilizing some of the commercially available programs (e.g., the phonics program called "Hooked on Phonics" [see the References]). Some children may, however, need more comprehensive speech and language therapy provided by a professional therapist.

Pediatric Intervention and Medications

Of course, one of the first steps in the evaluation process is to obtain a good physical, medical history, and, at times, basic assessment of body chemistry with lab work. Some of the medical conditions that can cause, mimic, or be associated with ADD symptoms include:

1. thyroid dysfunction

2. hypoglycemia (low blood sugar)

3. lead poisoning

4. sleep apnea

5. mild brain damage

6. brain infections (encephalitis)

7. many ear infections with high fevers

8. pinworms

9. some seizure disorders (e.g., epilepsy)

10. some medications prescribed for seizure disorders or asthma

Once these conditions can be ruled out and heredity factors (i.e., ADD-like behavior problems in the family history) are considered, a diagnosis of ADD may remain. Prior to medication trials, many pediatricians are now requesting complete psychological evaluations along with input from teacher ratings on that child's behavior. If there is an indication of ADD from medical history, behavioral observations, psychological testing and teacher ratings, then a trial on medication is indicated. The word "trial" is emphasized here because the guidelines for the most appropriate medication or combination of medications is not an exact science at this point, just as there are many antibiotics that may not work on a specific given infection, or may work for most people but not some. So there is a period of adjustment where the effects of the medication regime are monitored by the child's teachers and through parental reports. This feedback is critical to the pediatrician and will form the basis for a change in dosage or a change in medication. No attempt will be made to present an exhaustive review of all medications used to treat ADD; however, some of the most common ones are presented in Figure 13-1. (A more detailed explanation of medications for ADD is given in Books on Medications listed in Appendix B.)

Besides determining, prescribing, and monitoring any prescription medications for the treatment of ADD, the pediatrician is also responsible for explaining to you the use of these medications for ADD. A review of side effects for the most frequently used medications can be found in Figure 13-1 as well as other information helpful to both parents and teachers. It is also found in Appendix D and may be used as a handout for teachers and others involved in the care of the child. This chart is published by Specialty Press and distributed by the ADD Warehouse (1-800-233-9273); it is reprinted here with permission.

Figure 13-1. Medication Chart to Treat Attention Deficit Disorders**

Drug	Form	Dosing	Common Side Effects	Duration of Behavioral Effects	Pros	Precautions
Ritalin® Methylphenidate	Tablets 5 mg 10 mg 20 mg	Start with a morning dose of 5 mg/day and increase up to 0.3–0.7 mg/kg of body weight. 2.5–60 mg/day*	Insomnia, decreased appetite, weight loss, headache, irritability, stomachache.	3–4 hours	Works quickly (within 30–60 minutes); effective in 70% of patients; good safety record.	Not recommended in patients with marked anxiety, motor tics or with family history of Tourette syndrome.
Ritalin-SR® Methylphenidate	Tablet 20 mg	Start with a morning dose of 20 mg and increase up to 0.3–0.7 mg/kg of body weight. Sometimes 5 or 10 mg standard tablet added in morning for quick start. Up to 60 mg/day*	Insomnia, decreased appetite, weight loss, headache, irritability, stomachache.	About 7 hours	Particularly useful for adolescents with ADHD to avoid noontime dose; good safety record.	Slow onset of action (1–2 hours); not recommended in patients with marked anxiety, motor tics or with family history of Tourette syndrome.
Dexedrine® Dextroamphetamine	Tablet 5 mg Spansules 5 mg 10 mg 15 mg Elixir	Start with a morning dose of 5 mg and increase up to 0.3–0.7 mg/kg of body weight. Give in divided doses 2–3 times per day. 2.5–40 mg/day*	Insomnia, decreased appetite, weight loss, headache, irritability, stomachache.	3-4 hours (tablet) 8–10 hours (spansule)	Works quickly (within 30–60 minutes); may avoid noontime dose in spansule form; good safety record.	Not recommended in patients with marked anxiety, motor tics or with family history of Tourette syndrome.
Cylert® Pemoline	Tablets (Long Acting) 18.75 mg 37.5 mg 75 mg 37.5 mg chewable	Start with a dose of 18.75–37.5 mg and increase up to 112.5 mg as needed in a single morning dose. 18.75–112.5 mg/day*	Insomnia, agitation, headaches, stomachaches; infrequently, abnormal liver function tests have been reported.	12–24 hours	Given only once a day	May take 2–4 weeks for clinical response; regular blood tests needed to check liver function.
Tofranil® Imipramine Hydrochloride	Tablets 10 mg 25 mg 50 mg	Start with a dose of 10 mg in evening if weight < 50 lbs. and increase 10 mg every 3–5 days as needed: start with a dose of 25 mg in evening if weight is >	Dry mouth, decreased appetite, headache, stomachache, dizziness, constipation, mild tachycardia.	12–24 hours	Helpful for ADHD patients with co-morbid depression or anxiety; lasts throughout day.	May take 2–4 weeks for clinical response; to detect pre-existing cardiac conduction defect, a baseline ECG may be recommended. Discontinue gradually.

Medication	Dosage Forms	Dosage**	Side Effects	Duration	Helpful Notes	Cautions
		50 lbs. and increase 25 mg every 3–5 days as needed. Given in single or divided doses, morning and evening. 25–150 mg/day*				
Norpramin® Desipramine Hydrochloride	Tablets 10 mg 25 mg 50 mg 75 mg	Start with a dose of 10 mg in evening if weight < 50 lbs. and increase 10 mg every 3–5 days as needed: start with a dose of 25 mg in evening if weight is > 50 lbs. and increase 25 mg every 3–5 days as needed. Given in single or divided doses, morning and evening. 25–150 mg/day*	Dry mouth, decreased appetite, headache, stomachache, dizziness, constipation, mild tachycardia.	12–24 hours	Helpful for ADHD patients with co-morbid depression or anxiety; lasts throughout day.	May take 2–4 weeks for clinical response; to detect pre-existing cardiac conduction defect, a baseline ECG may be recommended. Discontinue gradually.
Catapres® Clonidine Hydrochloride	Tablets .1 mg .2 mg .3 mg — Patches TTS-1 TTS-2 TTS-3	Start with a dose of .025–.05 mg/day in evening and increase by similar dose every 3–7 days as needed. Given in divided doses 3–4 times per day. 0.15–.3 mg/day*	Sleepiness, hypotension, headache, dizziness, stomachache, nausea, dry mouth, localized skin reactions with patch.	3–6 hours (oral form) 5 days (skin patch)	Helpful for ADHD patients with comorbid tic disorder or severe hyperactivity and/or aggression.	Sudden discontinuation could result in rebound hypertension; to avoid daytime tiredness starting dose given at bedtime and increased slowly.

* Daily dose range

** Published with permission from Specialty Press (1995) and distributed by ADD Warehouse (1-800-233-9273)

How can medication help? There is emerging evidence to suggest that individuals with attention deficit disorders may have some form of dysfunction occurring in regions of the brain associated with the control and regulation of attention, arousal, and activity. The medications charted above fall into three classes: stimulants (Ritalin, Dexedrine, Cylert), anti-depressants (Tofranil, Desipramine) and anti-hypertensives (Catapres). These medications have all been shown to be effective in increasing attention and reducing impulsivity and hyperactivity. However, each individual responds in their own unique way to medication depending upon the person's physical make-up, severity of symptoms, and other possible problems accompanying the ADD. Therefore, careful monitoring should be done by a physician in collaboration with the teacher, therapist, parents, and patient.

Medications to treat attention deficit disorders and related conditions should only be prescribed by a physician. Information presented here is not intended to replace the advice of a physician.

Counseling and Other Therapies

Most children with ADD do not have just one problem. In addition to problems centering around the ADD condition, there may be sibling and peer problems, and problems stemming from a dysfunctional family where even a "normal" child placed in the family would manifest problems. In addition, many families with a child who has ADD may experience related family problems (e.g., marital difficulties) that may stem from the stress of dealing with the identified child's ADD behavior. Various types of therapies may be helpful and include *individual therapy* (for the child and one or both parents), *group therapy* (for the child to focus on social interpersonal problems), and *family therapy* (to focus on problems within the context of the family).

Individual Therapy

The child with ADD needs a structured therapy program to meet his/her specific individual needs, as well as to deal with problems common to most children with ADD. Generally, this therapy will focus on impulse control, social skills with peers and siblings, self-concept/self-esteem and, of course, ways of improving attentional skills. However, in addition to ADD-related difficulties, children can experience the whole myriad of problems that any other child might encounter. Also, children with ADD who are adopted, come into a blended family, or experience the stresses of a physically disabled parent or a physically disabled sibling, all have unique problems to be addressed.

Group Therapy

With ADD kids, there are numerous examples of problems manifested within the social context of small group play or work groups. Increasing demands are placed upon the child to fit into normal academic work or play activities. Providing a structured setting where appropriate social behavior may be modeled, imitated, and reinforced is very useful for the child to learn appropriate behaviors that will transfer to the normal social environment of the child. In short, it may be difficult for any behavior modification program to wait for appropriate or inappropriate behavior to occur in a natural social context in order to deal with it. Thus, having the child who has those problems participate in a therapy group of his/her peers will provide the context in a more controlled, structured situation and thus make behavior change easier to realize.

Family Therapy

Many problems of the child will affect the whole family. Over time, some parents and/or siblings may form rather rigid opinions about the ADD child (e.g., "the klutz," "dumbo," etc.) that are perpetuated by the whole family. Roles may be assumed within the family such that the child with ADD may sometimes be identified as the "scapegoat." Everything may be blamed on this child whether he/she is guilty or not. In time, the child may play the role of victim, harboring feelings of inadequacy and inferiority, which are often reinforced by other family members in their comments and their actions. Some dysfunctional, yet adaptive family patterns may therefore persist until these characteristics are observed and the family is confronted with them within the family therapy context. Awareness and confrontation in the context of the family is thus necessary for change.

Relaxation Training/Stress Management

The child with ADD encounters many stressors in attempts to adapt his/her unique physiological condition to the demands and expectations of those around him/her. Relaxation training and stress-management techniques have had widespread and successful application to various problems of childhood including fearful behavior, headaches, expressing anger, sleep problems, and a host of difficulties associated with school functioning. The child may experience many of these difficulties in addition to his/her ADD symptoms, but one of the most crucial difficulties for the child with ADD is poor sleep patterns. Many parents have often observed that their child is very restless during sleep, frequently noting, for example, "His bed is a disaster in the morning and sometimes I find him all turned around in bed." Problems are often compounded when the child's bedtime and time to awaken fluctuates. Consequently, some simple relaxation exercises at bedtime can be of great benefit to the child. A child psychologist/therapist can provide information and/or training in relaxation techniques for children as well as parents. It has also been interesting that kids seem to learn these techniques more easily than adults. Some excellent commercial relaxation tapes for children are available for professional use but few are available for home use. Informational and relaxation tapes for children may be obtained by writing the ADD Clinic, 983 Howard Avenue, Biloxi, MS 39530. However, some of the basic relaxation exercises are illustrated in some of the books that are especially designed for ADD children. A list of these is found in Appendix E focusing on recommended books for kids. One very useful book is by Moser (1988) entitled *Don't Pop Your Cork on Mondays: The Children's Anti-Stress Book.*

One of the easiest relaxation exercises to use with the child is what I call "R and R" (Relax and Recover). This is a very simple exercise the child can use in any stressful or frustrating situation. It has three steps:

1. Have the child say "STOP" to himself/herself while imagining a big red STOP sign.

2. Inhale through the nose and breathe out through the mouth.

3. Imagine being in a place that is "fun" or doing something that is "fun."

This exercise may be practiced once per day for two weeks so that it will become an almost automatic response when cued with, "This is a good time to use R and R" (e.g., when the child becomes frustrated and tense over homework). Thus, it is clear that each time the exercise is practiced during the first two weeks it is labeled "R and R." Periodically this may be reviewed with the child to maintain the relaxation skill. It is also emphasized that the child should never be forced to engage in this relaxation exercise. However, you can demonstrate the procedure and do it with the child in an attempt to get the child to model you.

Activities: Chores/Play

Parents can utilize both chores and play activities to foster behavior changes in their child.

Chores

Providing the child with opportunities to grow with regard to responsibilities is quite important. Carrying out chores may involve a whole series of critical training elements that can affect academic as well as social areas of the child's life through transference of learned practical skills. First, chores provide a situation where attention (listening skills), following instructions, and perhaps using a sequence of activities is involved. For example, putting out the trash involves emptying all waste cans into a bag, securing the bag, and taking it out to the garbage can. Usually, this task has to be done on a particular day (i.e., prior to garbage pick up). So, many factors are involved, just as in academic tasks.

A chores chart could be used showing each child in the family having responsibilities for a particular chore. Since some chores may be more undesirable than others, you should have open discussions about chores. Some children may wish to rotate undesirable chores instead of having consistent responsibility for them. Others, and especially the child with ADD, may wish to have a set routine because it may be easier to remember. Rotation of chores may ultimately be the better solution, however, as each child would get experience with a variety of chores that differ in their sequences of operation.

Play Activities

Many play activities could also provide opportunities to reinforce appropriate behavior. The importance of sharing and cooperating in play has been emphasized. Additionally, games have "rules" to be followed; game activities may also be selected that focus on an area of need for the child. A few commonly available games can be used to deal with some specific problems or to help the child develop different ways of thinking.

Checkers. This is an excellent game that involves rules, visual spatial and sequential judgment, thinking/planning before acting, and immediate feedback on mistakes of judgment. Additional components can be added, e.g., each player has to say something nice about the other player (i.e., give a compliment) before each move or after getting a king. Alternately, each player could boast of some thinking process or move of which he/she was proud of something he/she did before getting each king. Adults/parents monitoring this game, or while playing with the child, can provide tokens (poker chips or hand-made tokens of cardboard). These tokens can be saved or used as points to get some later privilege. You may also use the game of checkers as a procedure called "Think Ahead." Here you ask the child, "Where will you end up if you make that move?" After the child gives a mental guess, he/she may be shown the result of this move. Also, it would be important for the child to ponder, "If I end up there, what can my opponent do?" These questions result in the child learning to plan ahead mentally.

Legos®. This is an excellent activity that involves fine motor coordination, visual form judgment, sequencing, and planning skills. Frustration tolerance can also be reinforced when, in the face of frustration (i.e., can't find the right piece), the child is encouraged to persevere. When success is achieved, social praise and touch are delivered. Lego®-type activities can be performed alone, but are best done with the parent. You can provide verbal mediation and feedback on what the child is attempting to do. When the pieces do not match, questions can be suggested that may later be incorporated into the child's own cognitive thought sequences as a strategy for checking the accuracy of his/her own productions.

This activity is also good to reward the child for staying on task and for finishing his/her task. For children who have not experienced much success academically in completing tasks, finishing the Lego® production may result in a good feeling of accomplishment and success. When the child is successful at completing the production model, it allows you an opportunity to reinforce the child's completion by stating, "I really like the way you stayed with that until you finished." Also you may comment (when the smiling child presents the completed model), "It really feels good when you work on something and finish it." The child thus has a good model for what awaits him/her when academic tasks are completed more often. These activities are fun and the child, in the context of play rather than in the demands and pressure of the classroom, learns many skills. (The child may be totally unaware of how these skills may affect his/her academic work.)

Other Game-Like Activities. Other game-like play activities that may be used to help the child include:

❏ Crossword Puzzles—These are good for maintaining attention to words and sequencing.

❏ Picture Puzzles—The child may either have to find what's wrong with the picture (i.e., something's out of place) or may need to find some detail in a complex pictorial (i.e., find all the ducks).

❏ Dot-to-Dot Drawings—These are excellent to work on sustained attention as well as sequencing and work completion.

❏ Mazes—These are excellent for planning ahead and controlling impulsive responding by using a form of "mental exploration."

❏ "Simon Says"—This has been around for some time and is excellent to help the child focus attention to verbal cues.

❏ "Flinch"—This is a two-person game where players face each other with palms touching (one's palms face up; the other's palms are down). The one with palms up (on bottom) then must try to slap the other's hand. If successful, palm positions are reversed. "Flinch" provides a good procedure for the ADD child to become more sensitive to subtle nonverbal movement cues. It has been described by Shapiro (1994) as "a game to measure AD/HD." However, this game must be monitored; should the intensity of slaps increase or other inappropriate behavior occur, this game should not be allowed to continue.

Games may not only have some intrinsic value in skill building for the child with ADD, but may also be used as general awards for completing other tasks, academic or otherwise. (A game focusing on attention will be described in Chapter 14, as it is quite elaborate in detail; it is called "The Attention Training Game" and utilizes ordinary decks of playing cards.)

Diet

Much has been written of special diets for children with ADD. Hyperactive behavior was the initial focus of Dr. Ben Feingold (1974). In the past, food additives, such as dyes, were implicated as causes of hyperactive behavior. In actual clinical research, it has been found that less than five percent of hyperactive behavior can be attributed to this factor. Elaborate modification of diets is thus not justified to help children with this disorder. A good balanced diet, suitable for any child, would, however, be appropriate.

The most recent evidence from the work of Dr. C. Keith Conners (1989) suggests the following regarding dietary factors:

❏ Children with ADD may experience greater problems associated with missing breakfast than would normal children. They are also especially vulnerable to impairment in attention following a pure carbohydrate meal. Studies show that protein is very important in breakfast.

❏ A fall in blood sugar tends to be associated with more violent acting-out behavior, as well as with marked inattention.

❏ In contrast to megavitamins, regular multivitamin supplements can generally do no harm and may have a beneficial effect on the child's cognitive functions.

❏ There is an elimination diet that seems to help children with ADD. It is a high protein/low carbohydrate diet that is difficult to enforce.

However, Dr. Conners notes that it basically can't hurt to eliminate all unnecessary additives, most chocolate and other candy, to lower the sugar and carbohydrate intake for the ADD child.

A copy of this diet appears in Figure 13-2.

Free Play

Sometimes you may feel such a sense of urgency to deal with your child's problems that you believe every waking moment should be used in some type of training. In such instances, the normal free play—unstructured time for fun activities—is overlooked. Clearly, you need to find time for normal free play where there are no expectations other than to "have fun."

Family Programs

According to Drs. Sam and Michael Goldstein (1990), there are two ways to prevent a specific behavior from occurring: (a) educate the child, or (b) change the environment. Their behavioral concept is called "Preventive Education" or "Preventive Intervention." For example, if the child repetitiously leaves his/her homework at home, even though it's complete, parents may focus on two areas to prevent this problem. First, the child may be given both verbal and nonverbal cues. This combination may involve a verbal cue (i.e., "remember to pack your homework") or a nonverbal cue of having the child check off on the homework assignment sheet that homework was completed and filed in the appropriate place. Second, parents can position the book bag next to the child's desk by providing a small table for the bag.

Keeping a "scrap book" containing all papers with good grades and a diary of "good behaviors" will help to focus the emphasis on more positive consequences, point out important behaviors to maintain, and generally provide for more positive interactions between parent and child.

Figure 13-2. High-Protein, Low-Carbohydrate Diet

Food and drink allowed

Allowable proteins: All meats, fowl, fish, shellfish, cheese, nuts, soybean products, peanut butter.

Allowable vegetables: Fresh, frozen or canned: Artichoke, asparagus, avocado, beets, black-eyed peas, broccoli, brussels sprouts, cabbage, cauliflower, carrots, celery, corn, cucumbers, eggplant, garlic, kale, lentils, lettuce, lima beans, spinach, squash, string beans, sunflower seeds, tomatoes, turnips, water cress (corn, lima beans, lentils, and peas are least desirable).

Allowable fruits: Fresh, cooked or unsweetened, frozen or canned: Apples, apricots, berries, cherries, fresh coconut, grapefruit, kumquats, lemons, limes, mango, melon, papayas, peaches, pears, pineapple, and tangerines—with or without cream but *without* sugar. Sweeten with saccharin, Sucaryl, or Sweeta.

Allowable juice: The following if unsweetened: Apple, grapefruit, orange, pineapple, tomato, vegetable, V-8; Knox® gelatin may be added for protein.

Allowable beverages: Above juices; dietetic carbonated drinks except cola. Dietetic beverages must not have sugar in them; they should be 2 or less calories per serving. Herbal teas, milk, caffeine-low coffee (example: Sanka®), sugar-free broth.

Absolutely none of the following

Sugar: Honey, candy, including chocolate; other sweets such as: cake, chewing gum, Jello®, pastries, pie, pudding, sweet custards, sweet jelly or marmalade, and ice cream.

Caffeine: No ordinary coffee or tea (Sanka®, decaf, etc., and herbal teas are okay). Beverages containing caffeine, such as Coca Cola®, Pepsi®-Cola, other cola drinks, Ovaltine®, Postum®, hot chocolate are not allowed. No ordinary carbonated drinks: No grape, prune, or juices other than listed above.

Fruits: Bananas, dates, dried fruits, figs, grapes, persimmons, plums, prunes, raisins.

Starches: Macaroni, noodles, spaghetti, navy and kidney beans, potatoes, rice, ravioli.

Alcohol: Beer, cocktails, cordials, wine.

Medications containing caffeine such as: Anacin APC, 222's, A.S.A. Compound, etc., Caffergot, Coricidin, Empirin Compound, Fiorinal (plain aspirin or Bufferin permitted).

(Read the label on every can of juice, fruit, vegetable, meat, and other products. Select only those containing no syrup, honey, or sugar. These can be found at the dietetic counter in all large markets.)

Reprinted with permission from *Feeding the Brain: How Foods Affect Children* by Keith Conners (1989). New York: Plenum Publishing Corporation.

CALVIN AND HOBBES reprinted with permission from Universal Press Syndicate.

A variation of the "good behavior book" might involve using a video camera to record some of the child's appropriate behaviors such as helping, sharing, cooperating, showing good habits, and some of the other social graces previously noted. However, no attempt should be made to focus solely on the identified child with ADD or to tape behaviors that would be considered inappropriate (from our prior discussions, to do so would clearly reinforce such behavior). Should the child change from appropriate to some inappropriate behavior, the camera would be directed away from him/her. If the inappropriate behavior fails to stop within a few seconds, taping should be stopped.

SUMMARY OF CHAPTER 13

In addition to conventional medical and behavioral programs discussed thus far, there are many ancillary procedures that may be used with the child to facilitate the improvement of some specific problem area that may not be addressed by these primary procedures. These ancillary procedures may also complement and enhance the overall effectiveness of basic medical and behavioral programs. Educational procedures involving self-talk, self-instruction, self-monitoring, response cost, tape recorders, computers, and mnemonic devices may be beneficial. Speech and language procedures, pediatric interventions, counseling and other therapies including individual therapy, group therapy, family therapy, and relaxation/stress management are all often useful. Further activities such as chores or play with certain games can facilitate the development and/or enhancement of various types of appropriate behaviors that may have an impact on the child's adaptations to life situations and ultimately toward his or her successful competency in those situations. Diet, issues regarding free play, and family programs are all also critical for the child's desired development.

14

Playing the "Attention Training Game"

Previously, there was discussion of the use of games and play activities to bring about changes in certain areas in which the child is developmentally deficient. Such games, e.g., checkers, Legos®, Simon Says, etc., were not, by design, intended to train the child in a specific behavioral area. Playing those games or engaging in those activities may, however, serve to benefit the child by providing a variety of complex tasks that relate to behaviors the child will use in academic, play, and social situations. The following game, the "Attention Training Game," was designed to specifically improve various aspects of the child's attentional processes. (This game is based on a detailed analysis of the attentional processes as elaborated in Chapter 1.)

What You Need to Play the Game

"Attention Training Game" utilizes three decks of ordinary playing cards, a stopwatch, a timer, a dual cassette tape recorder, and recording sheets (found at the end of this chapter). These materials are used to conduct the game and to monitor the child's progress with the forms included. Only the most basic attention training is described in these game formats; more complex and systematic increases in difficulty level may be achieved by adding additional components to the game or by increasing the duration of each game. The simplest option for you would be to simply increase the time spent during each game. (Additional game formats may be obtained

Figure 14-1. The Attention Training Game

Game Type	Sensory Modality	
	Visual	**Auditory**
1. Focused Attention	Make mark every time RED card appears.	Make mark every time word "RED" is heard.
2. Sustained Attention	Make mark every time RED card FOLLOWS a BLACK card.	Make mark every time word "RED" is HEARD following word "BLACK."
3. Selective Attention	A 3 × 5 array of cards is put on the table. Make mark every time a RED follows a BLACK as cards are placed randomly on the 3 × 5 card array.	Make mark every time "RED" follows "BLACK" on tape recorder as second tape is played with random but different sequence of RED and BLACK. Must attend to one tape. Distraction tape names cards, e.g., RED Three.
4. Alternating Attention	Make mark every time a RED card comes after a BLACK (20″), then change to mark BLACK coming after RED (20″), then change back to RED coming after BLACK (20″).	Make mark every time word "RED" is heard to come after "BLACK" (20″), then change to "BLACK" after "RED" (20″), then change to "RED" after "BLACK" (20″). These sequences are different from ones used in visual format.
5. Divided Attention	Visual and Auditory are presented at same time. Child must mark on the left for Visual and the right for Auditory. When (a) a RED card is **seen** to come after a BLACK one, mark LEFT; and (b) when word "RED" is **heard** to come after "BLACK," mark RIGHT.	

by contacting the ADD Clinic in Biloxi, Mississippi.) A computerized version of the game will be available shortly from the ADD Clinic. An outline of each game component is provided in Figure 14-1. A Recording Sheet is reproduced in Figure 14-2 and also found in Appendix D.

Note that "paying attention" applies to both visual and auditory stimuli. Although tactile, olfactory, taste, and kinesthetic sensations are also important, they are much more limited in our daily lives, especially with regard to academic work situations. Clearly, the two most potent modes of information processing are the visual and auditory systems.

IMPORTANT: Training is designed to enhance attentional processes by first being more specific than other attentional tasks and thereby more likely to address the child's individual needs. Second, this procedure may reveal information that will possibly be helpful in other situations (e.g., in the classroom). However, this procedure is not intended to provide a "treatment program." Obviously, attentional disorders are far too complex to be addressed by these game-like tools. Additionally, if you do not wish to use playing cards for these games, you may cut up red and black cards of equal size with one color on one side (e.g., white) and the appropriate red or black on the opposite side, so that the child would not be able to see what card is next.

The Parts of the Game

The game is divided into the following parts:

Focused Attention (Visual)

Simply take three decks of cards, remove the jokers, and shuffle them. Deal single cards, piling them in a stack face up so that the child simply has to focus on the top of the stack to name the color. Place the cards at a rate of one per second (for those needing to practice their timing in putting the cards down, remember the traditional way of counting: One-Mississippi, two-Mississippi, three-Mississippi, etc.). Instruct the child to call out

Figure 14-2.   Attention Training Game Recording Sheet

Task	Visual	Auditory
Focused Attention		
Sustained Attention		
Selective Attention		
Alternating Attention		
Divided Attention		

"RED" as soon as a red card comes up and make a mark in the appropriate place on the recording sheet. Set the timer for one minute and stop when the bell rings. You can then count the number of correct responses and put this number on the chart. (The percentage correct can also be obtained by going back through and counting the total number of red cards presented to the point where the timer rang and divide the number of red cards called out (i.e. marked) by the total number of red cards presented.)

Focused Attention (Auditory)

Pre-record for exactly one minute a random series of the words "RED" and "BLACK" on the tape. Shuffle the three decks and read the color of the cards as you put them down, again at the rate of one per second. Now present this recording to the child and instruct him/her to put a mark on the recording sheet every time he/she hears the word "RED." Again, you can then count the total number of correct picks (subtract errors for those marked incorrectly). Knowing how many times the word "RED" was said on the tape, you can obtain a percentage of correct responses.

It should be obvious that this first game is very easy and few children should have trouble with it. However, some difficulty may be experienced by those with severe attentional impairments or when the length of the game is increased.

Sustained Attention (Visual)

Use three decks of well-shuffled cards. Tell the child to mark the recording sheet each time he/she sees a RED card that follows, or comes right after, a BLACK card. Place the card in a pile face up as you deal them at the rate of one per second for one minute. Count the number of errors and subtract this number from the total marks to get the number correct. A percentage may also be obtained.

Sustained Attention (Auditory)

Make a tape similar to but different from that in "Focused Attention (Auditory) above, as the child would have some familiarity with the first tape. Then, play the tape for one minute. Tell the child to mark the recording sheet every time he/she hears the word "RED" following, or coming right after, the word "BLACK." Subtract errors from the total marks to get the number correct and the percentage of correct responses over the one-minute period.

Selective Attention (Visual)

To set up this game, put some cards in an array of three rows by five columns. You will thus have a rectangular pattern of cards that will serve as distractors for the child when you lay down each card. Tell the child to mark the recording sheet every time a RED card follows, or comes right after, a BLACK card. Then each card is placed randomly over one of the cards on the 3 × 5 card array. Thus the child has to remember the color of the last card and just follow the next card placed without regard to the cards in the background. Again, count errors; subtract from the total marks to get the number correct, which allows calculation of the percent correct.

Selective Attention (Auditory)

Pre-record two tapes for this game. A dual cassette recorder capable with separate volume controls is preferable. First, record the Distraction Tape. Use the three decks of cards and speak *very softly* naming the cards more specifically (for example, "red three," "black king," "red five," "red two," etc.) as you go through them than you will when you record the Main Tape. Record one minute. Second, record the Main Tape in a normal volume of voice, saying only the colors as they come up in the deck (being sure to shuffle the deck prior to this recording so that a different sequence of colors will come up than on the Distraction Tape). For example, the only words on the Main Tape might be: Red, Black, Red, Red, Black, Red, etc. Record one minute of the Main Tape again at the rate of one per second. Put both tapes in the dual cassette recorder to play at the same time (or, you may use two separate tape recorders). Play both tapes and direct the child to mark the recording sheet when he/she hears the word "RED" following, or coming right after, the word "BLACK." Also tell the child to pay attention to the louder tape. (Use two other tapes with numbers recorded in very soft and normal louder voices to teach the difference between the two before actually starting this game.) It is most important during the game that when both Main and Distraction tapes are played, the Main tape be noticeable, i.e., stand out, against the background Distraction sounds. Count the errors as usual and calculate the percent correct over one minute.

Alternating Attention (Visual)

Shuffle the three decks of cards. Before starting this game, tape three 3 × 5 cards on the table in front of the child from his/her left to his/her right. Begin at the child's left. The first card (#1) should be marked (where you can read it) "R after B," which stands for "Red After Black." The next card (#2) is marked "B after R"; and Card (#3) is marked "R after B."

These are the three phases to the game. In the first phase, put the cards face up, one per second, for twenty seconds in a pile under Card #1. For this first phase, tell the child to mark the recording sheet every time he/she sees a RED card following, or coming right after, a BLACK card. Do this for 20 seconds. Then, after about 10 to 15 seconds, state that the rule has changed. Now the child should mark the recording sheet every time he/she sees a BLACK card following, or coming right after, a RED card. Place these cards in a pile face up, one per second, for 20 seconds under the card marked #2. After 20 seconds, again stop. During this 10- to 15-second break, state that the rule has changed again. Tell the child to mark the recording sheet every time he/she sees a RED card following, or coming right after, a BLACK card. Place these cards under Card #3 in a pile. At the end of the last 20-second phase, stop to check the number of errors written on cards #1, 2, and 3. For each pile subtract the errors from the total marks to get a total correct and calculate the percent correct.

Alternating Attention (Auditory)

Three phases are pre-recorded on tape, as read from the newly shuffled three decks of cards. Each phase will be 20 seconds; thus, ten pairs of ten cards, so ten pairs of cards should be placed on each pile for each phase. As in the previous game, 3 × 5 cards are taped to the table in front of the child, with Card #1 on the child's immediate left and marked "R after B"; Card #2 marked "B after R"; and Card #3 marked "R after B." For phase one, tell the child to mark the recording sheet every time he/she hears the word "RED" following, or coming right after, the word "BLACK." Phase one is played for 20 seconds and stopped. During a 10- to 15-second break, tell the child the rule has changed and now he/she should mark the recording sheet each time he/she hears the word "BLACK" right after the word "RED." Phase two is played for 20 seconds, then stopped. During the 10- to 15-second break, tell the child the rule has changed again and he/she should now mark the recording sheet each time he/she hears the word "RED" after the word "BLACK." Phase three is played for 20 seconds, then stopped. Subtract errors from total marks and calculate the percent correct as before.

Divided Attention (Visual and Auditory)

The last game involves divided attention; it is the most complex and per-haps, as a variant of alternating attention, it is comparable to a situation where you have two types of sensory input that are both relevant stim-uli, and where you must pay attention to both equally. For example, a pilot has to attend to both a beeping sound and a visual gauge, both of which are relevant to the safe operation of the plane. For the child, this situation may be one in which the child must watch a video, movie, or slides (visual input) and listen to the teacher's comments about what is being shown (auditory input).

You could devise a competition between two visual inputs or two auditory inputs, but the majority of situations will involve separate and distinct sensory inputs of visual and auditory information. Thus, only one task is presented here.

For this game, again pre-record a tape with the randomly shuffled three decks of cards for a one-minute time period. The same principle will be used for the visual and auditory sequences (i.e., red after black). Present the child with a divided page with VISUAL on the left and AUDITORY on the right and tell the child to mark the left side of the recording sheet when he/she **sees** a RED card following, or coming right after, a BLACK card and to mark the right side of the recording sheet when he/she **hears** the word "RED" following, or coming right after, the word "BLACK."

At the same time the tape is played, put the cards face up, one per second, in a pile to the child's left with the tape recorder on his/her right. After one minute, score the child's performance as usual by counting the total number of errors, subtracting from the total marked and calculating the percentage correct.

Recording the Child's Performance

Once you have all of the percent-correct estimates, based on data from the recording sheet, Figure 14-2, you can plot these separately for visual and auditory tasks on the graph provided in Figure 14-3. Each dimension of the attentional process may be plotted over time to note improvement. Therefore, you can compare visual and auditory attentional processes across tasks that increase in complexity from focused attention to alternating attention and ultimately to divided attention and record these on Figure 14-4. It is important to remember that **not all children will be able to do all these tasks.** Developmentally, some children may not be capable of alternating or divided attention. At present there are no strict developmental guidelines to recommend what is age-appropriate for each child. It is suggested that the child be the guide and if the task is strongly resisted or not comprehended after two explanations, proceed no further with that task or any task in the hierarchy more difficult than it. Restrict the training games for those tasks that appear to be developmentally appropriate and acceptable to the child, according to the child's reaction.

No attempt should be made to force the child to continue if the task is too difficult. It is equally important to state to the child that "Well, that one's a little too hard. We can do that one some other time in the future." Always reinforce the child's participation and improvement and avoid giving the child the impression that he or she has failed or not pleased the parent. Learning any task is generally a slow gradual process

Figure 14-3.   Attention Training Game Comparative Performance Record Attention Task (   )*

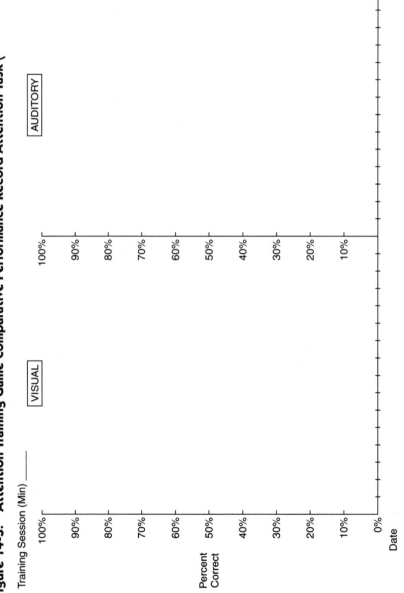

Training Session (Min) _____

VISUAL   AUDITORY

Percent Correct

100% 90% 80% 70% 60% 50% 40% 30% 20% 10% 0%

Date

Substitute: Focused, sustained, selective, alternating, or divided

Figure 14-4. Attention Training Game (   )* Attention (   )**

Training Session (Min) _____

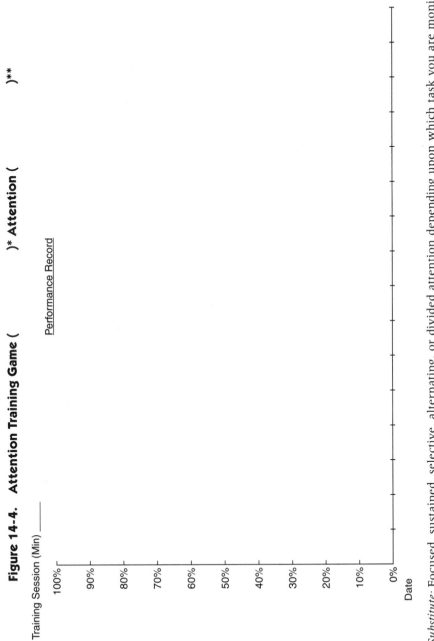

Performance Record

100%
90%
80%
70%
60%
50%
40%
30%
20%
10%
0%

Date

Substitute: Focused, sustained, selective, alternating, or divided attention depending upon which task you are monitoring

**Substitute*: Visual or auditory

with *plateaus* in learning (when it seems as if no progress is being made) or even *regressions* (when the child does more poorly after having good performance).

It is important to remember that for the child with ADD, performance is typically inconsistent. However, when improvements are shown, note this to the child. For example, "You did much better on that game compared to the last time we played it." Avoid giving negative comments, such as "You really messed up on that game and you did so well last time."

The graphs of the child's performance may be used to document improvement and to give feedback to the child on how well he or she is playing the game. When you point out the improvements over time, the child will be more motivated to continue to play and to deal with greater challenges.

To increase the difficulty level, two conditions may change: (1) Increase the duration of the game from one minute to two minutes. A maximum of five minutes should be imposed on all games. (2) An additional tape may be played in the background of noise from either (a) a typical classroom or (b) a playground. (All of these materials, charts, tapes, and information on the computerized attention games may be obtained from the ADD Clinic in Biloxi, Mississippi.)

Each task may be made more complex by changing the focus of the attentional processes (e.g., "mark the recording sheet whenever you see any red card followed only by a black queen or a red king"). However, this would be far too complex to systematically arrange without the supervision of a therapist trained in cognitive neuropsychological remediation. Thus, it is not recommended that the "Attention Training Game" be extended into this additional realm of complexity.

Last, **a word of caution:** When there is a child with ADD/ADHD in the family, there is a strong likelihood that one or both parents also have that condition. Should a parent find him-/herself confused by or having difficulty with some of the game formats, the parent may need to refrain from playing these games with the child. Simply stated, if the parent should provide feedback or information to the child on his or her performance that is *incorrect* because of the parent's own errors in recording, then the child would get distorted feedback and may obtain little benefit from this experience. In such cases, it would be far better for the parent or a relative who does not have ADD/ADHD to engage the child in these games. Alternately the child's teacher, or a guidance counselor at school, may become involved with the games.

The Point System. Use a different colored ink to draw in the child's performance of each game. Note that under each game a goal may be set based on the child's performance on the previous games. Goal setting is an excellent process, keeping in view that you might set a goal that is just slightly higher than the previous performance. This would make it more likely that the child will succeed. However, the key here is to set the goal just slightly higher and not too difficult for the child. A point system may be used such that the child gets ten points for meeting or exceeding his or her goal. Additional points may be earned by the percentage of correct responses on each game. Thus if the child gets 50 percent or greater, additional points may be awarded according to the following guide:

50 percent = 5 points

60 percent = 6 points

70 percent = 7 points

80 percent = 8 points

90 percent = 9 points

100 percent = 10 points

SUMMARY OF CHAPTER 14

Sometimes very crude attempts have been made to improve the attention span of the child with ADD. Concepts such as "paying attention" are generally poorly defined and usually involve the assumption that "everyone knows what paying attention means." However, several subtypes of attentional processes have been pointed out as initially described by neuropsychologists. A game has been proposed that involves both visual and auditory components of these attentional subtypes—focused, sustained, selective, alternating, and divided attention. You, the parent, can use some easily obtainable materials for this game, or materials may be ordered from the ADD Clinic in Biloxi, Mississippi. The game must be a fun activity and the child should be the guide for when to discontinue the game. (There will be available shortly some computer programs that will help to address some of these same needs for attention training. These computer-controlled programs will obviously be easier to use.)

15

What Does the Future Hold for the Child with ADD/ADHD?

Much has been discovered about ADD over the past 30 years. First, the name has changed several times over the years and may continue to change as more is learned about ADD behaviors. Second, there are now many follow-up studies on children who were formally diagnosed as having ADD and who were placed on Ritalin. As adults, persons with ADD continue to experience problems although in a modified form. We have learned that ADD is a lifelong "chronic disorder" for most all who have it. Third, we have learned much about the physiological nature of ADD that implicates a neurobiological basis for the disorder.

Genetic Factors

Many children who have ADD inherited it from one or both parents who also have it. Studies of identical twins adopted by different sets of parents (Cantwell, 1975) show that both twins developed similar ADD characteristics. However, nonidentical twins were not likely to show ADD characteristics. Several studies, notably Cantwell's (1972), have also implicated fathers and uncles of ADD children more so than other relatives as having related ADD problems. A rather comprehensive review of genetic studies by Dr. Lily Hechtman (1994) has suggested a genetic component from studies on twins, adopted children, and in families. Gaultheria (1991) has formulated a "two-stage model" that synthesizes both genetic and brain damage factors. The first stage is comprised of children who have ADD due to genetic factors. These factors are characterized primarily by polygenic inheritance pattern. This implies a number of individual genes contributing to the condition, as well as severity of the condition varying as a function of the number of genes involved. The second stage of this model is a comparatively smaller group of ADD children that has its etiology in brain damage easily caused by birth trauma or within the first year of life. These children are similar to the genetic group behaviorally, but some of their behaviors may show a differential response to treatment and perhaps an adverse reaction to stimulant medication.

A genetic deficit known as Fragile X Syndrome has been associated with ADD. (On the X chromosome, a fragile site on Q27 has been noted and thus provides its name.) Such children show physical characteristics of large ears and large testes in males, along with evidence of learning disabilities, possible retardation, as well as attentional problems (Hagerman, Kemper, & Hudson, 1985). However, chromosome studies are quite rare in the general ADD population, so there is no direct evidence at present to indicate that this gene may be responsible for other ADD characteristics in general.

Biological Factors

Prenatal conditions, such as use of alcohol during pregnancy, has been found to give rise to Fetal Alcohol Syndrome with its associated characteristics of learning and attentional difficulties. Other conditions, such as Perinatal Anoxia, have also been implicated. The finding of decreased cerebral blood flow, frontal lobe dysfunction, and various psychophysiological findings, all point to some form of central nervous system mechanism to account for the symptoms of ADD. Often, with a seizure disorder, there is also evidence of ADD. However, the focus has been to look for specific abnormalities in the EEG of many ADD children. The clinical electroencephalogram, or EEG, has been quite useful in the diagnosis of seizure disorder, but not generally with ADD, unless both coexist. What has been found in many recent computerized EEG studies is an excess of slow wave activity, specifically during periods when a shift to a more activated alert state should occur. Consequently, there has been direct neurophysiological evidence for a general drowsy state in the child with ADD. This pattern is also more specific and definitive in computerized EEG analyses and often overlooked in clinical EEG reports, since the primary focus of the clinical EEG is to look for specific abnormalities and not general background patterns. Similar findings have been reported for children with ADD from China, Korea, and Japan in a recent study by Matsuura, et al. (1993), thus again arguing for a biological, genetic basis for this disorder.

Innovative Therapies

Optimal Arousal Theory

This states that each individual has an optimal level of arousal that must be present to improve academic performance. For example, a study showed that by enhancing the difficult part of a word with color, the child with ADD learned the words better with the color helping to maintain the child's attention. Using bright colored pen markers can thus help maintain the child's attention while he/she is reviewing and studying words. Similar recommendations for using brightly colored mats on which the child may place materials for homework has been known for some time. A dissertation research study by Flick (1969) suggested that stimulus parameters of color, form, complexity, and brightness could be manipulated to enhance attentional processes in mentally disabled children.

Likewise, music can be used in the background while studying. For many normal children, rock music may be distracting. However, ADD kids may be more stimulated and may learn better with it. Other studies show that rock music was therapeutic for a small group of boys with ADD studied at the Oregon Health Sciences University. In the study, the researcher, F. Cripe (1986), hypothesized that the rhythmic beat increased central nervous system arousal (i.e., a kind of "driving effect" was achieved where the brainwave pattern becomes synchronized with the rhythmic beat), the music further masked other distractions, and its rhythmic beat also resulted in a reduction in tension, ultimately reducing overall motor activity for the student. The general consensus of the results was that most all of these boys improved their performance while studying under these conditions.

Other unpublished studies have shown that the use of auditory and visual stimulation may be most effective in creating a more normal internal neurophysiological state that would be more conducive to focusing and maintaining attention, thereby enhancing the processing of information and ultimately improving learning and performance. Use of tapes with pre-recorded natural sounds or "white noise" has been known to be of benefit for the child both in the classroom as well as at home doing homework.

Biofeedback

Recent research using a type of computerized EEG, or topographic brain mapping, has supported the general notion of excess slow wave activity in the frontal central regions of the brain of children with ADD. The work of Joel Lubar, Ph.D. (1991) has indicated that when the ADD child increases activation in areas that he/she was once deficient, there is improvement in symptoms. Combined with the biofeedback sessions are EMG (muscle) relaxation training to control for movement along with tutoring to deal with areas of academic deficiencies. This research generally has been consistent with other biological research findings by Dr. Alan Zametkin, et al. (1990) indicating a slowing down of brain activity in the frontal central regions as reflected by PET Scans, a kind of brain imaging procedure where a radioactive substance along with glucose is injected. When the brain takes up glucose, more is used by the more active parts of the brain. During a task requiring concentration, ADD individuals showed less activity in the frontal regions of the cortex of the brain. Dr. Lubar and other colleagues have employed EEG biofeedback to modify the brainwave response in a more normalized direction.

While this work appears promising, it is expensive and had, in the past, required up to 80 sessions of training that must be combined with other procedures to be effective. On the positive side, the technique is one that can be documented quite well, correlating changes in the EEG pattern with changes in behavior. It is also promising in that a large percentage of those ADD persons, treated as children, have been followed through adulthood and have experienced continued success in school. Most recently the first control study has appeared (Rossiter & LaVaque, 1995), indicating that EEG biofeedback, or neurotherapy as it is now called, was just as effective as Ritalin for treatment groups with 23 patients in each matched by age. Additional studies forthcoming may indicate whether this approach now with more efficient training protocols has been reduced to about 20 therapy sessions over a 4- to 8-week period. Replication of this study will determine whether neurotherapy may become a viable alternative to medication; it is, however, doubtful that other components of the treatment program (i.e., behavioral and educational) could ever be replaced. Thus, even if it should be possible to change the deficiency within the nervous system, there will still be a need for learned skills.

Hypnosis

From the limited research available on conventional hypnosis, there is little evidence to suggest that it would be a viable technique dealing with the complex pattern of symptoms exhibited by children with ADD. However, a recent report by Burte and Burte (1994) at the Milton Erickson Institute in Long Island, New York, indicates that use of Ericksonian hypnotic procedures can be a useful adjunct to the child's overall treatment program. The use of visualization techniques along with story metaphors may be used to address some of the behavior and feelings (such as impulsiveness, concentration problems, self-acceptance, and self-esteem difficulties that are often associated with ADHD) and have an impact on the child's academic and social skills. However, this represents only one component in a multi-modal treatment program that incorporates pharmacotherapy (medication), parent training/counseling, social skills, peer relations group work, and family counseling.

Using Ericksonian hypnosis, a very specific form of hypnosis, parents are aided in exploring their feelings and are assisted in "reframing" their perceptions of the child. Teachers, too, may be taught to reframe the ADD child's behavior of daydreaming, inattention, hyperactivity, and noncompliant behavior (as "boredom" or a "lack of stimulation"), and thereby devise ways of increasing "the child's stimulation or motivation" rather than punish the child. This may also include new materials, changing materials frequently, engaging the child more often, or utilizing the child's "imagination" more often. Hypnotic techniques with the child appear to involve primarily reinforcing "pro-social skills" taught during the group and employ the use of therapeutic stories (metaphor).

More specific treatment guidelines are needed to determine what part Ericksonian hypnosis actually plays in this overall program and what outcome figures are available. The authors state that the program is "still in its early stages, not yet systematically evaluated." It would appear impossible to determine the effectiveness of individual components and, unless more specific guidelines are made available for each component, it would be difficult to generalize results to any other setting. Perhaps future publications will present not only guidelines, but also outcome statistics so that, if clinically effective, those clinical practitioners who utilize Ericksonian hypnotic techniques may be able to make this available for the general public.

Habilitation

Neuropsychologists have, over the last ten years, been developing techniques to rehabilitate individuals (primarily adults, but some children) who have experienced some type of brain insult that produced impairments in specific skill areas involving attention, memory, visual motor skills, and other functions that have affected their adaptation to daily life routines. The emphasis in these techniques has been on rehabilitation as the attempt is made to regain or recover skills that have been lost or altered in some way. Some of these same techniques are beginning to be used with children who have ADD or LD (learning disabilities). While these children have not lost skills, they have failed to develop them. Consequently, their psychological test pattern looks similar to the adult or child with certain types of brain injury. While subtle differences in brain structure and function have been noted for children with the so-called "invisible handicaps," notably ADD and LD, no gross abnormalities of brain tissue or neurochemical processes have been fully "documented." "Documented" is emphasized as there are many sources pointing to a biological structural or neurochemical basis for the behavioral characteristics of ADD. There is a lack of definitive evidence. Nevertheless, there is such a similarity of behavioral characteristics with those individuals who have sustained actual brain injury that the application of cognitive neuropsychological remediation techniques to the child with ADD or ADD/LD seems clearly worthwhile. The bulk of outcome statistics are with individuals who have had actual brain damage, but these techniques have begun to be applied recently by several clinical researchers (including the author), and some results have been published.

One such program of training materials has been computerized and is entitled "Captain's Log.™" The program was developed by Dr. Joseph Sanford and R. J. Browne (1988). This system has been nicknamed a "mental gym." The explanation for this nickname is simple: The system provides a series of cognitive training exercises in several critical areas including modules for attention, visual motor skills, conceptual skills, numeric concepts/memory skills, and a newly added attentional program involving components that address visual scanning, concentration and inhibition, both visual and auditory attention (discrimination), as well as visual organization, memory, and attention to detail. The complete program is far too complex to explain in detail in this book and should be used only under the guidance of a clinical neuropsychologist familiar with such rehabilitation procedures. A recent study by Kotwal, et al.

(1994) has shown that such training ranging from 20 to 35 sessions in the cited studies resulted in some improvement on the Connor's Parent Rating Scale and structured questionnaire, along with general improvement in grades.

A recent article in *CHADD* Magazine (Fall 1994) pointed out the value of using computers to help children with ADHD. Other computerized cognitive neuropsychological programs are also available (e.g., NeurExercise™) which primarily have been used, to date, with adult head-injured patients, but have more recently been applied to ADD behavioral symptomatology. No research studies have been found with the NeurExercise™ program that was developed by Dr. Marvin Podd et al. (1989). Future studies, including research by the author, look quite promising and may become a useful tool in planning a comprehensive treatment program for children with ADD. Perhaps some training exercises may also be extended for use with home and school computers. This would certainly help to increase generalization of learning skills to those critical environments in which the child must function. However, these home and school programs should perhaps best be used as adjuncts to primary training programs that are conducted under the supervision of a clinical neuropsychologist experienced in the use of neuropsych rehabilitation programs.

Decision on Alternative Treatments

At present there is insufficient evidence on the recommended use of any alternative (non-drug) treatment with the exception of behavioral approaches to symptoms. Many parents who may feel desperate for some "quick fix" may be misled by anecdotal reports of success stories and "hype" over some novel approaches. Thus decisions regarding the use of alternative treatments should be made with much caution. Granted, there are some very promising approaches that have employed scientific standards that must be considered even more rigorous than those used during the initial medication trials with Ritalin. Some of these novel procedures were, of course, not ever intended to be used as a sole treatment of ADD and some of these would certainly be combined with other procedures in a typical multi-modal treatment program. In my clinic experiences, it's been rare that a child is seen with only ADD and no other problems. With the incidence of other problems such as learning disabilities, depression, anxiety, and conduct disorders so high, it is necessary to address each problem. Thus, a multi-modal treatment program is a generally accepted standard. Sometimes this occurs within one treatment center; an alternate approach would be to work with other professionals outside of the identified clinical practice to obtain some coordinated effort. Most treatment centers will provide combined programs as has been done at the ADD Clinic in Biloxi, Mississippi. For a description of the ADD Clinic, refer to Appendix A.

Will There Ever Be a "Magic Solution"?

Gene replacement or manipulation has been a focus of some innovative genetic research, but these studies have simply shown how complex the situation really is.

One day it may be possible to discover specific genes that are responsible for different kinds of attentional behavior. First, a more refined analysis of attentional behavior is needed similar to that described in Chapter 1 of this book. Attentional processes are really more complex than depicted in past studies and discussions. Second, larger numbers of cases will be required. Because of symptom overlap and the apparent variation in ADD clinical patterns, larger groups of clinical cases must be studied to isolate specific genetic patterns that relate to ADD alone.

There is no current treatment that is considered a "cure." At best, we are able to manage ADD symptoms. The fact that we are seeing ADD symptoms in adults would suggest that there is a lifelong battle for the child with ADD. We can, however, equip the child with skills that can substitute for pills, and certainly be aware of difficulties ahead allowing him/her to prepare for them. One day this may all change, but for now there is no "magic solution." A recent report by Dr. N. Alessi et al. (1993) states it all in the title, "The Gene for ADHD? Not Yet!"

SUMMARY OF CHAPTER 15

Every parent of a child with ADD probably secretly—or perhaps even openly—hopes that some "cure" will be discovered soon or at least that better preventive measures will be forthcoming. Well, there *is* hope in some of the amazing accomplishments in the area of genetics, yet any real breakthrough in this area may not come for many years. Various other innovative therapies may, at least partly, be employed at present (e.g., optimal arousal theory) while others, like biofeedback, hypnosis, and habilitation techniques, all offer promise. Of these, biofeedback and habilitation (behavioral training of neuropsychological functions) have the most impressive background of scientific research. As more research is published in major scientific journals and as these techniques and treatment protocols become more refined, there are, indeed, some very encouraging trends.

16
Final Words for Parents

As a parent of a child with ADD, you are faced with monumental challenges and awesome responsibilities that can affect many lives. While knowledge that you are not totally responsible for your child's behaviors is a giant step forward, this positive aspect is tempered by the fact that the way you respond to and raise the child will make a tremendous difference in the eventual outcome and how successful the child will be in life. While research has shown that many factors—personal, social, academic, and family characteristics—interact and may be additative in predicting outcomes, you—as parents—can play a significant role, especially during adolescence, in predicting aggression, delinquency and school performance, according to Loney et al. (1981).

It is therefore appropriate to conclude this book with some suggestions you can use to help your child through the critical years of early childhood through adolescence.

First, I must state from both a personal and clinical perspective, there is tremendous *stress* put on you and other family members by the child with ADD. Some families have reported that having a child with ADD was one of the prime reasons for their marital distress, separation, and divorce. Considering that the parent-child interaction is "two way," this is not unexpected. What, then, can you do to counteract this significant stress factor?

Suggestions for Parents

Focus on One Problem at a Time

Dealing with ADD problems can be overwhelming because there are so many. Just as we recommend with the child, take one step at a time. Break larger tasks into smaller units; deal with one or two behaviors, not all ten, that seem so urgent. A simple way to remember this item is the answer to an old question, "How do you eat an elephant? . . . One bite at a time."

Have Breaks in Routine Schedule

All family members, including the child, need a break from routine. I have talked to families where the child worked almost constantly during school and then at home for hours till he went to bed—even on weekends. Parents sometimes state that, "We need all this time just so he can keep up." Neglected, however, are the fun activities that everyone in the family needs for stress relief, as well as for normal development in family functioning. Many children and adolescents who are under such extreme pressures ultimately realize they can never achieve a satisfactory performance in school; they become very depressed, some to the point of contemplating suicide. These youngsters perceive that they can never meet the parent's or teacher's expectations that were set up for them; their lives become hopeless with no rewards or pleasures, and—for some—the only viable solution is perceived to be suicide.

Learn Stress Management/Relaxation Techniques

All family members can learn stress management and relaxation procedures. Many relaxation tapes exist. Short 5- to 10-minute tapes used daily may work best considering how hectic most families' schedules are today. A brief relaxation procedure is available for both children and adults. The one described in Chapter 13 could easily be adapted for adults. Many relaxation tapes have a soothing musical or nature sound (e.g., ocean waves) in the background; many of these tapes can now be found in local bookstores.

You are also urged to use the *self-talk method*, not only as a possible stress management technique, but to maintain the proper course in working with your child. As we have seen, it may be very difficult to use this technique of ignoring inappropriate behavior. You must engage in a pattern of self-talk that will keep your attention focused on something else, for example, reading a book or newspaper while a child has a temper tantrum. An internal parental dialogue might be as follows:

> "Okay. I know this is going to get worse, but I can handle it. It's important for me to keep my attention on this newspaper. I know I won't be able to concentrate very well, so I'm not concerned about learning anything from what I read—I just need to keep my attention on the paper." Following the behavior pattern is much like a sportscaster giving a play-by-play account: "O.K. It's getting louder now. He's thrashing his hands and feet and crying. I know this will continue for a while. I may even anticipate his choking or asking for help even though I know he's not in trouble. I'll just have to wait this out. I know if I attend to him now, I'll make things worse. If I give in, he'll just be more persistent next time and even more intense. I can handle this."

Daily Affirmations

Using daily affirmations can be very useful for any parent. Some of these may have a religious content, but others may simple reaffirm your desire to change the way you respond to your child. Some simple examples of these daily affirmations are:

> "I have the knowledge and the strength to deal with my child's difficult behavior."

> "In the past, I have been too harsh with my child's behavior. I can use other techniques that would be less emotional for both my child and myself."

"I am aware that my child's behavior will not change overnight. I can be patient and will continue to use techniques that I know will work in the long run."

A book of affirmations by Tian Dayton (1991) is now available and is listed as a reference.

Be Assertive

This is certainly crucial if you are to "survive" parenthood with your child. As has been pointed out numerous times, the ADD behavior pattern can be quite resistant to change. However, you will need to be just as resistant and persistent in not giving in to demands. For example, a technique known as the "Broken Record," as suggested by Cynthia Whitman, M.S.W. (1991), can be used when a child makes repetitive requests for something when in a store. Repeating over and over a statement such as, "I'm sorry that you can't get what you want," you must be prepared for the intensity of the child's response to escalate and yet maintain the same calm voice and tone.

It is important, too, to note here that you should also be assertive in not allowing the child to name call, curse, or threaten you. Being assertive is to request the respect you deserve, firmly stating, "I will not allow you to abuse me in this manner. It's okay to express your feelings but I will not tolerate abuse." It's important to then turn away from the child or perhaps even leave the room. Depending upon the intensity of abusive language, consideration should also be given to a more formal punishment (e.g., time out, or behavior penalty, or even the overcorrection procedure).

Join a Support Group

It is critical that you know you are not alone in dealing with your child. Many parents share the same struggles and can therefore benefit greatly from sharing and exchanging ideas, feelings, and common concerns. There are numerous support groups based locally in hospitals, clinics, schools, and churches, as well as national organizations such as CHADD. Some of these groups are listed in Appendix E. By joining one or more of these groups, you can keep informed of the latest research on diagnosis and treatment. At the same time, you reduce your feelings of isolation while developing common bonds that further enhance your sense of power in dealing with your child's ADD behavior.

Misconceptions

There are several beliefs parents often have about ADD. These include:

Misconception 1

He'll outgrow it. This is often stated when the child is young. As has been noted often, "ADD behavior begins in the *womb* and ends in the *tomb*." It's a lifelong process, though not unchangeable.

Misconception 2

The ADD child just needs a "good spanking" and "firm discipline." Many parents have tried this and few have succeeded with it. There are specific appropriate behavioral techniques involving nonpunitive punishments that work approximately 60 to 80 percent of the time when used consistently, and that percentage would be welcomed by most parents of children with ADD. **Spanking is ineffective!**

Misconception 3

The ADD behavior pattern dooms one to a maladjusted life. We now know of many successful adults who have had ADD and have developed ways of compensating for its difficulties. This impressive list of so-called "victims" of ADD includes Thomas Edison, Benjamin Franklin, Ernest Hemingway, Winston Churchill, and many others. In a very unique approach to ADD, focusing primarily on the adult with ADD, Thomas Hartmann, in his book *Attention Deficit Disorder: A Different Perception* (1993), makes an excellent case for the uniqueness of individuals with ADD in that many of their behavioral characteristics may be desirable for specific occupations. I have often stated that I would certainly want the pilot who is flying the plane I'm on to be "distracted" by an unusual sound in the engine or for him/her to be aware of the many gauges and instrument control positions at one time. The unfocused, or open focus, approach that such individuals possess can be a real asset in such a job.

Yet, one might say, "Yes, but what about the ADD person's impulsivity?" No problem. At this later stage of development many of these adult ADD patterns are replete with evidence of compulsive tendencies that have probably resulted from overcompensation of their impulsive ways of responding. Basically, some of these obsessive/compulsive strategies developed out of a need for rigid control and organization. While sitting in the plane awaiting take-off, I am also thankful that my pilot has acquired these obsessive/compulsive habits and goes through a routine checklist (developed with much practice). No, I wouldn't want to change any of my pilot's behavior!

When to Seek Professional Services

This parent's practical guide for dealing with ADD behavior problems is certainly not exhaustive, and is definitely not intended to take the place of a coordinated multidisciplinary treatment team approach. However, the book can certainly complement such an overall treatment program. Also, it is well known that the ADD behavior pattern varies considerably with regard to (a) the number of associated problems and (b) the severity of each behavioral component. In standard clinical practice it is often recommended that a behavioral intervention be tried before implementing a medication regime. Perhaps this manual can assist you in this procedure. Should you encounter continued problems, it would certainly be beneficial and even essential to seek professional help. Typically, you may consult with the child's pediatrician who may then suggest a psychological evaluation prior to considering or beginning a medication regime.

You can also find many innovative ways of helping your child. You are encouraged to participate in support groups (consult Appendix E for a list of national support groups), to stay current with new developments, and to continue to ask questions of the professionals you work with to get your own needs satisfied, as well as those of your child. One of the major groups is CHADD (Children and Adults with Attention Deficit Disorders) and may be contacted at (305) 587–3700 for information about a local chapter nearest you.

When you are aware of the most effective behavioral techniques and have a good understanding of the nature of the behavior you are dealing with, you will have the "power" to make effective changes in your child's ADD behavior.

SUMMARY OF CHAPTER 16

Several suggestions include:

1. focusing on one problem at a time,

2. having breaks in the routine schedule,

3. learning stress management/relaxation techniques,

4. using daily affirmations,

5. learning to be assertive,

and last, but most important,

6. joining a parent support group such as CHADD.

I have also noted several common misconceptions about ADD including: (a) the mistaken notion that "he'll outgrow it," (b) the erroneous conclusion that the ADD child "just needs a good spanking" and "firm discipline," and (c) the grossly wrong conclusion that the ADD behavior pattern "dooms one to a maladjusted life." To the contrary, there are many success stories with ADD kids, and we certainly know many ADD adults who have achieved "fame and fortune."

When using self-help–type programs such as this book, be sure to keep in mind that it is *not* intended to replace therapy or current conventional treatment. If anything, it should be treated as a useful resource. Should you not achieve desired results, you may need to consult your therapist or to seek the services of one familiar with current ADD treatment programs. Your situation may be more complex than others and may demand further evaluation and other treatment components from specialists.

The techniques outlined in this book may then be even more helpful and effective after some of the complex components of your child's problems have been addressed.

Stay on the positive track.

References

Alessi, N. et. al. "The Gene for ADHD? Not Yet," *Journal of American Acad. Child Adolescent Psychiatry,* 32(5) 1073–4, 1993.

American Psychiatric Association, *Diagnostic and Statistical Manual of Mental Disorders,* 4th Ed. Washington, D.C.: American Psychiatric Association, 1994.

Anesko, K. M. & Levine, F. M. *Winning the Homework War.* New York: ARCO/ Simon & Schuster, 1987.

Azrin, N. & Foxx, O. *Habit Control in a Day.* New York: Pocket Books, 1977.

Barkley, R. & Cunningham, C. *The Parent-Child Interactions of Hyperactive Children and their Modification by Stimulant Drugs in Treatment of Hyperactive & Learning Disabled Children,* edited by R. Knight & D. Baker. Baltimore: University Park Press, 1980.

Barkley, R.A. *Hyperactive Children,* 2nd Ed. New York: Guilford Press, 1986.

Burte, J.M. & Burte, C.L. "Eriksonian Hypnosis Pharmacotherapy and Cognitive-Behavioral Therapy in the Treatment of ADHD," *Australian Journal of Clinical Hypnotherapy and Hypnosis,* 15(1), 1–13, 1994.

Cantwell, D.A. "Genetics of Hyperactivity," *Journal of Child Psychology & Psychiatry,* 176, 261–264, 1975.

Cantwell, D.P. "Psychiatric Illness in the Families of Hyperactive Children," *Archives of General Psychiatry,* 27, 414–417, 1972.

Carlson, C.L., Pelham, W.E., Milich, R., Dixon, J. "Single and Combined Effects of Methylphenidate and Behavior Therapy of the Classroom Performance of Children with Attention Deficit Hyperactivity Disorder," *Journal of Abnormal Child Psychology*, 20:213–232, 1992.

Christophersen, Edward. *Little People: Guidelines for Common Sense Child Rearing*. Kansas City: Westport Publications, 1988.

Clark, Lynn. *SOS! Help For Parents*. Bowling Green: Parents Press, 1985.

Conners, C. Keith. *Feeding the Brain: How Foods Affect Children*. New York: Plenum Press, 1989.

Cripe, F.F. "Rock Music as Therapy for Children with Attention Deficit Disorder: An Exploratory Study," *Journal of Music Therapy*, 23(1), 30–37, 1986.

Dayton, Tian. *Affirmations for Parents: How to Nurture Your Children*. Deerfield Beach: Health Communications, 1991.

Feingold, Ben F. *Why Your Child Is Hyperactive*. New York: Random House, 1974.

Fine, A. & Goldman, L. "Innovative Techniques in the Treatment of ADHD: An Analysis of the Impact of EEG Biofeedback Training and a Cognitive Computer Generated Training." Paper presented at the American Psychological Association Annual Meeting, Los Angeles, 1994.

Flick, G.L. "Attention to Color-Form Stimuli as a Function of Stimulus Parameters and the Level of Adaptation in Normal and Mentally Retarded Children." Unpublished Doctoral Dissertation, University of Miami, Coral Gables, Florida, 1969.

Ford, M.J., Poe, V., & Cox, J. "Attending Behaviors of ADHD Children in Math and Reading Using Various Types of Software," *Journal of Computing in Childhood Education*, 4(2), 183–196, 1993.

Garber, Stephen W., Garber, Marianne D. & Spizman, Robyn F. *If Your Child Is Hyperactive, Inattentive, Impulsive, Distractible . . . Helping the ADD (Attention Deficit Disorder) Hyperactive Child*. New York: Villard Books, 1990.

Gaultheria, T. "Childhood Hyperactivity," in Thomas Gaultheria (Ed.) *Neuropsychiatry and Behavioral Pharmacology*. Berlin: Springer-Verlag, 1991.

Goldstein, S. & Goldstein, M. *Managing Attention Disorders in Children*. New York: John Wiley & Sons, Inc., 1990.

Gordon, M. & Mettleman, B.B. *Technical Guide to the Gordon Diagnostic System* (Syracuse: Gordon Systems, 1987).

Hagerman, R.J., Kemper, M. & Hudson, M. "Learning Disabilities & Attentional Problems in Boys with Fragile-X Syndrome," *American Journal of Diseases of Children*, 139, 674–678, 1985.

Hartmann, Thomas. *Attention Deficit Disorder: A Different Perception*. Penn Valley, CA: Underwood Books, 1993.

Hechtman, L. "Genetic and Neurobiological Aspects of Attention Deficit Hyperactive Disorder: A Review," *Journal of Psychiatry & Neuroscience*, 19(3), 193–201, 1994.

"Hooked on Phonics." Gateway Educational Products, Ltd., 1988.

Kid Works 2, Davidson & Associates, P.O. Box 2961, Torrance, CA 90509.

Kotwal, D., Montgomery, D. & Burns, W. "Computer Assisted Cognitive Training for ADHD: A Case Study." Presented at the Annual Convention of the APA, August, 1994 (accepted for pub. in *Behavior Modification*).

Levinson, S., Kopari, J. & Fredstrom, J. *The MotivAider® Method of Cue-Directed Behavior Change: Manual For Teachers*. Thief River Falls: Behavioral Dynamics, 1995.

Loney, J., Kramer, J., & Milich, R. "The Hyperactive Child Grows Up: Predictors of Symptoms, Delinquency, and Achievement at Follow-Up," in K.D. Gadow & J. Loney (Eds.) *Psychological Aspects of Drug Treatment for Hyperactivity*. Boulder: Westview Press, 1981.

Lubar, Joel F. "Discourse on the Development of EEG Diagnostic and Biofeedback for Attention Deficit Hyperactivity Disorders," *Biofeedback and Self-Regulation*, 16(3), 201–224, 1991.

Matsuura, M., Okubo, Y., Tora, M., Kojima, T., He, Y., Shen, Y. & Lee, C.K. "A Cross-National EEG Study of Children with Emotional and Behavioral Problems: A WHO Collaborative Study in the Western Pacific Region," *Biological Psychiatry*, 34, 59–65, 1993.

Moser, A. *Don't Pop Your Cork on Mondays: The Children's Anti-Stress Book*. Kansas City: Landmark Editions, 1988.

Olmi, J. "Home-Based Treatment for ADHD: Preventing the Bratty Kid Syndrome." Second Annual Conference: Attention Deficit Hyperactivity Disorders. Jackson, MS: November 15, 1993.

Parker, Harvey C. *Listen, Look & Think: A Self Regulation Program for Children*. Plantation, FL: Impact Publications, Inc., 1991.

Pelham, W.E., Bender, M.E., Caddel, J., Booth, S., & Moorer, S.H. "Methylphenidate and Children with Attention Deficit Disorder: Dose Effects on Classroom, Academic and Social Behavior." *Archives of General Psychiatry,* 42, 948–952, 1985.

Pelham, W.E. & Murphy, H.A. "Attention Deficit and Conduct Disorders," in M. Hersen (Ed.), *Pharmacological and Behavioral Treatments: An Integrative Approach.* New York: Wiley, 1986, pp 108–148.

Podd, M.H., Mills, M.W., & Seelig, D.P. "A Manual for NeuroXercise™." Published and distributed by Dr. Podd, 1989.

Rossiter, T.R. & LaVague, T.J. "A Comparison of EEG Biofeedback and Psychostimulants in Treating Attention Deficit/Hyperactivity Disorders." *Journal of Neurotherapy,* 1,1,48–59, 1995.

Sanford, J.A. "Improving Cognitive Behavioral Psychotherapy Treatment of ADHD and ADD Disorders with the *Captain's Log:* Cognitive Training System." Accepted for publication in the Fall-Winter *Newsletter of the Society for Cognitive Rehabilitation,* 1995.

Shapiro, L. *Tricks of the Trade: 101 Psychological Techniques to Help Children Grow and Change.* King of Prussia: The Center for Applied Psychology, Inc., 1994.

Sohlberg, M.M. & Mateer, C.A. *Introduction to Cognitive Rehabilitation.* New York: Guilford Press, 1989.

"TV Allowance." Manufactured by Mind Master, Inc., 7400 Red Rd., Suite 21, South Miami, FL 33143.

Whitman, C. *Win the Whining War and Other Skirmishes: A Family Peace Plan.* Pasadena: Perspective Publishing, 1991.

Williams, Carl D. "The Elimination of Tantrum Behavior by Extinction Procedures," *Journal of Abnormal Social Psychology,* 59, 269, 1959.

Zametkin, A. J. et al. "Cerebral Glucose Metabolism in Adults with Hyperactivity of Childhood Onset," *New England Journal of Medicine,* 323; 1361–66, 1990.

APPENDIX **A**

The ADD Clinic

ADD Clinic

983 Howard Avenue
Biloxi, MS 39530

T he ADD Clinic provides comprehensive programs for children, adolescents, and adults who present attentional, learning, or behavioral-emotional problems. Following a comprehensive behavioral/psychological assessment, a multi-component treatment program is available to address each person's individual needs. Behavioral and cognitive therapies are emphasized but traditional psychotherapy, play therapy, and various group therapies are offered. While behavioral counseling is the primary orientation of treatment for parents of children with ADD, cognitive/behavioral strategies are also used with the child, adolescent, or adult who has ADD. Additional cognitive neuropsychological remediation is employed for the person with ADD.

Assessment of Attentional Behavior

Attentional behavior is evaluated in three ways. First, an objective computer-based procedure is used to assess the child's general level of self-control, his/her sustained attention and his/her ability to attend in the presence of distractions. This provides valid information regarding a person's ability to focus attention (i.e., vigilance) over time and his/her ability to inhibit or suppress his/her responses (i.e., avoiding impulsive responding)—two fundamental feature characteristics of ADD. In addition, a measure of the child's ability to focus under conditions of distraction is obtained. A person's scores, objectively recorded by the computer, are then compared to those of a normative group of same-aged peers. Both auditory and visual attention may be assessed. This data would then be combined with historical background information and parent/teacher ratings on ADD behavior to provide a comprehensive assessment of attentional behavior. **There is no specific test for ADD.** Assessment and ultimate diagnosis of ADD thus depend upon the use of background historical information and clinical judgment along with objective test data and behavioral observations, especially from teachers in the classroom.

Neuropsychological Assessment and Diagnosis

A comprehensive neuropsychological evaluation involves assessment of the child's basic abilities, achievements, effective control functions, social skills, emotions, and behavior. In addition to an objective assessment of attentional behaviors, particular emphasis is placed upon the child's classroom behavior where considerable information is obtained using teacher ratings of attention, activity, social skills, and other potential behavior problems. When necessary, a personal school consultation may be scheduled to observe and monitor the child's behavior directly in the classroom. Diagnostic impressions are therefore based on data obtained from several sources.

Diagnosis is, however, frequently complicated by a complex array of behaviors exhibited by most children with attention, learning, and/or behavior problems. It is, therefore, important to separate their primary, secondary, and tertiary diagnoses. For example, a child with an "attention deficit disorder" may develop a secondary "learning disorder" because of basic attentional difficulties and tertiary "behavioral/emotional" problems from long-standing frustration and failure. Additional stress reactions and depression, or a generally negative self-concept, would not be atypical. Consider also a child with a learning disability who experiences similar frustration and failure, with associated development of a negative self-concept, who may have difficulty attending because of excess anxiety and tension, and, who may also show *behavioral/emotional* problems. When evaluating a child, it is, therefore, important to determine which factors—attention, learning, or behavior—may be the primary problem and those that are secondary and tertiary in the overall diagnostic impression. Treatment programs of the ADD Clinic are designed with this diagnostic sequence in mind.

ADD Clinic Treatment Program

Cognitive Behavioral Program: Initially the individual is introduced to various strategies of attentional control using a variety of techniques directed at those ADD characteristics that are of primary importance for the child. Included in this compendium of techniques are self-awareness training and cognitive mediation procedures involving self-instruction, self-monitoring, and the basic strategies of "stop, look, listen, and think" before acting. Medical and psychiatric consultation is also available through the ADD clinic.

Neuropsychological Remediation Training

This component involves a relatively new clinical field that cuts across a variety of health disciplines including psychology, psychiatry, special education, vocational rehabilitation, occupational therapy, and speech pathology. Its general aim is to rehabilitate the cognitive functioning of individuals who have cortical brain dysfunction. Individuals treated with cognitive rehabilitation techniques include those with head injuries, learning disabilities, cerebral infarction (strokes), mental retardation, and attention deficit disorders. These same techniques may also be used to facilitate early learning in young normal individuals. In other words, neuropsychological cognitive rehabilitation can be used with individuals who have *lost or who have not achieved* their full mental abilities. "Captain's Log™" has been the prime source for training programs at the ADD clinic.

The First Phase of Treatment

The first phase of treatment typically focuses upon strengthening or enhancing attention, concentration, and memory skills. Without adequate levels of functioning in each of these areas, other aspects of the habilitation or rehabilitation process are often frustrated. The *Attention Skills Module* is designed to enhance the patient's ability to attend and concentrate on auditory and visual stimuli for increasingly extended periods. The 22 programs in this module cover such cognitive skills as visual and auditory perception, visual and auditory discrimination, timed reaction to visual and auditory discrimination, timed reaction to visual and auditory stimuli, and inhibition of response. There is also available software developed at the ADD clinic providing attention training exercises for home use.

The Focus of Subsequent Treatment

After the initial phase, the focus turns to the establishment of restoration of verbal language skills. The amount of attention paid to these skill areas depends upon the nature of the individual's deficits or weaknesses. A critical aspect with respect to the rehabilitative/habilitative process is the provision for training in the areas of reasoning, abstraction, and logical analysis. When these higher level cognitive functions are emphasized, they seem to have a synergistic affect upon the rest of the neuropsychological rehabilitation process.

The general purpose of the *Visual/Motor Skills Module* is to improve the patient's skills in a variety of visual-motor areas. Such areas include fine motor speed, spatial orientation, visual tracking, and memory for visual-spatial events. The *Conceptual Skills Module* focuses on improving patient skills in conceptualization by utilizing numbers, patterns, symbols, and sequences.

Finally, the *Numeric Concepts/Memory Skills Module* covers fundamental quantitative concepts in a framework that emphasizes cognitive strategies and information processing techniques.

How the Goals of Treatment Are Achieved

The programs in this system are designed to provide enjoyable and motivating practice material that gives immediate feedback on performance within an individualized behavioral therapy format for both children and adults. Through a behavioral procedure called "shaping," the patient is able to gradually develop those cognitive functions that have either been delayed in maturation or impaired through trauma or other disease process. Special devices are also available so that motor coordination problems will not prevent a patient from using this system. An individual's progress will therefore build upon success achieved on each task. This is accomplished by beginning each task at a level the person can handle successfully. Once that performance is strengthened through reinforcement, the task may be made slightly more difficult until all deficit areas are covered and the patient has achieved maximum gains.

Social Skills Group Program

Many children with ADD have problems in their social relationships. This program is behaviorally-based and designed to establish and/or enhance further development of a variety of social skills that relate to problem areas in the child's classroom, as well as in his/her play activities.

Child Behavior Management for Parents

Concurrent with the child's program, behavior management techniques are taught to those care givers who must deal directly with ADD behaviors in the home situation, as well as in other outside situations. The most effective behavioral strategies for use with ADD behaviors are discussed.

Mini-Classroom Program

One of the most difficult problems in the treatment of ADD behaviors involves the transfer of what the child learns during individual therapy to the classroom setting. This program was therefore initiated to assist in the child's utilization of the various strategies for coping with distractions and to strengthen his/her "on task" behavior in a small classroom-type environment. This would ultimately bridge the gap between his/her individual acquisition of coping strategies and their utilization in the regular classroom. A second work situation in which these skills could be potentially transferred is during homework sessions.

The ADD Clinic offers year-round assessment and treatment of ADD behaviors in children, adolescents and adults as well as ongoing research programs. For information about an intensive Summer Program, workshops for parents of children with ADD, as well as regular year-round programs, call 1-800-962-2673 or write the ADD Clinic, 983 Howard Avenue, Biloxi, MS 39530.

CH.A.D.D. Fact Sheet on ADD

The Disability Named ADD:
An Overview of Attention Deficit Disorders

Children and Adults With Attention Deficit Disorders

Attention Deficit Disorder (ADD) is characterized by attention skills that are developmentally inappropriate, impulsivity, and, in some cases, hyperactivity. ADD is a neurobiological disability that affects up to 5% of all American children. Without early identification and proper treatment ADD can have serious consequences including school failure and drop out, depression, conduct disorders, failed relationships, and even substance abuse.

Until recently, it was believed that ADD symptoms disappeared in adolescence. It is now known that many symptoms continue into adulthood for 30-70% of individuals with ADD. Adults with ADD may

---

Note: In this fact sheet, the term Attention Deficit Disorder (ADD) is used to include the distinct categories of Attention Deficit Hyperactivity Disorder and Undifferentiated Attention Deficit Disorder.

© 1993 CH.A.D.D.
Reprinted with permission of CH.A.D.D.

experience difficulties at work and in relationships. They may also exhibit other emotional difficulties.

Medical science first noticed children exhibiting inattentiveness, impulsivity, and hyperactivity in 1902. Since that time, the disorder has been given numerous names, including Minimal Brain Dysfunction and The Hyperkinetic Reaction of Childhood. In 1980, the diagnosis of Attention Deficit Disorder was formally recognized in the *Diagnostic and Statistical Manual, 3rd edition (DSM III)*—the official diagnostic manual of the American Psychiatric Association (APA).

The Disorder

ADD is a neurobiological disability that interferes with a person's ability to sustain attention or focus on a task and to delay impulsive behavior.

ADD characteristics often arise in early childhood. It is marked by behaviors that are chronic, lasting at least six months with onset before age seven. Characteristics of children with ADD can include:

❏ fidgeting with hands or feet

❏ difficulty remaining seated

❏ difficulty following through on instructions

❏ shifting from one uncompleted task to another

❏ difficulty playing quietly

❏ interrupting conversations and intruding into other children's games

❏ appearing to be not listening to what is being said

❏ doing things that are dangerous without thinking about the consequences

Students with ADD have a greater likelihood of grade retention, school drop out, academic under-achievement, and social and emotional adjustment difficulties. This is probably because ADD makes children vulnerable to failure in the two most important arenas for developmental mastery—school and peer relations.

A significant percentage—perhaps as many as 50%—of children with ADD are never properly diagnosed.

ADD is often inaccurately portrayed as a type of specific learning disability (SLD). It is not. Children with ADD are not unable to learn, but they do have difficulty performing in school due to poor organization, impulsivity, and inattention. However, some children with ADD also have a learning disability, further complicating identification and treatment.

Children with ADD do not routinely show signs of serious emotional disturbance (SED). However, if not properly diagnosed and treated, children with ADD can develop significant emotional difficulties, such as behavioral disorders, depression, and even substance abuse.

Many adults with ADD were never properly diagnosed as children. They grew up struggling with a neurobiological disability they didn't even know they had. Others were diagnosed as "hyperkinetic" or "hyperactive" and told their symptoms would disappear in adolescence. As a result, many developed other problems which masked the ADD.

Most adults with ADD are restless, easily distracted, have difficulty sustaining attention and concentrating, are impulsive and impatient, have frequent mood swings and short tempers, are disorganized and have difficulty planning ahead.

Adults with ADD often experience career difficulties. They may lose jobs due to poor job performance, attention and organizational problems, or relationship difficulties. On the other hand, adults who learn to adapt to their disability and to harness the energy and creativity that often accompanies ADD can thrive professionally.

The Cause

In 1990, the *New England Journal of Medicine* published the results of a landmark study in which researchers at the National Institute for Mental Health used advanced brain imaging techniques to compare brain metabolism between adults with ADD and adults without ADD. The study documented that adults with ADD utilize glucose—the brain's main energy source—at a lesser rate than do adults without ADD. This reduced brain metabolism rate was most evident in the portion of the brain that is important for attention, handwriting, motor control and inhibition of responses.

These brain metabolism studies, combined with other data including family history studies and drug response studies, have convinced researchers that ADD is a neurobiological disorder and not caused by a chaotic home environment.

Diagnosis and Treatment

Determining if a child has ADD is a multifaceted process. Many biological and psychological problems can contribute to symptoms similar to those exhibited by children with ADD. For example, anxiety, depression and certain types of learning disabilities may cause similar symptoms.

A comprehensive evaluation is necessary to establish a diagnosis, rule out other causes and determine the presence or absence of co-occurring conditions. Such an evaluation will often include intelligence testing plus the assessment of academic, social and emotional functioning and developmental abilities. Measures of attention span and impulsivity will also be used, as well as parent and teacher rating scales. A medical exam by a physician is also important.

Diagnosing ADD in an adult requires an examination of childhood, academic and behavioral history.

Treating ADD in children requires medical, psychological and educational intervention, and behavior management techniques. A multimodal treatment approach includes:

❏ parent training in behavior management

❏ an appropriate educational program

❏ individual and family counseling when needed

❏ medication when required

Psychostimulants are the most widely used medication for the management of ADD related symptoms. Between 70-80% of children with ADD respond positively to psychostimulant medications. These medications decrease impulsivity and hyperactivity, increase attention and, in some children, decrease aggression.

Behavior management is an important intervention with children who have ADD. The most important technique is positive reinforcement, in which the child is provided a rewarding response after a particular desired behavior is demonstrated.

Classroom success may require a range of interventions. Most children with ADD can be taught in the regular classroom with either minor adjustments to the classroom setting, the addition of support personnel, and/or "pull-out" programs that provide special services outside of the classroom. The most severely affected may require self-contained classrooms.

Adults with ADD can benefit from learning to structure their environment. Psychostimulant medications can also be effective with adults who have ADD. Vocational counseling is often an important intervention. Short-term psychotherapy can help the patient identify how his or her disability might be associated with a history of sub-par performance and difficulties in personal relationships. And extended psychotherapy can help address any mood swings, stabilize relationships, and alleviate guilt and discouragement.

Prognosis

Children with ADD are "at-risk" for school failure and emotional difficulties. However, with early identification and treatment, these children can succeed.

From 30-70% of children with ADD will continue to exhibit symptoms of ADD in adulthood.

Once properly diagnosed, adults with ADD can learn to adapt to their disability. Armed with an understanding of the disability and its implications, and with appropriate treatment, adults with ADD can succeed.

Suggested Reading

❏ Barkley, R. (1990). *Attention Deficit Hyperactivity Disorders: A Handbook for Diagnosing and Treatment.* New York: Guilford Press.

❏ Greenberg, G.S. & Horn, W.F. (1991). *Attention Deficit Hyperactivity Disorder: Questions and Answers for Parents.* Champaign, IL: Research Press.

❏ Parker, H.C. (1988). *The Attention Deficit Disorder Workbook for Parents, Teachers and Kids.* Plantation, FL: Impact Publications.

Need more information about Attention Deficit Disorders or the national organization dedicated to helping children and adults with ADD succeed? Call Children and Adults with Attention Deficit Disorders (CH.A.D.D.) at 305-587-3700, or write CH.A.D.D. at 499 Northwest 70th Avenue, Suite 109, Plantation, Florida 33317.

APPENDIX C

Information for Teachers

Critical Factors in Working with ADD/ADHD Children

There are many critical factors to consider when working with ADD/ADHD students. I have attempted to provide a list that is as useful and complete as possible—one that I hope will make a difference in the way students learn and teachers teach.

1. **Teacher flexibility, commitment, and willingness** to work with the student on a personal level. This means putting forth the time, energy, and extra effort required to really listen to students, be supportive, and make changes and accommodations as needed.

2. **Training and knowledge about ADD/ADHD.** It is essential that teachers are aware that this problem is physiological and biological in nature. These children are not "out to get us" deliberately. Their behaviors aren't calculated to make us crazy. This awareness helps

---

Reprinted with permission from *How to Reach and Teach ADD/ADHD Children* by Sandra F. Rief, 1993. West Nyack, NY: The Center for Applied Research in Education.

us maintain our patience, sense of humor, and ability to deal with annoying behaviors in a positive way. Every school site (elementary and secondary) should have inservicing to educate staff about ADD/ADHD, the effects of the disorder on the child's learning and school functioning, and appropriate intervention strategies.

3. **Close communication between home and school.** It is very important to increase the number of your contacts and establish a good working relationship with this population of parents. If you are to have any success with ADD/ADHD students, you *need* the support, cooperation, and open line of communication with their parents.

4. **Providing clarity and structure for the students.** This guide emphasizes the need for structure. Students with attentional problems need a structured classroom. A structured classroom need not be a traditional, no-nonsense, rigid classroom with few auditory or visual stimuli. The most creative, inviting, colorful, active, and stimulating classroom can still be structured.

   Students with ADD/ADHD need to have structure provided for them through clear communication, expectations, rules, consequences, and follow-up. They need to have academic tasks structured by breaking assignments into manageable increments with teacher modeling and guided instruction, clear directions, standards, and feedback. These students require assistance in structuring their materials, workspace, group dynamics, handling choices, and transitional times. Their day needs to be structured by alternating active and quiet periods. No matter what your teaching style or the physical environment of your classroom, you can provide structure for student success.

5. **Creative, engaging, and interactive teaching strategies** that keep the students involved and interacting with their peers are critical! All students need and deserve an enriched, motivational curriculum that employs a variety of approaches. If you haven't had training in multisensory teaching strategies, cooperative learning, reciprocal teaching, learning styles, or the theory of multiple intelligences, you

Used with permission from Decker Forrest.

need to update your teaching skills and knowledge for today's classroom. These are good topics for staff development days.

6. **Teamwork** on behalf of the ADD/ADHD student. Many teachers find team-teaching extremely helpful. Being able to "switch" or "share" students for part of the school day often reduces behavioral problems and preserves the teacher's sanity. It also provides for a different perspective on each child.

Teachers cannot be expected to manage and educate these very challenging students without assistance. A proper diagnosis is needed. With many ADD/ADHD students, medical treatment is critical to the child's ability to function in school. Management of the social/behavioral problems these children often exhibit requires help from counseling (in school and often privately). In-school counseling centers can assist in many ways, such as: behavior modification (charts, contracts), time-out/time-away, conflict resolution, training in social skills, relaxation techniques, controlling anger, and cooling down. You need cooperation and partnership with parents and support and assistance from administration. You are all part of the same team!

Elicit the assistance and expertise of your site resources. Refer the child to your site consultation team or student study team. Members of the team will probably observe the student in your classroom or other school settings. They can be of great support by attending meetings with you and parents to share concerns, provide information, and brainstorm "creative" solutions. Many outside referrals for medical/clinical evaluations are initiated at the school site. Your communication with the team is very important.

You can facilitate matters before coming to your team by:

— **Saving work samples** (Any papers or work that reflects the child's strengths and weaknesses) Collect a variety of written samples.

— **Documenting specific behaviors you see** (e.g., falling out of chair, writing only one sentence in 20 minutes of independent work, blurting out inappropriately in class). It is important that teachers document their observations and concerns about these students. This documentation is crucial for many children to get the help they need. Teachers are in a position to facilitate the necessary medical/clinical evaluation and intervention that may be needed for student success.

NOTE: Many times parents don't recognize that their child is experiencing the problems that we are seeing in school. Children with ADD/ADHD present their pattern of behavior year after year. It often takes parents a few years of hearing similar comments from different teachers to become convinced that they should pursue some sort of treatment for their child.

There is another reason for teacher documentation to be placed in the student's records. Physicians will often see the child during a brief office visit, not notice anything significant, and conclude that the student doesn't have a problem. Often the implication is that the problem is with the teacher/school. When the school records show a history of inattention, distractibility, impulsivity, hyperactivity, a physician would be more prone to take the school/parent concerns seriously. The physician/clinician needs to determine that the child's problems are pervasive (visible in a number of settings over a period of time). Good documentation (observations and anecdotal records) help supply the necessary evidence.

— **Communicating with parents.** It is important to share positive observations about their child along with concerns. Be careful how you communicate and voice concerns. Never tell parents, "I'm sure your child has ADD." Communicate your concerns by sharing specific, objective observations. "Becky is very distractible in my class. I have noticed that she . . ." Tell parents the strategies you are using to deal with the problems in the classroom. Then tell parents that you are involving your site team for assistance, and let the school nurse or counselor make recommendations for outside evaluations if deemed necessary.

7. **Administrative support.** It is critical that administrators be aware of the characteristics and strategies for effectively managing ADHD students so they can support the teacher in dealing with disruptive children. Some of these students are extremely difficult to maintain in the classroom and require highly creative intervention. You will certainly need administrative support (e.g., having a student removed from class when behaviors interfere with ability to teach or other students' ability to learn). Some intervention for highly disruptive children include: time-outs, suspensions, half-days, cross-age tutors rotating into the classroom to keep the child on-task, and having parents spend the day in class with the student and meeting with the consultation team.

It is important to distribute these students and avoid placing a large group of ADD/ADHD students in the same classroom. Loading one classroom with a high number of ADHD students would burn out the best of teachers and push them to seek another profession.

However, it is rare to find a classroom without at least a few ADD/ADHD students (as well as students with learning disabilities).

One of the keys to success is home-school communication and co-operation. When parents are difficult to reach and won't come to school, follow through with home-school contracts, monitor their child's homework, and so on; administrative assistance is also very much needed.

8. **Respecting student privacy and confidentiality.** It is important that a student's individual grades, test results, special modifications of assignments or requirements, as well as medication issues are not made common knowledge.

9. **Modifying assignments, cutting the written workload!** What takes an average child 20 minutes to do, often takes this student hours to accomplish (particularly written assignments). There is no need to do every worksheet, math problem, or definition. Be open to making exceptions. Allow student to do a more reasonable amount (e.g., every other problem, half a page). Accept alternative methods of sharing their knowledge such as allowing a student to answer questions orally or to dictate answers to a parent, and so on.

   Ease up on handwriting requirements and demands for these students. Be sensitive to the extreme physical effort it takes these children to put down in writing what appears simple to you. Typing/word processing skills are to be encouraged.

10. **Limit the amount of homework.** If the parent complains that an inordinate amount of time is spent on homework, be flexible and cut it down to a manageable amount. Typically, in the homes of ADHD children, homework time is a nightmare. Many teachers send home any incomplete classwork. Keep in mind that if the student was unable to complete the work during an entire school day, it is unlikely that he/she will be able to complete it that evening. You will need to prioritize and modify.

11. **Providing more time on assessments.** These students (often very intelligent children) frequently know the information, but

can't get it down, particularly on tests. Be flexible in permitting students with these needs to have extra time to take tests, and/or allow them to be assessed verbally.

12. **Teacher sensitivity about embarrassing or humiliating students in front of peers.** Self-esteem is fragile; students with ADD/ADHD typically perceive themselves as failures. Avoid ridicule. Preservation of self-esteem is the primary factor in truly helping these children succeed in life.

13. **Assistance with organization.** Students with ADD/ADHD have major problems with organization and study skills. They need help and additional intervention to make sure assignments are recorded correctly, their work space and materials are organized, notebooks and desks are cleared of unnecessary collections of junk from time to time, and specific study skill strategies are used.

14. **Environmental modifications.** Classroom environment is a very important factor in how students function. Due to a variety of learning styles, there should be environmental options given to students that consider where and how they work. Where the student sits can make a significant difference. Lighting, furniture, seating arrangements, ventilation, visual displays, color, areas for relaxation, and provisions for blocking out distractions during seatwork should be carefully considered. Organize the classroom with the awareness that most ADD/ADHD students need to be able to make eye contact with you, have you close by to step forward and cue, be seated near well-focused students, and be given a lot of space. There are many environmental factors that can be regulated and modified to improve ADD/ADHD students' classroom functioning considerably.

15. **Value students' differences and help bring out their strengths.** Provide many opportunities for children to demonstrate to their peers what they do well. Recognize the diversity of learning styles and individual approaches in your classroom.

16. **Belief in the student—not giving up when plans A, B, and C don't work.** There are always plans D, E, F, . . . Success will require

going back to the drawing board frequently. These children are worth the extra time and effort.

AN INTERVIEW WITH JOE

(41 years old, California)

"Watch Joseph. He's one of the most intelligent children I've ever seen." This was the comment made to Joe's parents when he and his siblings were tested at a young age by their neighbor, a professor of psychology in New York—Joe, who never received higher than a *D* from sixth grade through high school. Joe, who was constantly ridiculed by his teachers and was "a big disappointment to his parents."

Joe was "left back" in seventh grade while living in Connecticut. He remembers the trauma of all his friends moving on to another school when he repeated seventh. Joe flunked algebra four times. He graduated from high school "dead last" in his class. "After a while I had defaulted into a discipline problem. You gravitate towards those students who have absolutely no respect for the system. Otherwise, you have to agree that the only other thing that could be wrong is YOU."

Junior College was an uphill battle all over again. He saw his classmates "cruise through all their subjects" to get their degree. "The only difference between them and me was that I never knew what to do with numbers. Reading is extremely difficult for me. I have to do it very slowly and put everything into my own translator to assimilate the material and have it make sense." Joe's adult life was "a patchwork of jobs." Up until a few years ago, the average time he stayed with a job was one year. "There were so many days I was beaten to a pulp, and completely down and out until I was thirty years old. I knew there was something wrong with me, but no one knew what it was."

One significant change came in his adult life when a friend took him 'under his wing' and mentored him for three years in his business. Now I have "a good job as a technician in a good company. But it never lets up, I can't get a reprieve. In the real world of high tech, it requires constant training and schooling." Joe was identified as an adult as having learning disabilities and attention deficit disorder.

What would you like to do?

"I'd like to finish school and go to grad school. I've only started. I'll never give up."

What would have made a difference for you growing up?

"No one saw or was interested in my strengths. The spoken word came easily to me, the written word was very difficult. I was able at a young age to take an engine apart and put it back together. I have an excellent understanding of mechanical things. I was always musically talented . . . and I know everything there is to know about reptiles and amphibians.

"If one person would have interceded on my behalf. If one person would have said, 'This is not a stupid person we're dealing with . . . There's something more involved here that we need to get to the bottom of.' The weight of the world would have been lifted from my shoulders."

Forms, Charts, and Graphs

Home Situations Questionnaire

Child's Name _____ Date _____

Name of Person Completing This Form _____

Instructions: Does your child present any problems with compliance to instructions, commands, or rules for you in any of these situations? If so, please circle the word Yes and then circle a number beside that situation that describes how severe the problem is for you. If your child is not a problem in a situation, circle No and go on to the next situation on the form.

Situations	Yes/No (Circle one)		If yes, how severe? Mild (Circle one) Severe								
Playing alone	Yes	No	1	2	3	4	5	6	7	8	9
Playing with other children	Yes	No	1	2	3	4	5	6	7	8	9
Mealtimes	Yes	No	1	2	3	4	5	6	7	8	9
Getting dressed/undressed	Yes	No	1	2	3	4	5	6	7	8	9
Washing and bathing	Yes	No	1	2	3	4	5	6	7	8	9
When you are on the telephone	Yes	No	1	2	3	4	5	6	7	8	9
Watching television	Yes	No	1	2	3	4	5	6	7	8	9
When visitors are in your home	Yes	No	1	2	3	4	5	6	7	8	9
When you are visiting someone's home	Yes	No	1	2	3	4	5	6	7	8	9
In public places (restaurants, stores, church, etc.)	Yes	No	1	2	3	4	5	6	7	8	9
When father is home	Yes	No	1	2	3	4	5	6	7	8	9
When asked to do chores	Yes	No	1	2	3	4	5	6	7	8	9
When asked to do homework	Yes	No	1	2	3	4	5	6	7	8	9
At bedtime	Yes	No	1	2	3	4	5	6	7	8	9
While in the car	Yes	No	1	2	3	4	5	6	7	8	9
When with a babysitter	Yes	No	1	2	3	4	5	6	7	8	9

- - - - - - - - - - - - - - - - - -For Office Use Only -

Total number of problem settings _____   Mean severity score _____

The Home Situations Questionnaire. From *Defiant Children: A Clinician's Manual for Parent Training* by R. A. Barkley, 1987, New York: Guilford Press. Copyright 1987 by The Guilford Press. Reprinted by permission of the publisher.

Child Behavior List

Undesirable Behavior— Inappropriate Behavior	Desirable Behavior— Appropriate Behavior
1. _____	1. _____
2. _____	2. _____
3. _____	3. _____
4. _____	4. _____
5. _____	5. _____
6. _____	6. _____
7. _____	7. _____
8. _____	8. _____
9. _____	9. _____
10. _____	10. _____
11. _____	11. _____
12. _____	12. _____
13. _____	13. _____
14. _____	14. _____
15. _____	15. _____
16. _____	16. _____
17. _____	17. _____
18. _____	18. _____
19. _____	19. _____
20. _____	20. _____
21. _____	21. _____
22. _____	22. _____

School Note
(Ages 4-7)

Name _____   Date _____

Dear Teacher: Please put an (X) over the face that best describes this child's class behavior for each item.

Morning	Yes	Partially	No
Followed instructions	☺	😐	☹
Completed work	☺	😐	☹
Obeyed class rules	☺	😐	☹
Got along with peers	☺	😐	☹
Time Outs _____	☺	😐	☹

Afternoon			
Followed instructions	☺	😐	☹
Completed work	☺	😐	☹
Obeyed class rules	☺	😐	☹
Got along with peers	☺	😐	☹
Time Outs _____	☺	😐	☹

Comments _____

_____

_____

_____

_____

_____

School Note
(Ages 8-12)

Name _____   Date _____

Dear Teacher: Please put an (X) over the number that best describes this child's class behavior for each item.

Morning	Yes	Partially	No
Followed instructions	2	1	0
Completed work	2	1	0
Obeyed class rules	2	1	0
Got along with peers	2	1	0

Time Outs _____   Detentions _____

Afternoon			
Followed instructions	2	1	0
Completed work	2	1	0
Obeyed class rules	2	1	0
Got along with peers	2	1	0

Time Outs _____   Detentions _____

Comments _____

_____

_____

_____

_____

_____

_____

Homework Assignment Sheet

Date: _____

Subject	Assignment	Teacher Initials	Books/ Materials Needed	In Bag	Finished Filed	Parent Initials	In Bag

Special projects to be completed	
Tests to study for tomorrow or future date (specify)	
Materials/clothes needed for special events	
Teacher notes or requests	

Homework Check Card

Working	Monday	Tuesday	Wednesday	Thursday	Friday	Saturday	Sunday
"On Task"							
"Off Task"							
Net Totals							
Grand Totals							

Behavior Check Card

Behavior	Monday	Tuesday	Wednesday	Thursday	Friday	Saturday	Sunday
Working Cooperatively							
Playing Cooperatively							
Cumulative Totals							
Date				Point Total Goal This Week			

Social Graces Checklist

DATE: _____

NAME: _____

Social Skill	Monday	Tuesday	Wednesday	Thursday	Friday	Saturday	Sunday
Greet others							
Say goodbye							
Say thank you							
Introduce others							
Give compliments							
Thanks for compliments							
Offer to help							
Recognize others' feelings							
Apologize							
Neat/clean appearance							

Attention Training Game Recording Sheet

	Visual	Auditory
Focused Attention		
Sustained Attention		
Selective Attention		
Alternating Attention		
Divided Attention		

Attention Training Game Comparative Performance Record Attention Task ( )*

Training Session (Min) _____

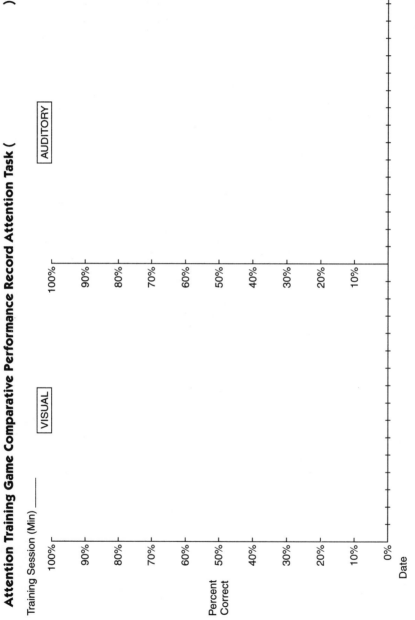

| VISUAL | AUDITORY |

Percent Correct

100%
90%
80%
70%
60%
50%
40%
30%
20%
10%
0%

Date

Substitute: Focused, sustained, selective, alternating, or divided

Attention Training Game (_____)* Attention ( )**

Training Session (Min)

Performance Record

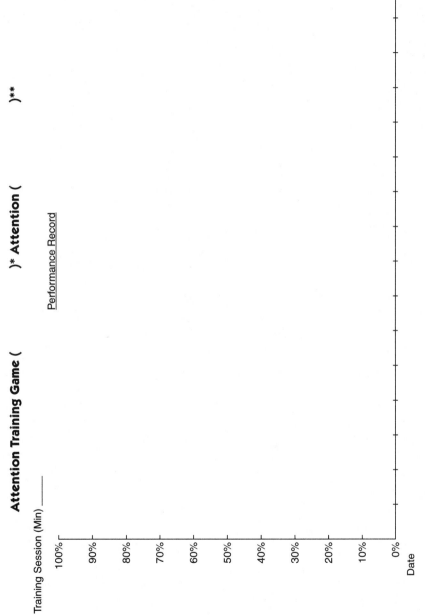

100%	
90%	
80%	
70%	
60%	
50%	
40%	
30%	
20%	
10%	
0%	

Date

* *Substitute*: Focused, sustained, selective, alternating, or divided attention depending upon which task you are monitoring
** *Substitute*: Visual or auditory

Recommended Resources

O ther sources of help are listed here and are organized in these categories:

❑ **Recommended Resources for Kids** (see also Videos & Newsletters categories)

❑ **Recommended Resources for Teens and Adults**

❑ **Recommended Resources for Parents**

> *Books*
>
> *Legal Resources*
>
> *Videos*
>
> *ADD Resource Catalogues*
>
> *Newsletters*
>
> *Computer Software Resources*
>
> *Organizations/Support Groups*

❑ **Recommended Resources for Teachers** (see also Videos category)

Recommended Resources for Kids

Bauer, K. *Active Andy: An Elementary School Child's Guide to Understanding ADHD.* Wauwatusa: IMDW Publications, 1993.

Corman, C. and Trevino, E. *Eukee the Jumpy Jumpy Elephant.* Plantation: Specialty Press, 1995.

Galum, M. *Otto Learns About His Medicine.* New York: Imagination Press, 1988.

Gehret, J. *I'm Somebody, Too!* New York: Verbal Images, 1992.

Gehret, M. *Eagle Eyes: A Child's Guide to Paying Attention.* New York: Verbal Images Press, 1991.

Gordon, M. *I Would If I Could: A Teenager's Guide to ADHD/Hyperactivity.* New York: GSI, 1991.

Gordon, M. *Jumpin' Johnny Get Back to Work: A Child's Guide to ADHD/Hyperactivity.* New York: GSI, 1991.

Gordon, M. *My Brother's a World Class Pain: A Sibling's Guide to ADHD.* New York: GSI, 1992.

Moss, D. Shelby. *The Hyperactive Turtle.* Rockville: Woodbine House, 1989.

Nadeau, K. and Dixon, E. *Learning to Slow Down and Pay Attention* (Revised Edition). Ammandale: Chesapeake Psychological Publications, 1993.

Parker, R. *Making the Grade: An Adolescent's Struggle with ADD.* Plantation: Specialty Press, 1994.

Parker, R. *Slam Dunk: A Young Boy's Struggle with ADD.* Plantation: Specialty Press, 1995.

Quinn, P. and Stern, J. *Putting on the Brakes: Young People's Guide to Understanding Attention Deficit Hyperactivity Disorder (ADHD).* New York: Magination Press, 1991.

Quinn, P. and Stern, J. *The "Putting on the Brakes" Activity Book: For Young People with ADHD.* New York: Magination Press, 1993.

Shapiro, L. *Jumpin' Jake Settle Down: A Workbook to Help Impulsive Children Learn to Think Before They Act.* King of Prussia: The Center for Applied Psychology, 1994.

Shapiro, L. *Sometimes I Drive My Mom Crazy, But I Know She's Crazy About Me.* King of Prussia: The Center for Applied Psychology, 1993.

Recommended Resources for Teens and Adults

Dendy, C.A. *Teenagers with ADD: A Parent's Guide*. Rockville: Woodbine House, 1994.

Hallowell, E. and Ratey, J. *Driven to Distraction: Reorganizing and Coping with Attention Deficit Disorder from Childhood through Adulthood*. New York: Pantheon, 1994.

Hartmann, T. *Attention Deficit Disorder: A Different Perception*. Penn Valley: Underwood Books, 1993.

Hechtman, L. and Weiss, G. *Hyperactive Children Grown Up*. New York: Guilford Press, 1986.

Kelly, K. and Ramundo, P. *You Mean I'm Not Lazy, Stupid, or Crazy? A Self-Help Book for Adults with Attention Deficit Disorder*. Cincinnati: Tyrell and Jerem Press, 1993.

Murphy, K. and LeVert, S. *Out of the Fog: Treatment Options & Coping Strategies for Adult Attention Deficit Disorder*. New York: Hyperion, 1995.

Nadeau, K. *A Comprehensive Guide to Attention Deficit Disorder in Adults*. New York: Brunner Mazel, 1995.

Quinn, P. *ADD and the College Student: A Guide for High School and College Students with Attention Deficit Disorder*. New York: Magination Press, 1994.

Weiss, L. *Attention Deficit Disorder in Adults: Practical Help for Sufferers and Their Spouses*. Dallas: Taylor Publishing Co., 1992.

Weiss, L. *"Attention Deficit Disorder in Adults" Workbook*. Dallas: Taylor Publishing Co., 1994.

Wender, P. *Attention Deficit Hyperactivity Disorders in Adults*. New York: Oxford University Press, 1995.

Wender, P. *The Hyperactive Child, Adolescent and Adult: Attention Deficit Disorder Through the Lifespan*. New York: Oxford University Press, 1987.

Recommended Resources for Parents

Books

Alexander-Roberts, C. *The ADHD Parenting Handbook*. Dallas: Taylor Publishing Co., 1994.

Anderson, W. Chitwood, S. and Hayden, D. *Negotiating the Special Education Maze: A Guide for Parents and Teachers.* Rockville: Woodbine House, 1990.

Bain, L. *Attention Deficit Disorders.* New York: Dell Publishing Co., 1986.

Barkley, R. *Attention Deficit Hyperactivity Disorder: A Handbook for Diagnosis and Treatment.* New York: Guilford Publications, 1990.

Colemann, W. *Attention Deficit Disorders, Hyperactivity and Associated Disorders: A Handbook for Parents & Professionals,* 6th Ed. Madison: Calliope Books, 1993.

Conner, C. *Feeding the Brain: How Foods Affect Children.* New York: Plenum, 1989.

Copeland, E. and Love, V. *Attention, Please!* Plantation: Specialty Press, 1995.

Cutler, B. *You, Your Child and Special Education: A Guide to Making the System Work.* Baltimore: Paul H. Brooks, 1993.

Fontenelle, D. *Understanding and Managing Overactive Children.* Englewood Cliffs: Prentice-Hall, Inc., 1983.

Fowler, M. *Maybe You Know My Kid: A Parent's Guide to Identifying, Understanding and Helping Your Child With Attention-Deficit Hyperactivity Disorder.* New York: Birch Lane Press, 1990.

Friedman, R. and Dogal, G. *Management of Children and Adolescents with Attention Deficit Hyperactivity Disorder.* Dallas: Pro-Ed, 1992.

Garber, S. W. et al. *If Your Child is Hyperactive, Inattentive, Impulsive, Distractible . . . .* New York: Villard Books, 1990.

Goldstein, S. and Goldstein, M. *A Parent's Guide: Attention Deficit Disorder in Children.* Salt Lake City: Neurology Learning and Behavior Center, 1995.

Goldstein, S. and Goldstein, M. *Hyperactivity: Why Won't My Child Pay Attention.* New York: Wiley-Interscience, 1992.

Greenberg, G. and Herm, W. *Attention Deficit Hyperactivity Disorder: Questions and Answers for Parents.* Champaign: Research Press, 1991.

Hallowell, E. and Ratey, J. *Driven to Distraction: Recognizing and Coping with Attention Deficit Disorder from Childhood through Adulthood.* New York: Pantheon, 1994.

Hartmann, T. *Attention Deficit Disorder: A Different Perception.* Navato: Underwood-Miller, 1993.

Hechtman, L. and Weiss, G. *Hyperactive Children Grown Up.* New York: Guilford Press, 1986.

Impersoll, B. *Your Hyperactive Child: A Parent's Guide to Coping with ADD.* New York: Doubleday, 1988.

Isaacs, S. and Ritchey, W. *I Think I Can, I Know I Can.* New York: St. Martin's Press, 1989.

Kelly, K. and Ramundo, P. *You Mean I'm Not Lazy, Stupid, or Crazy? A Self-Help Book for Adults with Attention Deficit Disorder.* Cincinnati: Tyrell and Jerem Press, 1993.

Kennedy, P., Terdal, L. and Fusetti, L. *The Hyperactive Child Book.* New York: St. Martin's Press, 1993.

Latham, P. S., *Succeeding in the Workplace: Attention Deficit Disorder & Learning Disabilities in the Workplace.* Grawn: JKL Communications, 1994.

Levine, M. *Keeping A Head In School.* Cambridge: Educator Publishing Service, 1990.

Maxey, D. *A Different Way of Dealing with ADHD: 365 Daily Meditations for Encouragement.* Roanoke: AAAD Support Groups, 1993.

Maxey, D. *How to Own and Operate an Attention Deficit Kid.* Roanoke: AAAD Support Groups, 1993.

Moss, R. *Why Johnny Can't Concentrate.* New York: Blanton Books, 1990.

Paltin, D. *The Parent's Hyperactivity Handbook: Helping the Fidgety Child.* New York: Plenum Press, 1993.

Phelan, T. *All About Attention Deficit Disorder* (Revised). Glen Ellyn: Child Management, 1993.

Silver, L. *Dr. Larry Silver's Advice to Parents on Attention Deficit Disorder.* Washington: American Psychiatric Press, 1993.

Sloane, H. *The Good Kid Book: How to Solve the 16 Most Common Behavior Problems.* Champaign: Research Press, 1988.

Taylor, J. *Helping Your Hyperactive Child.* Rochlin: Prima Publishing, 1994.

Legal Resources

Horovitz, I., King, T., and Meyer, E. "Legally Mandated Options Available to Children with ADHD within Public Education," *Clinical Pediatrics,* 1993, Vol 32(11) 702–704.

Latham, O.S. and Latham, P.H. *Attention Deficit Disorder and the Law.* Washington: JKL Communications, 1992.

Videos (Those with * Are for Kids; Those with ** Are for Teachers)

Barkley, R. *ADHD in Adults.* New York: Guilford Press, 1994.

**Barkley, R. *ADHD in the Classroom: Strategies for Teachers.* New York: Guilford Press, 1994.

Barkley, R. *ADHD—What Can We Do?* New York: Guilford Press, 1992.

Barkley, R. *ADHD—What Can We Know?* New York: Guilford Press, 1992.

**Goldstein, S. and Goldstein, M. *Educating Inattentive Children.* Salt Lake City: Neurology Learning and Behavior Center, 1990.

*Goldstein, S. and Goldstein, M. *It's Just Attention Disorder.* Salt Lake City: Neurology Learning and Behavior Center, 1991.

Goldstein, S. and Goldstein, M. *Why Won't My Child Pay Attention?* Salt Lake City: Neurology Learning and Behavior Center, 1989.

*Gordon, M. *Jumpin' Johnny Get Back to Work: The Video.* New York: GSI, 1991.

Phelan, J. *Adults with Attention Deficit Disorder: ADD Isn't Just Kids Stuff.* Glen Ellyn: Child Management, 1994.

Phelan, J. *Attention Deficit Hyperactivity Disorder.* Glen Ellyn: Child Management, 1990.

Phelan, T. and Bloomberg, J. *Medication for Attention Deficit Disorder: All You Need to Know.* Glen Ellyn: Child Management, 1994.

**Rief, S. *ADHD Inclusive Instruction and Collaborative Practices.* New York: National Professional Resources, 1993.

Robin, A. *ADHD in Adolescence: The Next Step—A Video Guide for Clinical Description, Diagnosis and Treatment of Adolescents with ADHD.* Worcester: Madison Avenue Marketing, 1993.

Robin, A. *ADHD in Adulthood: A Clinical Perspective.* Worcester: National Professional Resources, 1992.

ADD Resource Catalogues

ADD Clinic
Resources for Parents
983 Howard Avenue
Biloxi, MS 39531
1-800-962-2673

ADD Discount Books
312 Riley Circle
Gadsden, AL 35901
(334) 543-1170

ADD Warehouse
300 Northwest 70th Avenue
Suite 102
Plantation, FL 33317
(305) 792-8944

Attention Deficit Resources Center
1344 Johnson Ferry Road
Suite 14
Marietta, GA 30068

National Professional Resources, Inc.
Dept. C95, 25 South Regent Street
Port Chester, NY 10573
914-937-8879, FAX: 914-937-9327

Newsletters (Those with * Are for Kids)

ADD Forum (CompuServe)
800-524-3388 (Representative 464)

The ADHD Report
Guilford Publications
Russell Barkley, Editor
800-365-7006

ADDendum
c/o C.P.S.
5041-A Backlick Road
Annandale, VA 22003
Paul Jaffe, Editor

The ADDed Line
3320 Creek Hollow Drive
Marietta, GA 30062
800-982-4028

ADDult News
c/o Mary Jane Johnson
ADDult Support Network
2620 Ivy Place
Toledo, OH 43613

ATTENTION (magazine)
CH.A.D.D. National Headquarters
499 Northwest 70th Ave., Suite 308
Plantation, FL 33317
305-587-3700, FAX: 305-587-4599

*BRAKES: The Interactive Newsletter for Kids with ADHD
Magination Press
19 Union Square West
New York, NY 10003
800-825-3089

CH.A.D.D.E.R. and *CH.A.D.D.E.R. BOX*
CH.A.D.D. National Headquarters
499 Northwest 70th Ave., Suite 308
Plantation, FL 33317
305-587-3700, Fax: 305-587-4599

Challenge
P.O. Box 448
West Newbury, MA 01985

Electronic Bulletin Boards
(a) American On-line
(b) Prodigy
(c) Disabilitier Forum
(d) ADD Bulletin Board

HAAD ENOUGH (Bi-Monthly)
HAAD Support Groups
P.O. Box 20563
Roanoke, VA 24018

The Rebus Institute Report
1499 Bayshore Blvd., Suite 146
Burlingame, CA 94010

Computer Software Resources

ABLEDATA
National Rehabilitation Information Center
Catholic University of America
4407 Eighth St., NE
Washington, D.C. 20017
(202) 635-5822

"Following Directions" (Grades 3-6)
Lawrence Productions
1800 S. 35th Street
Galesburg, MI 49053
(800) 645-6564

Kids Works 2
Davidson and Associates
P.O. Box 2961
Torrance, CA 90509
(800) 545-7677

Miranker, C. and Elliot, A.
The Computer Museum Guide to the Best Software for Kids
New York: Harper Collins Publishers, Inc., 1995

"Test Taking Made Easy" (Grades 2-5)
Lawrence Productions
1800 S. 35th St.
Galesburg, MI 49053
(800) 645-6564

Organizations/Support Groups

ADDA (Attention Deficit Disorder Association)
4300 West Park Boulevard
Plano, TX 75093

ADDAG (Attention Deficit Disorder Advocacy Group)
8091 South Ireland Way
Aurora, CO 80016
(303) 690-7548

ADDendum (quarterly newsletter for adults who have Attention
  Deficit Disorder)
Box 296
Scarborough, NY 10510

ADDult Support Network (for ADD Adults)
Mary Jane Johnson
2620 Ivy Place
Toledo, OH 43613

Adult ADD Association
1225 East Sunset Drive
Suite 640
Bellingham, WA 98226-3529
(206) 647-6681

Adult Attention Deficit Foundation
132 North Woodward Avenue
Birmingham, MI 48009
(313) 540-6335

Attention Deficit Resource Center
(Special Focus on ADD Adults)
Lawrence L. McLear, Ph.D, Director
1344 Johnson Ferry Rd., Suite 14
Marietta, GA 30068
(800) 537-3784

Children with Attention Deficit Disorders (CHADD)
499 Northwest 70th Ave., Suite 308
Plantation, FL 33317
(305) 587-3700

Learning Disabilities Association (LDA)
4156 Library Road
Pittsburgh, PA 15234
(412) 341-1515

National Network of Learning Disabled Adults (NNCDA)
808 West 82nd St., F-2
Scottsdale, AZ 85257

Recommended Resources for Teachers

Barkley, R. *ADHD in the Classroom: Strategies for Teacher (Video)*. New York: Guilford Press, 1994.

Copeland, E. and Love, V. *Attention Without Tension*. Atlanta: 3 C's of Childhood, 1990.

Goldstein, S. and Goldstein, M. *A Teacher's Guide: Attention Deficit Hyperactivity Disorder in Children*. Salt Lake City: Neurology Learning and Behavior Center, 1987.

Goldstein, S. and Goldstein, M. *Educating Inattentive Children (Video)*. Salt Lake City: Neurology Learning and Behavior Center, 1990.

Parker, H. *ADAPT: Attention Deficit Accommodation Plan for Teaching*. Plantation: Specialty Press, 1992.

Parker, H. *The ADD Hyperactivity Handbook for Schools*. Plantation: Impact Publications, 1992.

Pierangelo, R. and Jacoby, R. *Parents' Complete Special Education Guide: Tips, Techniques, & Materials for Helping Your Child Succeed in School and Life.* New York: The Center for Applied Research in Education, 1996.

Rief, S. *ADHD Inclusive Instruction and Collaborative Practice (Video).* New York: National Professional Resources, 1993.

Rief, S. *How to Reach and Teach ADD/ADHD Children.* New York: The Center for Applied Research in Education, 1993.

Swanson, J. *School-based Assessments and Interventions for ADD Students.* Irving: KC Publishing, 1992.

Glossary

ACHIEVEMENT: The successful reaching of a goal, usually academic.

ACTING OUT: The expression of a wish, need or motivation in overt behavior.

ACTIVITY LEVEL: Generally refers to the amount and frequency of movement that a person exhibits.

AGGRESSION: When a person makes a hostile physical attack either verbally (hostile comment) or in action (hitting).

ANCHOR: Any stimulus eliciting or associated with a specific feeling state.

ANTICIPATORY RESPONSE: A preliminary adjustment that facilitates the reaction to an expected stimulus event.

ANTISOCIAL: Behavior that violates the rights of others.

ANXIETY DISORDER: General term for psychological disorders in which chronic anxiety is a prominent feature, and usually involves body symptoms such as rapid heartbeat, sweaty palms and excess muscle tension.

ASTHMA: Condition of the lungs characterized by a decrease in the diameter of some air passages, causing difficulty in breathing.

BEHAVIOR MODIFICATION: Techniques of treating psychological problems through the maladaptive behavior they produce.

BEHAVIOR PENALTY/RESPONSE COST: Withdrawal or discontinuation of a reward that follows an inappropriate behavior.

BEHAVIOR REPERTOIRE: A group of behaviors that have been "learned" to varying degrees and may be elicited or emitted.

BEHAVIORAL CONTRACT: An agreement between two persons, usually parent and child, such that when the parent gets a desired behavior, the child receives something he/she wants.

CENTRAL NERVOUS SYSTEM (CNS): Neural tissue comprised of the brain and spinal cord.

COGNITIVE SET: A thought pattern that dictates a readiness to respond in a specific and consistent manner.

CONDUCT DISORDER: Persistent violation of others' rights with behaviors such as stealing, running away, lying, truancy, and destructive acts towards people or animals.

CONNER'S PARENT & TEACHER RATING SCALES: Rating on ADD characteristics provided by parents and teachers to aid in diagnosing and monitoring ADD/ADHD.

CONTINGENT REINFORCEMENT: Any case in which one event has an increased probability of being followed by reward, usually by design.

CONTINUUM: A field of experience that, though it may be broken into elements, is a whole.

DELUSIONAL: Holding a belief that is contradicted by evidence and logic.

DEPRESSION: A reduced state of both physiological and mental functioning, usually associated with feelings of unhappiness and sad affective expression.

DIFFERENTIAL REINFORCEMENT: Selective reinforcement/reward of one behavior where another behavior (sometimes an alternative one) may not be reinforced/rewarded.

DYSFUNCTIONAL: Working or operating in a manner as to be a handicap to the individual, or group.

DYSGRAPHIA: Impairment of well-established fine-motor movements, specifically affecting handwriting.

DYSLEXIA: Reading disorder characterized by the inability to identify letters or words or by distorted reading and sometimes characterized by letter reversals beyond the age of six.

EEG (ELECTROENCEPHALOGRAM): Record of the electrical charges of the brain.

ENCEPHALITIS: Inflammation of the brain.

ENIGMA: Something that appears to be a puzzle, seemingly inexplicable.

EPILEPTIC/SEIZURE DISORDER: Involves a rapid and unpredictable electrical discharge in the brain causing temporary changes in mental state.

ERIKSONIAN HYPNOSIS: Specific hypnotic techniques formulated and described by Milton Erickson, M.D.

EXTINCTION: A decrease in and elimination of behavior that occurs because it is no longer reinforced.

FETAL ALCOHOL SYNDROME: A combination of physical and psychological defects including learning and attentional problems caused by heavy maternal drinking during pregnancy.

FINE MOTOR: Activities such as handwriting that involve specific muscles of the hand for small movements and smooth actions.

FOCUSED ATTENTION: The most basic form of attention that involves one's ability to respond to a specific stimulus without a shift in attention.

FRAGILE X SYNDROME: A genetic disorder associated with a defect in the X chromosome that often results in mental retardation, but also may be manifested by LD and ADD characteristics.

FRONTAL LOBE DYSFUNCTION: Damage or impairment of function of the frontal lobe that may produce behavioral, emotional, and cognitive problems and especially difficulty with executive (control) functions.

GAIN (ELECTRONIC):   An increase in signal strength when transmitting from one point to another.

GENERALIZATION: The process by which a learned response will occur in more situations than those in which it was first learned.

GROSS MOTOR: Activities such as walking, throwing, running, etc., that involve the large skeletal muscles of the body.

GROUNDING: Similar to behavior penalty where the child must remain at home and thereby lose the privileges associated with events outside the home. Typically used with older children and teenagers.

HYPOGLYCEMIA: A condition in which the level of blood sugar is abnormally low or abnormally reduced.

INTELLIGENCE: Involves the ability to learn and adapt to new situations, understand both verbal and nonverbal concepts, and ranges from the lowest level of retardation to the highest level of genius.

LEARNING DISABILITY: Disorder of psychological processes related to the understanding or expression of language manifested by problems in basic skills of reading, writing, spelling and/or arithmetic.

MENTALLY RETARDED: A general term for limited intelligence with Intelligence Quotients (IQ) below 70.

METAPHOR (ERIKSONIAN):   Stories that have meanings at different levels—conscious and unconscious.

MNEMONIC DEVICE: A cognitive strategy used to assist memory.

MODELING: Learning through imitation.

MULTI-MODAL: Usually refers to treatment programs that have several components and involve several disciplines, or several different approaches to a problem situation.

NEUROBIOLOGICAL: Biological processes involved in the nervous system.

Neurodevelopmental Lag: Usually refers to a specific part of the central nervous system (brain) and related functions that are delayed in their development.

Neurolinguistic: Term used to describe the connection and interaction between language and other internal (neurological) processes.

Neurophysiology: Physiology of the nervous system in the body.

Neurotransmitter: A chemical that facilitates the transmission of electrical impulses between nerve endings in the brain.

Overcorrection: A technique in which a person tries to make an inappropriate behavior better than normal through positive practice.

Perinatal Anoxia: Loss of oxygen to fetus (newborn) around the time of birth.

PET Scan: A means of examining the brain by tracing the path of radioactive particles through the brain.

Physiological: Concerning body function.

Pinworms: Parasite found in the intestines and around the anus.

Polygenic Inheritance: Resulting from the action of many genes.

Premack Principle: States that an action with a high probability of occurrence can be used to reinforce an action with a low probability of occurrence.

Psychosomatic: Real physical symptoms that are caused by psychological factors.

Public Law 94–142: Created by Congress in 1975 to assure that all handicapped children (to age 21) be able to avail themselves of free public education, especially special education and related services needed to meet the child's needs, and to provide these in an atmosphere that is as normal as possible.

Punishment: A consequence that decreases the likelihood of a behavior occurring again.

Q 27 (GENETIC TERM):   A specific site on the X chromosome in the Fragile X Syndrome.

REFRAME: To look at or consider a specific situation or event within a different context.

REWARD: Something that is provided for a person after a desired behavior has occurred and is something the person wants, needs, or likes.

RISK TAKING: Situations where there is a desired goal and a lack of certainty that it can be attained within the presence of some danger.

SELECTIVE ATTENTION: Attention that is channelled towards certain stimuli and ignores the presence of others.

SELF CONCEPT: How we see or describe ourselves.

SHAPING: Reinforcing behaviors that lead up to or approximate the desired behavior.

SLEEP APNEA: A respiratory sleep disorder in which breathing repeatedly stops for ten seconds or more during the night.

SOCIALIZATION: Learning to accept the rules and expectations of society and acquiring appropriate social behavior in the process.

SOCIOECONOMIC STATUS (SES):   Classification of family status according to various social and economic factors.

STROKE (PSYCHOLOGICAL):   Verbal or physical recognition for certain behaviors.

SUSTAINED ATTENTION: An extended period of concentration on a relatively simple task.

TARGET BEHAVIOR: A specific behavior that is identified to be modified through the use of behavioral techniques.

THEOPHYLLINE: A commonly used bronchodilator.

THYROID DYSFUNCTION: Deregulation of the thyroid gland that may result in increased activity (overactive thyroid) or being sluggish and day-dreaming behavior (underactive thyroid), all ADD-like behaviors.

TIME IN: Positive reinforcement given when the child is doing appropriate behavior or at least no inappropriate behavior.

TIME OUT: A procedure that decreases undesirable behaviors by removing all reinforcements.

TRANSFER OF TRAINING (POSITIVE): A phenomenon in which the learning of one particular task in one situation helps the learning of a subsequent task (in another situation).

VIGILANCE: Alertness to respond to a specific stimulus over an extended period of time.

VISUAL-MOTOR: Skills that involve making a motor response such as speaking, drawing, writing or movement activities in response to a visual stimulus.

VISUAL-SPATIAL: Refers to the awareness and identification of the spatial orientation of stimuli.

Index

A-B-C behavioral program principles, 31–32; *See also* antecedents, behaviors, consequences.
accommodating special needs students, viii, 99
active vs. passive learning, 126
ADD Clinic, 136, 181–186
treatment programs, 183–186
adolescents with ADD/ADHD, 11, 31
predictors of outcome, 11–12
adults with ADD/ADHD, 11, 173, 159, 189
aggression, xxv, 74, 76–77, 87, 115
alcoholism, 11
allergies, 21
alternating attention, 2
attention training game, 151
alternative treatments, 166–167
Anesko, K., & Levine, F., 109, 112
angry parent, xiii, 29
antecedents, 31–32, 35–45

appropriate behavior, xix, 48–52, 67–72
creating new, 63, 65, 67–72, 83
punishing, 58, 65
repetition, 84
rewarding, 58
appropriate behavior diary, 60
assessment techniques, 100, 181–183
attention, types of, 2
Attention Deficit Disorder/Attention Deficit Hyperactivity Disorder (ADD/ADHD)
assessment and diagnosis, 3–5, 10–12, 13–15, 100, 181–183, 190
CH.A.D.D. overview, 187–192
characteristic behaviors, vii, 1–8, 12, 23, 30, 67–68, 100, 188
effect on family, 7, 16
effect on teachers, vii, 8, 16
origins, 189

Attention Deficit Disorder/Attention
    Deficit Hyperactivity Disorder
    (ADD/ADHD) *(Continued)*
  primary problems, 67
  symptomatic treatment approach,
    16
attention meter, 41
attention span, increasing, 41–44,
    145–157
attention training game, 145–157
  components, 146
  recording performance, 153
auditory and visual stimulation,
    162

behavior
  acting out, xxv, xxxi, 77
  appropriate, xix, 48, 67–72
  check card, 188
  defined, 47
  describing, 49
  desirable/undesirable, 48–52
  distinction from person, 120
  inappropriate, xix, xxxiii, 48, 51,
    73–76,
  morals, 52
  safety, xviii, 51–52
behavioral characteristics, vii, xi, 1–8,
    67–68, 188
  in classroom setting, 100
  inconsistent behavior, 12, 30
  learned component, 23
  neurophysiological origins, 6,
    19–21
behavioral modification programs,
    xxiii–xxxv, 58–63, 69–71, 73–76,
    81–83

A-B-C principles, 31–32
  advice for parents, xix–xxii
  behavioral contract, 92
  behavior penalty, xix, xxxiv, 81–82
  beyond home, 91, 94
  duration, 95
  monitoring and recordkeeping, xx
  rapid changes, 91
  right/wrong approach, xxiv
  strengthening/weakening
    behaviors, 58, 62, 73
  termination, 94–95
  use with medication, 8, 101
bi-directional pattern of parent-child
    relationship, 26–27
biofeedback, 162
biological origins of ADD, 19, 30, 161
brain damage, xii, 160
brain injury, 165
brain wave patterns, 20, 161
Broken Record technique, 172

Captain's Log, cognitive training, 165
case studies, xxiv–xxxv
central nervous system, 161
CH.A.D.D. fact sheet, 187
chores, 83, 137
  as restitution, 83, 84
  unpleasant, 93
church, 97
clowning behavior, 104
cognitive rehabilitation, 185
cognitive self-talk, 76
communication
  with ADD/ADHD child, 39
  between home and school, 93–96
  from teacher, 111

computers, 129
    use with neuropsychological
        programs, 166
consequences, 31–32, 55–65
contracts between parent and child,
    92–93
control, giving to child, xiii, 62
cooperation, 118
counseling, 134–135
creating appropriate behavior, 67–72
cues, direct vs. indirect, 86
cure for ADD, 167

daily affirmations, 171
developmental history, 10–11
diagnosis of ADD
    criteria, 3–5, 10–12, 190
    Gordon Diagnostic System, 13–15
    and learning disabilities, 14–15
    teacher's role, 100
    and treatment overview, 190
Diagnostic and Statistical Manual
    (DSM) 3–5, 13, 188
    coding for ADD/ADHD, 5
diary of good behaviors, 141
diet, high protein/low carbohydrate,
    142
dietary factors, 140
differential reinforcement, 70
direct cues, 86
disrespect to parents, 84
distancing, parent from child, 71
distractibility, *See* off task behavior.
distraction and deficiency of positive
    strokes, 72
divided attention, 2
    attention training game, 152

dress-rehearsal for time out, 77–78
DSM, *See* Diagnostic and Statistical
    Manual.
dysfunctional families, 134

ear infections, 21
EEG studies, 20, 161
extinction of undesirable behavior,
    62, 63, 65, 74–84

failures, and self-image, 122
family history, *See* heredity.
family therapy, 135
Fetal Alcohol Syndrome, 20, 160
focused attention, 2
    attention training game, 147
following instructions, 116
Fragile X Syndrome, 160
frontal lobe activity, 20

games as intervention tools, 137
    Attention Training Game, 145–157
    Checkers, 138
    Flinch, 139
    Legos, 138–139
generalization of behaviors, 96
genetic engineering, 19, 167
genetic factors, 19, 159–160
genetic studies, 167; *See also* identical
    twins.
glucose in diet, 140
glucose metabolism, 20
goal setting, 97
Gordon Diagnostic System, 13–15
Grandma's rule, 61, 65, 92
grandparents, 96
grounding, 82–83

group therapy, 134
guidelines for teachers, 193
guilty parent, 29

habilitation, 164
head injury, 10
hearing defects, 21
heredity, 6, 19, 131; *See also* genetic
    factors.
hindered parent, 29
hitting, 76, 78–79; *See also*
    inappropriate behavior.
Home-School Behavior chart, 94
Home-School Behavior Chart for
    point system, 88
home and school programs,
    coordinating, xxxiii, 91–96
Home Situations Questionnaire,
    xviii, 204
homework, 91–92, 105–114
  forgetting, 114
  prioritizing and scheduling, 110
  rules, 114
  setting routines, 109–110
  supervision, 112–113
  taking too long, 108
homework assignment book,
    107–108
hopeless parent, 28
hyperactivity, symptoms of, 4
hypnosis, Ericksonian, 163

identical twins with ADD, 159–160
imitation, in modeling, 69
immaturity, 68
impulsive behavior, xxviii, 4–5,
    22–23, 174

inappropriate/appropriate behavior,
    69, 83, 85, 87, 205
inappropriate behavior
  aggressiveness, 74
  development of, 74
  ignoring, xix, 74, 75
  removing or decreasing, 73–76
  whining, xxvii, 75
inattention, symptoms of, 3–4; *See
    also* off task behavior.
inconsistent performance, 156
increasing behavioral repertoire,
    67–72
indirect cues, 86
individualized education plan (IEP),
    101
individual therapy, 134
instrumental procedures, 61; *See also*
    Grandma's rule.
Intermediate Visual and Auditory Test
    (IVA), 14
internal dialogue, 121

lead poisoning, 20
learning disability, 14, 15
learning opportunities, increasing, 91
lecturing, 79
less responsive parent, 29–30
listening, 116
low-arousal state, 6, 20, 161
low-energy parent, 28

magic solution, 167
manipulation of parents, xxvii, 57, 60
marital problems, 134, 169
medications, 7–8, 21, 130–133
  and behavior modification, 8, 101

dosage study, 101
  information for teachers, 101
  monitoring response to, 101
  side effects, 102
  termination of, 101
medication trials, 131
memory aids, 129
misconceptions, 173
misidentification of child with ADD, 6
mnemonic devices, 129
modeling, 63–64, 65, 69–70, 85
  modeling behaviors from television, 115
MotivAider®, 44, 127
multidisciplinary treatment approaches, 125
music, use in therapy, 162

name-calling, 77, 87
  effect on ADD child, 121–122
National Joint Committee for Learning Disability, 14
negative attention, 56–57
negative consequences, 73
nerve cell structure, 20
neurochemical factors, 20
neurophysiology of ADD/ADHD, xii, 6, 19–21, 30, 68
neuropsychological remediation techniques, 165, 183
neurotherapy, 163
non-confronting parent, 28

off task behavior, 42–43, 68–69
  teacher monitoring, 100
opposite behavior, 83, 85, 87, 205

optimal arousal theory, 161
overcorrection, xxxiv, 83

parental attention
  balancing, 74
  power of, 74
  shifting negative to positive, 75
parental control, xiii, 75–76, 170–173
  inconsistency in, 82
  parents who don't discipline, 28–29
parent-child relationship, xiii, 25–31, 74–76
  abuse toward parent, xiv, 172
  factors affecting, 27, 28
  suggestions for parents, 170–172
parents as homework consultants, 112
paying attention, 40–41
peer pressure, 114
perinatal anoxia, 160
physical fighting, 80; *See also* aggression.
physical punishment, 23, 28, 55, 65, 173
play activities, 137–140
point systems, xx, 85–89
  recording points, 88
  set up for success, 87
polygenic inheritance pattern, 160
positive/negative consequences, 58–60
positive practice and restitution, 83, 84
positive statements, 62
pouting, 77

praise, 59–60, 65, 72, 108
  with physical contact, 72
predictors of outcome for ADD
    adolescents and children, 11–12
preferential seating in classroom, 102
Premack Principle, 102, 110–111
preventive education, 141
problem areas, three most common,
    105
problem behavior vs. alternative good
    behavior, 48–52, 85; *See also*
    opposite behavior.
problem-oriented treatment, 47
prognosis, 191
progress reports, 111
protein in diet, 140
psychological evaluations, 13, 131
punishing appropriate behavior, 58,
    65
punishment, 56, 57, 59, 65
  physical, xix, 23, 28, 55, 65, 173
  used alone, 85

"R and R" relax and recover exercise,
    136
rating scales in diagnosis, 16
reactions to behavioral procedures,
    xix, 81
reading to ADD children, 116
rehabilitation, 165
reinforcement, 58–59, 63
  differential, 70
  physical contact, 71
  selective, 70
  stroking, 71–72
relationships with others, 51
  parents, 26, 27, 51

peers, 114–120
  siblings, 51, 114, 117
relaxation training, 135
repetition of appropriate behavior, 84
reports from teachers, 93–94, 206–207
resistant behaviors, 81, 84
response cost, 81–82, 128
response cost procedure, 103
responsibility, 86
  for completing chores, 137
restitution, xxxiv, 84
rewarding inappropriate behavior,
    58, 65
rewards, 57, 58, 60, 65
  for chores, 93
  for completing tasks, 138–140
  removing, 76
right brain/left brain dysfunction, 15
Ritalin, 132–133, 159
role playing, 96
routines, breaks in, 170
rule-governed behavior, 36
rules, 35–39
  age appropriateness, 37
  optimum number, 37
rules and expectations, 35, 38–39

school behavior programs, 87
schoolwork, failure in, 87
seizure disorder, 161
selective attention, 2
  attention training game, 150
selective reinforcement, 70
self-concept, 120–123
  modifying, 123
  weakened by behavior programs, 87
self-esteem, 120–123

self-monitoring procedures, 103, 109, 127
self-talk, 127
    for parents, 75, 171
sensory stimuli, response to, 6
shaping, 63–64
sharing, 64, 117, 118
sibling rivalry, 117
sleep problems, 135–136
sleepy state, 161; *See also* low arousal state.
social graces, 119
social problems, 114, 120
social skills, categories, 115
    deficiencies, 64
speech and language problems, 130
stimulants, 7–8, 20, 21, 130–133
stress, 28
    on family, 169
    symptoms of, 135
stress management, 135–136
    for family members, 170–171
stroking, in reinforcement, 71–72
structural abnormalities in anatomy, xii, 20
support groups, viii, 172
sustained attention, 2
    attention training game, 149
symptomatic treatment approach, 16
symptoms, conditions that mimic, 8, 130–131

tantrums, xxvi, 62, 74
tape recorders
    in classroom, 102, 129
    at home, 128–129
    for spelling, 128

target behaviors for time out, 77–78
teacher-child relationship, 100–104
    flexibility, 193
    involvement in behavior programs, 91
    suggestions for teacher, 103
teacher-parent communication, 194, 197
    reports from teacher, 93–94, 206–207
teacher ratings
    rating schoolwork, 91–92
    rating sheets, 93, 94
    role in assessing ADD, 100
    on task behavior, 94
teacher's role in ADD assessment, 100
teaching strategies, 194–199
    saving time, 92
television
    disputes with siblings, 118
    parental monitoring of programs, 115
    TV Allowance™, 118
    violence, 115
tests for ADD/ADHD, 13, 14
Tests of Variables of Attention (TOVA), 14
therapy, 134–135
thyroid, 21
time in, 70–71
time out, xix, 57, 70–71, 76–81
    conditions of, 76
    guidelines, 77–78
    recommended duration, 76, 78

time out *(Continued)*
   resistance to, 81
   target behaviors, 77–78
   for toys, 79
   for two, 80
   young children, 81
token economy; *See also* point
   systems.
   age appropriate to, 86
transfer of training, 96–97
troubled parent, 29
TV Allowance™, 118

unidirectional pattern of parent-child
   relationship, 26
unstructured play time, 141

video camera, 143

whining, xxvii, 77
Winning the Homework War, K. Anesko
   & F. Levine, 109
write-say method, 129